UNDERCOVER

The Men and Women of
the Special Operations Executive

Other titles by Patrick Howarth

History and Criticism

The Year is 1851
Questions in the House
Squire: Most Generous of Men
Special Operations (*Editor*)
Play up and Play the Game
When the Riviera was Ours

Novels

The Dying Ukrainian
A Matter of Minutes

Life-boat Service

The Life-boat Story
The Life-boat Service
How Men are Rescued from the Sea
Life-boats and Life-boat People

Poems Broadcast

Play Back a Lifetime
The Four Seasons

PATRICK HOWARTH

UNDERCOVER

The Men and Women of
the Special Operations Executive

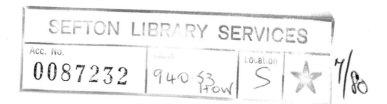

Routledge & Kegan Paul
London, Boston and Henley

To my many friends and colleagues in SOE
and, in particular,
to the memory of Christine Granville

First published in 1980
by Routledge & Kegan Paul Ltd
39 Store Street, London WC1E 7DD,
Broadway House, Newtown Road,
Henley-on-Thames, Oxon RG9 1EN and
9 Park Street, Boston, Mass. 02108, USA
Set in Linocomp Plantin by
Rowland Phototypesetting Ltd
Bury St Edmunds, Suffolk
and printed in Great Britain by
Unwin Bros Ltd

British Library Cataloguing in Publication Data

Howarth, Patrick

Undercover
1. Great Britain. Army. Special Operations
Executive
2. World War, 1939–1945 – Secret service –
Great Britain
I. Title
940.54'86'41   D810.S7

ISBN 0 7100 0573 3

Contents

Illustrations

Acknowledgments

Many people have helped me with my researches. I would like to convey my special thanks to those who read chapters or sections of my typescript and, from their expert and first-hand knowledge of events, offered me their criticisms, suggestions and corrections. They were Joan Bright Astley, John Bowen, Maurice Buckmaster, John Davis, Sir William Deakin, J. E. B. Finlay, Professor M. R. D. Foot, Henrietta Gregorius, G. A. Holdsworth, David Howarth, Peter Kemp, Michael Lis, Vera Long, Marjorie, Lady Marling, A. M. Rendel, Jack Smith-Hughes, Reginald Spink, Sir Peter Wilkinson and the Hon. C. M. Woodhouse.

I am also very grateful for help given in various ways by Lord Allerton, J. C. Andrews, Jean-Bernard Badaire, Georges Bégué, Micheline Borochovich, Richard Broome, Sir Olaf Caroe, Humbert Clair, Frazer Crawford, Hugh Crosland, Lady Dean, Christopher Elliott, Robert Gabion, Maurice Gourdin, Joseph Gambier, Mary Holdsworth, Baroness Hornsby-Smith, D. T. Hudson, Peggy Jones, Andrew Kennedy, Peter Lake, Alastair Macdonald, Charles MacIntosh, Leonard Manderstam, Alun Morgan, Gordon Nornable, Colonel J. D. Parker, Colonel Jean Pochard, Robert Poirson, Anne Pollak, Arthur Radley, Michael Reynolds, S. L. Roberts, T. H. Shufflebotham, David Smiley, Faith Spencer Chapman, J. A. True-love, Peggy Venner, Lois Watson and Rosen Yaakov.

I am most grateful too to Olive Walker for her expert typing.

Photographs are reproduced by kind permission of the BBC *Radio Times* Hulton Picture Library (nos 6, 8, 22 and 23) and the following individuals: Maurice Buckmaster (no. 14); Faith Spencer Chapman (no. 11); John Davis (no. 24); Lady Dean (no. 17); Henrietta Gregorius (no. 7); G. A. Holdsworth (no. 5); Mary Holdsworth (no. 15); The Rt. Hon. Baroness Hornsby-Smith (no. 20); Peter Kemp (no. 21); Andrew Kennedy (nos 2 and 3); Michael Lis (no. 16); Marjorie, Lady Marling (no. 10); David Smiley (no. 25); Sir Peter Wilkinson (nos 18 and 19); The Hon. C. M. Woodhouse (nos 1, 4, 9 and 13).

Chapter I

Founder Members

On a dark December morning in 1941 I reported as instructed to the offices of the Inter-Services Research Bureau at Norgeby House in Baker Street in London. My acceptance into this organization had followed an interview in a room off the Horse Guards' Parade, where I had been confronted by Major Peter Wilkinson, whom I had last seen when we had been boys together in Rugby School. Now an officer in the Royal Fusiliers he revealed in his shoes and his Sam Browne belt that peculiar shine which habitually indicates the regular soldier.

Wilkinson was evidently well informed about my recent activities. For the last ten months before war broke out in September 1939 I had acted as editor of a quarterly magazine of high academic standards known as *Baltic and Scandinavian Countries* and published, somewhat improbably, in Gdynia in Poland. My predecessor in this post had been Denis Hills, who was later to achieve considerable distinction as a writer and, more spectacularly, through being incarcerated by President Amin of Uganda.

When it had become clear beyond all further doubt that German troops were about to invade Poland I had received a summons to the British Vice-Consul, who was named Ronald Hazell. I found him a short, rather dapper man, correct, almost formal, in manner and wearing a black jacket and striped trousers. He was also the representative in Poland of the United Baltic Corporation, in whose ships I had travelled between England and Poland.

Hazell informed me that I must leave Poland and that he had arranged a passage for me in the SS *Batory*, which would be leaving Gdynia for Copenhagen the next day. When I asked him what he proposed to do he told me that he had diplomatic immunity. I swallowed this without question.

My interview with Peter Wilkinson was a short one. So far as I can recall he asked only two questions. One was how well I spoke Polish. To this I replied as truthfully as I could. Polish is a difficult language for western Europeans to master. To those who have tried it comes as no surprise that it was a Pole who invented Esperanto. However in ten months I had naturally acquired a certain competence. The other question was whether I was willing to jump out of an aircraft. In the circumstances I felt I could give only one answer, though I was later to learn that there were men, much braver than I am, who were not prepared to give any such assurance at a first interview.

At one stage my interview was interrupted by a telephone conversation in which Wilkinson appeared to be addressing the man at the other end of the line as 'Alf cock'. Whoever 'Alf cock' may have been, he was evidently in urgent need of some military stores, and Wilkinson disposed of the problem by saying: 'Get them at Lillywhite's and put them down to my account.' As one who had been long enough in the Army to know something of the normal system of indenting I found this a refreshing way of dealing with supply problems. An organization which operated in this manner was, I felt already, one in which I would wish to serve.

One of the first people I encountered after arriving in Norgeby House was Ronald Hazell, who had an office two doors away from the one in which I was to work. He was now dressed in the uniform of a major in the British Army. Understandably I began to wonder what had lain behind the shipping and consular activities I had witnessed in Gdynia.

My own office I shared with a dark-haired girl named Althea Trevor and with Marjorie Stewart, who was already an actress of some distinction. She had a rather deep voice and an evidently warm and sympathetic nature and even in her twenties would have been described more readily as a beautiful woman than as a pretty girl. Her conversation tended to be studded with references to a bewildering number of brothers and sisters, with whose identity one was somehow expected to be familiar. Theatrical habits persisted with her at least to the extent that she found it necessary, even in wartime London, to come to work by taxi.

One inner office leading off ours was occupied by Peter Wilkinson. A second was shared by two curiously contrasting figures. Frank Keary, who was one of them, was a rather frail-looking man who wore civilian clothes and evidently spoke excellent Czech. The other now revealed to me the identity of 'Alf cock'. This was Captain Alfgar Hesketh-Prichard, a tall young man with a broken nose which he had acquired as an amateur steeplechase rider, a sallow complexion, restless movements and a frequently conspiratorial air. He also had very striking eyes. Air Chief Marshal Sir Philip Joubert de la Ferté, the Commander-in-Chief of Coastal Command, with whom, I was soon to discover, Hesketh-Prichard tended to deal directly, described him as 'the man with the pleading eyes'. Much of the pleading seemed to me to be directed towards Marjorie Stewart.

Along the corridor, in an office next to Hazell's, there was an enormous man named Harold Perkins, who had been both a master mariner and a factory-owner in Poland. He spoke execrable but confident Polish. The evident warmth of his personality was transmitted by an exceptionally engaging smile which somehow shone through exceptionally discoloured teeth.

Others to whom I was introduced included a tall, bald master-printer with a deep bass voice named Jack Ince, who had been recruited in order to occupy himself largely with forgery, and a girl with china-blue eyes and a gentle, almost demure, manner named Vera Long, who was, it transpired, nearly a founder member of the organization to which I had now been admitted.

The organization was the Special Operations Executive, although the name at that time was seldom used much below ministerial or permanent-secretary level, a variety of cover-names being adopted instead. The particular group which I had joined formed the Polish and Czechoslovak sections, both of which were under the control of Peter Wilkinson.

Before I was allowed to begin work I had to undergo one more interview. This was with a brigadier, a shortish, dark man with clipped speech, clipped moustache and brisk movements. I already knew enough of the Army to recognize these as some of the hallmarks of the regular officer. I did not at that stage know enough to appreciate that behind the conventional façade there were sometimes to be found men with a rich capacity for inventive and original thought and consummate powers of leadership. One such was the brigadier who now interviewed me. He was Colin McVean Gubbins, the value of whose contribution to the achievements of the Special Operations Executive it would be difficult to overestimate.

The Special Operations Executive, or SOE as it came to be generally called, may be said to have come formally into being on 16 July 1940, when the control of a committee 'to co-ordinate all action by way of subversion and sabotage against the enemy overseas' was entrusted to the Minister of Economic Warfare, Dr Hugh Dalton. Winston Churchill defined the purpose more succinctly when he instructed Dalton to 'set Europe ablaze'. As a consequence organized resistance in territories occupied by the Axis powers was to be created, directed and supplied from outside in a manner unprecedented in any major war in history, for to sabotage and subversion was soon to be added the conduct of guerrilla warfare.

Although SOE was not formally established until the war had lasted more than ten months and after all British regular forces, apart from those stationed in Gibraltar, had been expelled from the continent of Europe, its origins may be traced to the period before the Second World War, and its roots were various. One of the more intangible of its roots was a literary tradition which fostered and expressed the desire of an appreciable number of British people to engage in a particular kind of clandestine activity and to belong to a particular kind of élite brotherhood.

When Rudyard Kipling's Kim was subjected to initiative tests by Lurgan Sahib, trained to give a detailed account of everything he had seen in a day and instructed in the use of disguises, he was also told that 'from time to time God causes men to be born – and thou art one of them – who have a lust to go abroad at the risk of their lives'. Kim, in short, was being initiated into 'the Great Game that never ceases day and night, throughout India'.

In *The Seven Pillars of Wisdom* T. E. Lawrence described the force he had helped to create as a self-centred army without parade or gesture, devoted to freedom. He also wrote of his British associates in Egypt, Clayton, Storrs, Sykes and the others, that they were 'intrusives', who wanted to 'break into the accepted halls of English foreign policy'.

Kim was the creation of a great literary artist. So arguably was the public figure known as T. E. Lawrence. But there were plenty of lesser figures in English fiction in the 1920s and 1930s who carried on their tradition. John Buchan's Sandy Arbuthnot, who hobnobbed with Albanian bandits and was the first white man to ride through the Yemen, could be regarded as the perfect prototype of an SOE officer. Indeed Richard Usborne, who wrote a scintillating study of the heroes of Buchan, Sapper and Dornford Yates and who himself served for a number of years in SOE, stated that almost every officer he met in the organization pictured himself, just as he did, as either Richard Hannay or Sandy Arbuthnot.

There were also social factors, some of them peculiar to Britain, which helped to shape much of the human material on which SOE was to draw. In the 1930s, as in earlier decades, the public schools, with their adherence to the prefect system and to the concept of the survival of the fittest, continued to turn out men who would think it natural that, while still in their twenties, they should be given almost total responsibility over areas of colonial territory the size of several

English counties. The habits of mind and conduct inculcated by these schools, particularly the more rugged ones, much of whose curriculum was a kind of prolonged assault course, were to help a number of SOE officers not only to survive, but to act in quasi-ambassadorial, quasi-military capacities over large areas in which guerrilla warfare was being waged.

Nor was it fortuitous that the nation which gave birth to the Scout movement also created SOE. Baden-Powell was a highly eccentric general who delighted in disguises and had a habit, when on leave, of engaging in private espionage missions. It was his unorthodoxy as a soldier which caused him to formulate various disciplines, including fieldcraft, which were intended for Scouts in peacetime but which were also to form an important part of the para-military training in the SOE schools. The choice as director of SOE training of Colonel J. S. (Jack) Wilson, Director of the Boy Scouts International Bureau from 1924 to 1939 and formerly of the Indian police, was an inspired one. Wilson was later in charge of SOE's Scandinavian sections. While filling both posts with distinction he continued to concern himself with the international Scout movement and to feel a direct responsibility for Scouts in allied, neutral and enemy countries.

Although the British had no experience of fighting against an occupying power in their own country, their armed services and police forces had already by 1940 a long history of dealing with resistance in various forms, including guerrilla warfare. It has been estimated that in the reign of Queen Victoria the British Army was engaged in no fewer than eighty-two campaigns, most of them against irregular troops. In the major war at the end of the Queen's reign the British commanders in South Africa repeatedly had the bewildering experience of not themselves being able to choose the sites of battles. In the First World War the German commander in East Africa, Lettow-Vorbeck, with a tiny force and a perpetual shortage of ammunition, harassed and tied down troops under British command which were vastly superior to his in numbers and did not surrender until after the armistice had been declared in November 1918. In Ireland the British encountered a masterly resistance leader in Michael Collins, who was capable of such a coup as the seizing of all the secret files of the Special Branch in Dublin. The exercise of the mandate in Palestine gave further evidence of how vulnerable occupation troops can be.

It might therefore have been expected that leading British military strategists and Staff College instructors in the 1930s would have been seriously concerned with some of the problems which SOE would eventually have to face. In fact they were not. Some insight into orthodox military thinking may be gained from the fact that the War Office did not even think it necessary to produce a manual on the lessons to be learnt from the South African war.

Nevertheless there were a few Army officers of relatively lowly rank who chose to depart from the prevailing orthodoxy and give serious thought to the problems of irregular warfare. One of these was Major J. C. F. (Joe) Holland of the Royal Engineers, who in 1938 was posted to a small branch of the War Office known as GS(R), the R standing for 'research'. Later it was to be renamed MI(R). The research to which Holland devoted his energies was into the practice of guerrilla warfare. In this task he was soon joined by Major Colin Gubbins.

Colin Gubbins was a Scotsman, his mother's family, the McVeans, being Highlanders, a lineage of which he was extremely proud. He was commissioned in the Royal Artillery in 1914. He fought with distinction on the Western Front, being awarded the MC. He served under General Ironside in Russia when attached to General Denikin's forces and later, like Holland, in Ireland.

GS(R) when Gubbins joined it was a tiny and obscure section. Among its early members was Joan Bright, later Joan Astley, who in the 1970s was to be accorded the distinction of being appointed Gubbins's biographer. Joan Bright recognized Holland as the driving force of their organization and described him as a man with an independent mind, an acute brain and 'a loving and poetic heart'. Of Gubbins when she first met him she wrote that he was quiet-spoken, energetic and charming, with 'just enough of the buccaneer' in him to make lesser men underrate his gifts, particularly that of leadership.

Many people have commented on Gubbins's zest for living. Hugh Dalton recorded that he enjoyed life to the full, never forgot a face or a name, and had a gift for inspiring confidence in those who worked under him. Kim Philby, the Soviet intelligence officer, who served for a time in SOE as an instructor in propaganda before joining the Secret Intelligence Service, where he did his serious damage, had a warm admiration for Gubbins, a compliment he did not extend to many of his colleagues in SIS. The air of Gubbins's office, he wrote, crackled with energy and his speech was both 'friendly and mercifully brief'. He added that it was rumoured that Gubbins could only find time for his girl-friends at breakfast, yet was man enough to keep them. John Goldsmith, the racehorse trainer, who was parachuted by SOE into France, recalled entering a FANY mess with Gubbins at eleven o'clock in the evening for a proposed ten-minute visit and finding him doing handstands in the same place at five o'clock the next morning.

While serving in MI(R) Gubbins made a reconnaissance of Germany's eastern frontiers. He also visited an Anglophile ship-owner in Yugoslavia to discuss the possibility of filling barges with explosives so that, in the event of war, they could be blown up in the narrows of the Iron Gates on the Danube, the object being to impair the flow of Roumanian oil to Germany. But much of his time was devoted to writing, under Holland's general guidance and in collaboration with one of two other officers, a series of pamphlets setting out the principles of guerrilla warfare and sabotage. These were later to be translated into a number of languages and dropped from the air into enemy-occupied countries. If distributed today they would probably be described as terrorists' handbooks.

The pamphlets for which Gubbins was largely responsible offended against many of the principles of chivalry in warfare as well as the tradition of dogged determination embodied in the concept of the thin red line. Guerrillas were instructed not to undertake an operation unless certain of success, to ensure that a good line of retreat was always available, and never to engage in a pitched battle unless in overwhelming strength. They were advised to use women and children as couriers because they were less likely to be stopped and searched. Among targets recommended were cinemas in which occupation troops were being entertained, as they would be highly inflammable. Instructions were given in the use of the various explosives then available – ammonal, gelignite and dynamite – with detailed calculations of the quantities required to destroy railways, bridges and buildings. Informers in the service of the enemy must, it was pointed out firmly, be killed promptly and, if possible, a note was to be pinned to the body explaining the reasons for death.

The pamphlets also contained observations on the personal qualities required in guerrilla leaders, the part which regular officers could play and the support of guerrilla forces from outside. 'In guerrilla warfare', it was stated, 'it is the personality of the leader that counts', for the leader would have to make decisions on his own responsibility and lead his men in each enterprise. Regular officers would, it was thought, be needed as a leaven and to carry out staff duties when guerrilla movements spread, but such officers must 'clear their minds of all pre-conceived ideas regarding military procedure'.

Gubbins also gave much thought to the role to be played by a nation which supported resistance from outside. Such a nation would want to have its own mission at the headquarters of a guerilla movment, and the officers forming such a mission must, he wrote, have a knowledge of the ethnological, political and religious groupings of the country to which they were sent, of its history and aspirations, its heroes of the present and its martyrs of the past. In addition to studying language and topography they must be prepared 'at the risk of future regrets and disillusion' to identify themselves with the people they came to serve. It was in this mould that some of the best of SOE's liaison officers with guerrilla forces were to be shaped.

Finally the pamphlets made a plea for preparations for supporting guerrilla movements to be made before, and not after, war had broken out. In at least partial recognition MI(R) was allowed discreetly to train a few carefully selected individuals: regular officers, mountaineers, explorers, linguists. Among those to receive such early training were Peter Wilkinson; Douglas Dodds-Parker, who was later to hold ministerial office in a Conservative administration; and the son of Axel Munthe, author of *The Story of San Michele*. This was Malcolm Munthe who was later to be involved with resistance in both Scandinavia and Italy.

The British secret service in its modern form was largely the creation of the sixteenth-century statesman Sir Francis Walsingham. When the Second World War broke out it enjoyed a high reputation internationally, though, contrary to popular belief both at home and abroad, it was not staffed predominantly by men of independent means with a taste for adventure. It had, and has, a number of cover-names, but for purposes of clarity it may be conveniently referred to as SIS or Secret Intelligence Service.

SIS is under the control of the Foreign Office, an arrangement which serves as a safeguard, in theory at least, against the danger of secret servicemen operating a foreign policy of their own. Its task is the collection of intelligence, partly by espionage. Sabotage is not its concern, and it is often argued that, because of the alarm and counter-measures they give rise to, acts of sabotage actively hamper the smooth and secret gathering of intelligence.

The attitude of professional secret servicemen and members of the Foreign Office staff towards suggestions that there was a need, even in embryo form, for the kind of organization SOE was to become tended therefore to be one of caution, tinged, more or less heavily, with disapproval. Nevertheless a small section of SIS known as Section D was set up shortly before war broke out. For a time it operated on lines roughly parallel with those of MI(R). The distinction in theory between the two was that MI(R) had some concern with actions which could be publicly admitted. Section D had none. Before long the two organizations were merged, Section D having the controlling interest.

The first head of Section D, Major Lawrence Grand, was a regular soldier who, like Holland, had been commissioned in the Royal Engineers. Elegant and distinguished in appearance, he made a practice, even after war had broken out, of wearing civilian clothes, usually embellished by a red carnation and enhanced by a long cigarette-holder. Joan Bright called him 'a volatile dreamer'. Julian Amery, an early recruit to Section D, described him as a man gifted with unusual powers of persuading his superiors and enthusing his subordinates. He was certainly far-sighted and imaginative, and he suffered from the unwillingness of the British government to provide him with the funds needed for the projects he conceived. To help overcome this he persuaded the mining magnate Chester Beatty, with whom he was on friendly terms, to attach mining engineers and others to Section D while keeping them on his own payroll.

Grand's unorthodoxy gave Section D much of its early impetus, but his methods were not always acceptable to his superiors. Like Holland he was to revert to normal Army duties at a fairly early stage in the war, both subsequently rising to the rank of major-general.

The second most important figure in Section D's early days was an Australian named George Taylor. Bickham Sweet-Escott, another early recruit to Section D, who was later to become one of SOE's abler staff officers, described him as 'brilliant but ruthless' and regarded him as a major influence in shaping both the theory and practice of SOE. Dalton described Taylor as 'belligerent, persistent and ingenious'.

A number of people have paid tribute to Taylor's intellectual powers. These were needed, for to formulate the strategy and tactics of an organization which had so few precedents to draw on required penetrative minds as well as the kind of imagination Grand offered. As an immediate measure much had to be done to make good the shortcomings of untrained novices, of which in Section D's formative days there was plenty of evidence.

On one occasion a telephone call from a police officer was received in Section D's offices in the St Ermin's Hotel in Caxton Street. The officer said he had a man in custody who had been proclaiming publicly that he was going to blow up the Roumanian oil wells. The man had given the police Section D's telephone number. In fact Section D did have plans for destroying the oil wells in the event of a German invasion; the man was on its payroll; and very little could be done about his indiscretions because no one had remembered to make him sign the forms required by the provisions of the Official Secrets Act.

There was a courier who, on being sent abroad by Section D, decided he must bear as strong a likeness as possible to Sherlock Holmes. There was another courier whose instructions were to go to a certain hotel in a Balkan capital, order scrambled eggs and hot chocolate for breakfast and read the London *Times*. The first recognition signal would come when the agent he was to meet would ask if he could borrow the *Times*. The courier duly went to the hotel, ordered scrambled eggs and hot chocolate and waited. Nothing happened. He ordered more scrambled eggs and hot chocolate and continued to wait. Just as he had placed a third order an infuriated agent came up to him and hissed: '*You're* supposed to be reading the *Times*.'

This sort of thing had to be worked out of the system, and with commendable speed much of it was. Section D could also claim a number of positive exploits before it was merged into SOE, the best of them being defensive in kind. Louis Frank, a Belgian banker with a scintillating mind, prevented a large quantity of Belgian gold from falling into German hands after Belgium had been invaded. Tommy Davies, a director of Courtauld's and an early recruit to MI(R), went over to Calais shortly before the Germans arrived there and removed several hundred thousand pounds' worth of platinum from Courtauld's factory.

After the German invasion of the Netherlands in May 1940 plans which had been prepared for extracting the bulk of the industrial diamonds held in Amsterdam had to be put into effect hurriedly because of the speed of the German advance. A Dutch-speaking officer of Section D, Major E. R. Chidson, was in charge of the operational party. He was assisted by two civilian diamond merchants, one Dutch and one English. Such was the importance attached to their mission that a destroyer, HMS *Walpole*, was made available to transport them to and from the Dutch coast.

Ymuiden, where they disembarked, was being bombed by German aircraft and traffic was in a state of general confusion. They therefore commandeered a car driven by a pretty girl, relying on the instinct of the Dutch member of the operational party, Jan Smit, that they could trust her. The girl was Jewish and had just brought her family to the coast in the hope that they would be able to escape. She agreed to remain with them while they carried out their mission in Amsterdam and bring them back that evening to Ymuiden.

In Amsterdam they visited the offices of J. K. Smit & Zonen, whose head, Jan Smit's father, had already sent most of his industrial diamonds to Britain. He agreed to try to persuade the other leading merchants to follow his example. But it took time to contact them on a day which, as it happened, was a public holiday, and the decisions they faced were not easy ones. Was it wise to place their entire stock on board a British vessel which might well be sunk by the Luftwaffe? Could they not be sent to Paris or retained and used as bargaining counters? After some debate nearly all the merchants agreed to hand over their whole stock to the British operational party. They did not even ask for receipts.

Meanwhile the girl driver, who worked in a branch of the Dutch War Office, had visited her colonel and obtained the passes which would now be needed at road-blocks on the road to Ymuiden. The colonel also sent a small detachment of troops to guard Chidson's party discreetly while they remained in Amsterdam.

When the party reached Ymuiden again they found that the boatman who had agreed to ferry them to HMS *Walpole* had been killed in the bombardment. They therefore commandeered a tug; a revolver was placed in the tugmaster's back; and the rendezvous with the destroyer was kept, the canvas bag containing the diamonds being got aboard with some difficulty because of the swell. The destroyer reached Harwich without further incident.

At home progress was made at the research establishments with the development of plastic explosive (PE) – a much more suitable material for sabotage than the explosives listed in Gubbins's pamphlets – time fuses, limpet mines and weapons which were small and easily portable.

Perhaps most important of all, in spite of a few unfortunate early choices, Section D had formed a nucleus around which people of the calibre SOE was to need could be assembled. Recruiting for Section D was on what is sometimes called the 'old boy network'. There was no other acceptable method. Secrecy had to be preserved, and it would have been disastrous if SOE had applied to other branches of the services for staff, thereby affording them the chance to offload, in accordance with established practice, those officers whom they could most readily spare.

The senior ranks of Courtauld's provided one valuable source of manpower for Section D, Hambros Bank another, the legal firm of Slaughter and May a third. These were the men of whom Philby wrote that 'they brought with them a style of strained improvization as they left their tidy offices in the City and the Temple to spread disorder and financial chaos throughout Europe, gamekeepers turned poachers'. They had a leavening of regular soldiers and some sailors. There were scarcely any airmen. This was to have unfortunate consequences.

During his years in the political wilderness in the 1930s Winston Churchill, as is well known, developed a kind of private intelligence service whose main task was to keep him informed of German military strength and intentions. Much of the information received was channelled through an industrial intelligence centre, which was the creation of Major Desmond Morton, a personal aide of Churchill's. Among the recommendations which this body made was the establishment, when war came, of a Ministry of Economic Warfare. Those who communicated with the centre included Charles Hambro, then the youngest man ever to have been appointed a director of the Bank of England and himself a future head of SOE, and George Courtauld. Another informant was a Canadian, William Stephenson, who by the time he was thirty had already made himself a dollar millionaire.

Stephenson had volunteered for the Royal Flying Corps in the First World War. He won the DFC and the MC, crashed behind the German lines, was wounded and captured, and escaped. He had a considerable talent for abstract mathematics and became amateur light-weight boxing champion of Britain.

In the years immediately after the First World War Stephenson, who decided to settle in Britain and became a test pilot, made a study in his spare time of the possible applications of radio and even television. An invention of his made possible the first publication in a newspaper of a photograph transmitted by radio. This appeared in the *Daily Mail* in December 1922. With a small amount of capital Stephenson acquired interests in two radio companies. Before long he owned the largest film and recording studios outside Hollywood, and he extended his interests to steel and cement. It was through one of his companies, Pressed Steel, which made 90 per cent of the car bodies for the leading British motor-car manufacturers, that he obtained a detailed knowledge of just how much of Germany's steel production was being used for weapons of war. This he communicated to Churchill.

In the winter of 1939–40 Stephenson went to Sweden and drew up a plan for the destruction, with the help of certain pro-British Swedes, of cranes and harbour installations at Oxeloesund in order to prevent the transport of iron ore to Germany. King Gustav of Sweden became aware of the project and made a direct appeal to King George VI. When Lord Halifax, who was then Foreign Secretary, learnt, evidently for the first time, what was intended, he promptly exercised his power of veto.

In Churchill's judgment Stephenson was a man who could be entrusted with the gravest responsibilities, and in 1940 he sent him to the United States as a kind of personal emissary to President Roosevelt with the specific task of establishing a base from which clandestine warfare could continue to be conducted if Britain were overrun.

Stephenson was a small man physically who conveyed to those who met him a feeling of drive and authority. He had a capacity for going straight to the heart of any problem and an inclination to go straight to the top of any organization with which he had to deal. With the President of the United States he soon established a *rapport*, and he realized that his most important immediate task was to convince the President that the British had both the will and the capacity to continue fighting. The United States Ambassadors in Paris and London, William Bullitt and Joseph Kennedy, had been sending persistently disparaging reports about Britain's prospects, Kennedy doing so with undisguised glee.

In 1916 Stephenson had met William J. Donovan, a much-decorated American soldier, who later became a Wall Street lawyer and also a millionaire. They formed a close friendship, and in 1940 Stephenson suggested to Roosevelt that if he wanted a first-hand appraisal of how the war in Europe was likely to develop he might be well advised to send Donovan on a special mission. Roosevelt agreed. On 15 July 1940, the day before SOE came formally into being, Stephenson sent a signal to London announcing that Donovan was coming and that the purpose of his mission was not being disclosed to the United States Embassy.

Donovan paid more than one exploratory visit to Europe, and in March 1941 he was shown what was happening in the SOE training schools. He declared himself considerably impressed. Not only did the United States forces have nothing comparable, but the training methods employed and the people being trained provided indisputable evidence of an intention to hit back aggressively on the continent of Europe.

When President Roosevelt decided that new machinery must be created in the United States for the collection of secret intelligence and the conduct of clandestine warfare he again sought Stephenson's advice. Again Stephenson suggested Donovan as the right man to head the new organization, and again Roosevelt agreed.

The new organization became known as the Office of Strategic

Services (OSS) and was to be the forerunner of the future Central Intelligence Agency. Ray S. Cline, historian and future Deputy Director of the CIA, was to write of OSS that 'it might never have come into being if it had not been urged upon the United States by the British and fashioned after the British intelligence system'. This he described as a classic example of the best kind of covert action. Donovan himself, whose commanding personality was to dominate OSS throughout the rest of the war, was generous enough to admit that most of his instruction in secret service work came from Stephenson.

Stephenson's role in the United States was an unusual one in a number of respects. Nominally he was head of British Security Co-ordination, whose ostensible task was the protection of British shipping and of cargoes of war material being sent to Britain. In practice he was the chief representative of SIS, SOE and other secret organizations, for which duties he accepted no salary throughout the war.

This partial integration of secret services was not part of the usual British pattern. A similar arrangement was made when a mission was sent to the Soviet Union after the German invasion of that country, but there any similarity between the two missions ended. If, as seems unlikely, the mission to the Soviet Union under George Hill did achieve – or, to be fair, could have achieved – anything of value, the evidence remains hidden in the secret files. The mission which Stephenson, operating under the code-name 'Intrepid', continued to lead in the United States was to achieve a great deal.

There were two other important roots from which SOE was to grow. One was the result of the decision to send a British military mission to Poland shortly before war broke out. The head of the mission, Major-General Adrian Carton de Wiart, who was of Belgian origin, was the holder of the VC. He had lost a hand and an eye, he was described by Churchill as 'a model of chivalry and honour', and when he received an honorary degree at Oxford University it was said of him that he had fought in more campaigns than others had even read about.

After the First World War, which he admitted to having enjoyed in spite of spending most of it on the Western Front, he had led a military mission to the Polish armies which were fighting against advancing Soviet forces and had formed a close friendship with their commander, Józef Piłsudski. He had then become the unpaying tenant of a half-million-acre estate on the Prypet Marshes belonging to Prince Charles Radziwill where he became, as he put it, 'very out of touch with world affairs'.

The members of his mission who came out to Poland to join Carton de Wiart in the late summer of 1939 included Colin Gubbins as GSO(I) and, as a staff captain, Peter Wilkinson. Others joined the mission locally. One who did so was Harold Perkins, whom Carton de Wiart chose to accompany him on most of his tours of duty and whom he described as 'a very good officer'. Another was Ronald Hazell, who had set out to join the mission immediately after despatching me to Copenhagen. Another was a small man with a barely audible voice who pointed out that he was a British subject in spite of his name, which was Richard Truszkowski, and who volunteered his services as a driver. He was in fact an exceptionally brilliant bio-chemist, who was to become a member of SOE's Polish section and subsequently a professor in a New Zealand university.

SIS already had valuable links with Polish intelligence. Through these it had been able to receive and transport to Britain a machine of the kind known as Enigma, which Polish experts had built after the skilful abstraction of the parts of an actual model made for the Germans. This machine played a major part in the process whereby the British were able to read all the German top-grade ciphers for the greater part of the war.

In the field of conventional warfare by contrast there was little the members of the mission could achieve. They were all too aware of the inadequacy of Marshal Śmigły-Rydź's strategic plans. Heroics before reason, Carton de Wiart called them. They could have had no doubts about the effectiveness of the German war machine, and it was not long before they were forced to escape, with some difficulty, into Roumania. Yet even in the short time available Gubbins and Wilkinson were able to form some links which would be of lasting value.

Poland had a long tradition of underground struggle against occupying powers, extending into the twentieth century. Drawing on the experience of the past therefore the Polish government, before going into exile in 1939, made provision for the organization of a resistance movement within Poland. Major-General Michał Tokarzewski, who was to be arrested the next year, not by the Germans but by the Russians, was appointed the first commander, and he quickly enrolled 200 officers to serve as the nucleus of a national resistance force. An underground political committee was also formed, at first only with members of the peasant and socialist parties, but later embracing all parties which enjoyed widespread support among the Polish people. Regular liaison was maintained by courier between the underground movement and the Polish government in France, and in 1940 a conference was held in Belgrade between underground and government representatives.

By maintaining contact with the Polish leaders in France who were concerned with the resistance movement Gubbins and Wilkinson laid the foundations for the future co-operation between SOE and the Polish Home Army. The lesson had also been learnt that what had been started in Poland could be attempted elsewhere, although for success to be achieved the help of SOE would, in most places, be needed. As Gubbins expressed it in a lecture he gave in 1948 to the Royal United Service Institute, in occupied Europe in 1940 'only the Poles, toughened by centuries of oppression, were spiritually uncrushed'.

Gubbins was to serve under Carton de Wiart once more. This was in the Norwegian campaign in 1940, when he was given command of the so-called 'independent companies'. These units, which had been trained to fight and maintain themselves independently of the main body of the Army, were another brainchild of MI(R). They were later, following the Boer example, to be called Commandos. In Norway, in a campaign which did little to enhance British military prestige or British prospects of being able to overcome German land forces, the independent companies fought with distinction. The part which Gubbins personally played was recognized by the award of the DSO.

After the military disasters in Norway and France General Andrew Thorne, a far-sighted corps commander stationed in the south-east of England, persuaded the War Office that in the event of a German invasion some effective provision must be made for harassing the enemy behind his lines. As a result an organization was brought into being which gave Britain, for the first time in her history, the nucleus of an underground resistance movement.

Gubbins, instead of being allowed to remain with the Commandos, was given the task of creating the new body, in which capacity he was directly responsible to Ironside as Commander-in-Chief, Home Forces. The principal officers were chosen by Gubbins himself, Wilkinson acting as his chief staff officer. Civilians, who were later given Home Guard uniforms, were recruited from poachers, game-keepers, ghillies, fishermen and coal-miners. In order to attract as little attention as possible the new organization was given the unromantic name of 'auxiliary units'.

Gubbins's gravest problem was that of arming the new units, as he was told no weapons or equipment could be made available from normal Army stocks. He therefore approached his former associate in Section D, Lawrence Grand, and was pleasantly surprised to discover how many anti-tank mines, Molotov cocktails and explosives could be made available from Section D's research establishments. The auxiliary units did therefore have a number of weapons with which the great bulk of the regular soldiery were still wholly unfamiliar.

The auxiliary units were happily never required to go into action, but the training they received, partly from the Lovat Scouts, in fieldcraft generally and in stalking and silent killing in particular, was to benefit and indeed save the lives of a number of them, particularly those who were to serve in SOE or the Commandos.

The area commanders whom Gubbins chose and who were to continue to serve under him in SOE included several men who had already achieved distinction in civilian life: Andrew Croft as explorer, Peter Fleming as writer and traveller, both of them early MI(R) recruits, and Anthony Quayle as actor.

In deciding to place SOE under the control of the Minister of Economic Warfare Churchill was no doubt influenced by the thinking of his pre-war industrial intelligence centre. He was also influenced by the personality of the minister. Hugh Dalton was a man of exceptionally combative nature. He had a large frame, a first-class mind, a booming voice, almost limitless energy and a virtual inability to conceive that in any circumstances he could be wrong. Although these qualities did not endear him to the senior officials of such long established departments as the Treasury and the Foreign Office, with whom he gleefully entered into confrontation whenever the opportunity arose, they were not amiss in the unique new post to which Churchill appointed him. He was also formidably hideous, Storm Jameson in a memorable passage of English prose likening his appearance to that of a Chinese executioner.

In pre-war years, while principal Labour opposition spokesman on foreign affairs, Dalton had persistently opposed his party's traditional practice of voting against the service estimates, describing it as a 'narrow-minded and nonsensical negation'. On taking over the Ministry of Economic Warfare he had made a practice, as he put it, of giving less power within the ministry to the fearful and more to the bold. He certainly had no doubt that his was the right ministry and he was the right man to control SOE. When a proposal was put forward for War Office control he pointedly asked the Director of Military Intelligence whether he really thought subversive activities could be directed by disciplined soldiers such as himself.

In his immediate entourage as the minister responsible for SOE Dalton had a future Prime Minister, Hugh Gaitskell, whom he had appointed to act rather as a French *chef de cabinet*, and a future Ambassador in Paris, Gladwyn Jebb, who provided the principal regular link between SOE and the Foreign Office. The choice of the first head of SOE seems to have been suggested by SIS. This was Sir Frank Nelson, who had had wide commercial interests in India, had been a backbench Conservative Member of Parliament and had performed consular duties in Switzerland. He was nearing sixty when appointed. He worked prodigiously long hours, but the qualities required of the controller of a secret intelligence service, of which anonymity is one, were not altogether those needed for such a combative service as SOE.

Dalton had met Gubbins in November 1939, when he had sat next to him at a dinner party given by the Polish Ambassador, Count Edward Raczyński. He was much impressed by what Gubbins told him about Poland and Czechoslovakia and went so far as to describe him as 'a most intelligent British soldier'. Thoughout 1940 Gubbins's services were much in demand, but once the threat of a German invasion had receded Dalton secured his appointment as SOE's director of operations and training. With this the framework on which SOE was to be built might be said to have been completed.

Those who were in office during the first two or three months of SOE's existence tended, because of the method of recruiting, to be socially fairly homogeneous. The social range was soon to widen greatly as more and more specialists were needed. When Harry Ree, a schoolmaster of pacifist convictions, underwent training for his mission as an SOE agent in occupied France those who took part in courses with him included a Canadian academic, a Cook's courier, a small businessman, an unsuccessful artist, a deb, a nurse and a rep from Coty's. That the talents of such diverse beings were eventually used as they were was due, in the first instance, to the qualities of foresight, imagination and vigour which the founder members of SOE possessed, as those of us who joined them later were to discover, in an unusually high concentration.

Chapter 2

Early Exploits

The impression I had rapidly formed that the Polish and Czechoslovak sections of SOE contained a number of individuals of exceptional calibre was strengthened in the weeks which followed my initiation. A few new recruits were drawn in shortly after I was, two of them being friends of Alfgar Hesketh-Prichard. One of these, Squadron-Leader Lord Allerton, a tall, blond man, prematurely a little bald, had an abundance of easy charm, though the reason for his presence was not apparent to me until I had learnt a little more of the complexity of Hesketh-Prichard's mind. The other was Gavin Maxwell, later to achieve fame as a writer as well as becoming a successful portrait painter. In SOE he was to be employed, very properly, in training others in fieldcraft.

Gavin Maxwell was a witty *raconteur* who adopted a manner suggesting a caricature of a Guards officer. In his autobiographical work, *The House of Elrig*, he described vividly his somewhat unusual childhood. The families of both his parents were aristocrats, his mother being a daughter of the Duke of Northumberland. Both families belonged to an esoteric sect known as the Catholic Apostolic or Irvingite Church. In their home in Galloway the young Maxwells rarely met any other children and, except among themselves, became, as he put it, 'as shy as wild animals'. He himself, as a result of an up-bringing which made him rather better equipped to understand and enjoy the company of otters and other wild creatures than that of his fellow humans, came to acquire what he called 'verbal armour'. Years later I was to read Kathleen Raine's anguished memoir of Gavin Maxwell, and only then did I learn that he had, or at least proclaimed he had, homosexual inclinations. For my part I found him a prickly character, but I probably lacked the capacity to establish a *rapport* with a rare spirit.

Another newcomer was appointed my secretary. This was an exceptionally pretty girl with a peaches-and-cream complexion and a tinkling voice named Patricia Jackson. She quickly decided, on her own initiative, that a necessary part of her duties was to darn my socks. This was very helpful. She later became British Ambassadress in Washington, having married Patrick Dean, one of the more influential members of the Foreign Office staff in the war and immediate post-war periods.

There was also an occasional visitor, a tall man with a sun-tanned complexion, a stammer and a generally distinguished appearance of the kind most readily described as soldierly. This was Major Gus March-Phillipps. It soon became apparent that his visits were mainly for the purpose of seeing Marjorie Stewart, and I began to feel my presence was something of an embarrassment to them. In this I was right.

The most ebullient member of the section was Harold Perkins, generally known as 'Perks', whose physical strength was such that Bickham Sweet-Escott recorded having actually seen him bend a poker in two with his bare hands. Perkins had run away to sea at the age of sixteen and gained his master's ticket when he was twenty-three. Wanting to marry and have a stable home, he decided that the best prospects for him during the slump at the end of the 1920s might be with a British engineering company in Czechoslovakia, with which he had family connections. For two years in Czechoslovakia he studied engineering and foundry and workshop practice. He then opened up a subsidiary company in Poland, eventually controlling the Benn-Bielsko factory in Upper Silesia, where industrial and management practices were introduced of a modernity little known in Poland at that time.

There were cleverer men in SOE than Perkins, but there were few who commanded the loyalty of their subordinates more spontaneously and persistently than he did. In his dealings with the Polish Sixth Bureau, a body more or less corresponding with SOE, and with the many Poles who were parachuted into Poland he was the exemplar of the liaison officer, who, Gubbins had prescribed, must identify himself with the people he served at the risk of future regrets.

One of these Polish parachutists, recalling his experiences later, described Perkins as 'our British guardian angel'. He went on to recount affectionately how Perkins used a stick, from which he would not be parted, as a conductor uses a baton and said: 'Tell the Polish people that here in England live their true friends, who will never desert Poland.'

No doubt Perkins meant what he said. He had neither the prescience nor the cynicism to foresee the magnitude of the disaster which was to overwhelm, and indeed be contrived for, a resistance movement which was the first to come into effective action against the

Germans and which remained perhaps the best disciplined and organized of any in the world.

Alfgar Hesketh-Prichard, whose lean body and restless nature contrasted stongly with Perkins's reassuring solidity, had also gravitated to Czechoslovakia and had also studied engineering.

As a boy Alfgar Hesketh-Prichard seems to have been inspired by the image of a father whom he barely knew. The father survived the First World War, in which he was awarded the DSO and the MC, only to linger on, a bedridden casualty, for another two years. His son was only four when he died. The father had been an exceptional shot and had founded the Army school of sniping. He had also played cricket for the Gentlemen against the Players. The family *ambience* was of the kind which caused Alfgar Hesketh-Prichard to be appointed a page of honour to King George V at the age of eleven.

At Stowe School Hesketh-Prichard suffered from a series of illnesses. For the rest of his life he was liable to be afflicted with violent stomach cramps and at the beginning of the Second World War was to be declared unfit for military service. Nevertheless by the time he went up to Cambridge in 1935 he had become an outstandingly good yachtsman and skier. He had also worked in two German factories, one of them belonging to the Caspari family. His contemporary, Fritz Caspari, an Oxford Rhodes scholar, was to have a distinguished record of refusing to compromise with the Nazi regime.

At Cambridge Hesketh-Prichard read mechanical sciences. He won first-class honours in the first part of the tripos. That he did not do so in the second may well have been attributable to illness, for his tutor wrote of him: 'I don't suppose there is a better mathematical brain of his age in England today.' He joined the University Air Squadron, took his duties seriously and became a skilled pilot.

In 1938 Hesketh-Prichard began work in Prague with the Sigmund engineering group, for whom he helped to establish a factory in England the next year. He was also in contact with the highly professional Czechoslovak intelligence service.

To his medical board's refusal to allow him to join the Army Hesketh-Prichard reacted in characteristic fashion by contriving to have himself appointed, as a civilian aged twenty-three, to teach guardsmen at Pirbright his father's methods of sniping. In time he was directed along the informal lines of communication which already existed to Peter Wilkinson and so to the Czechoslovak section of SOE. He was no longer considered medically unfit.

The Czechoslovak Second Bureau was organized according to the

French model. It had therefore no exact counterpart in Britain, but it corresponded more closely to SIS than to SOE. Its wartime head, Colonel (later General) Frantisek Moravec, with whom Hesketh-Prichard would have to deal, was a man of considerable achievement. When he was appointed head of a section of the Bureau he was told his country's intelligence service was probably the worst in the world. He soon transformed it into one of the best. He had an agent in the German Abwehr who was for years one of the most valuable of the Allies' high-grade sources of information. After the Munich agreement he successfully transferred, with the help of SIS, thirty agents and all his files to Britain, where he continued to work closely with SIS, for which he had a high regard. The military intelligence which Moravec's service provided during the war was of a consistently high order, not the least important of it coming from a painstaking study of local German newspapers carried out in a house in the Bayswater Road. Moravec never forgot the lesson he had learnt as a young intelligence officer when, after he had obtained through an agent a description of a German weapon, his superior officer had tossed him a German military magazine which described the weapon in equal detail, adding: 'The subscription is only twenty crowns a year.'

Czechoslovak co-operation with SOE was less smooth, largely because of the hold which the Germans had over the country and the consequences of such acts of resistance as did occur. The effect of the Munich agreement of 1938 and the German occupation the next year on most of the people of Czechoslovakia was stunning, and there was no stay-behind resistance organization of the kind set up in Poland. Sabotage did occur in the early years of the war, much of it of an undetectable kind, and caused the Germans real concern. After Reinhard Heydrich was appointed 'Protector' of Czech lands in September 1941 he even referred to an 'obviously large-scale resistance movement'. Yet production for the German armed forces continued in the Czech factories, and there was effective government, much of it provided by Czechs. Some three years after war broke out there were more than 350,000 Czech employees in the office of the Protector, with less than 750 Germans to supervise them.

Undetectable acts of sabotage are in some respects the most desirable of all. They give rise to far fewer reprisals than the more obvious kind, and it can happen that the forces of the occupying power find their weapons of war are faulty only when they go into battle.

There is however nothing spectacular in undetectable sabotage, and as head of the government in exile Dr Edvard Beneš was determined to give the world unmistakable evidence of effective Czechoslovak resistance. It was this consideration which led to the decision that Heydrich must be assassinated.

Two Czechs, Jozef Gabcik and Jan Kubiš, were chosen for the task from a number of volunteers. They went through SOE training schools and were dropped by parachute from an RAF aircraft in December 1941. Soon after their arrival in Czechoslovakia a signal was sent to London stating that an attempt on Heydrich's life would be of no use to the Allies and that the consequences for the Czechs would be immeasurable. Nevertheless Beneš confirmed the order that the assassination must take place. In May 1942 therefore Gabcik and Kubiš carried out their attack by sub-machine gun and grenade while Heydrich was being driven in an open car. He was not killed immediately but died in hospital a week later. Debris found in his car showed the grenade to have been of British manufacture.

Hitler immediately ordered massive arrests, and it is believed that 5,000 people, including the whole population of the village of Lidice, were killed as a direct reprisal for the assassination. Gabcik and Kubiš were betrayed by an informer, whose sole motive seems to have been financial greed, and although the Czech resistance movement was not destroyed it suffered a grave setback. There were certainly no prospects of a British officer seeing action in Czechoslovakia for a long time to come.

A major rising did take place in Slovakia in August 1944 involving some 65,000 men. It was ordered in the hope, and belief, that the Red Army would reach the scene of action before, and not after, the Germans were able to crush the revolt. This hope was no more to be fulfilled than the similar expectations of the Polish Home Army during the Warsaw rising. A British officer, John Sehmer, did operate with the Slovak insurgents but was captured and killed. Perkins, who by then had taken over the Czechoslovak and Hungarian sections of SOE as well as the Polish, did enter Prague shortly before the Germans left and was appointed British acting Chargé d'Affaires until it was thought fit to send a professional diplomat to take over. But all these were far too distant prospects for Hesketh-Prichard, who was determined to go into action soon. In the meanwhile he was also determined to improve some of the services and supplies on which SOE was dependent.

One of Hesketh-Prichard's operational plans was to be parachuted into France to steal a German night-fighter which he would then fly back to Britain. He therefore approached Dr R. V. Jones the scientist who, with the relatively modest title of Assistant Director of Intelligence on the Air Staff, did so much to harness the talents of acute scientific minds to the conduct of the war against the Luftwaffe. (To Kim Philby he was 'the formidable Dr Jones'.) Jones dissuaded Hesketh-Prichard from trying to steal the night-fighter, but when Hesketh-Prichard, as Jones put it, 'pleaded' to be given a target he showed him a picture of a new radio navigational beam station in France and suggested he might try to find his way into the control room.

A few days later Hesketh-Prichard reappeared in Jones's office and told him the plan Jones had put forward had been approved and the code-name for the operation was Pineapple. 'From now on,' he added, 'I'm Pineapple.' From then on to Jones and other members of Jones's unit he was Captain Hesketh-Pineapple.

Jones briefed Hesketh-Prichard on the technical instructions to be transmitted to the French resistance group which was to co-operate in the raid. There followed a report from France of such excellence that, in Jones's opinion, it made Hesketh-Prichard's proposed operation redundant. The sender of the report was Yves Rocard, Professor of Physics at the Sorbonne, whom SOE later brought out of France. In Jones's judgment it was the best piece of technical observation on the part of an agent on the ground he had ever seen.

During their initial discussion Hesketh-Prichard had told Jones that his air intelligence unit was doing more than any other to win the war. That he was able to make such a judgment – indeed that as a junior officer employed elsewhere he even knew what Jones's unit was doing – revealed one of the characteristics which distinguished Hesketh-Prichard most clearly from other people around him. This was a persistent and intelligently directed curiosity. One way in which he tried, probably without success, to satisfy his curiosity was to play backgammon at White's Club with the head of SIS, Sir Stewart Menzies. He also frequented White's for another reason. His step-father was mortally ill and could eat little except white fish, which was not easily obtained in wartime. Hesketh-Prichard would therefore visit the kitchens at White's as they were about to close, collect any white fish that was available, take it down to his stepfather in Hertfordshire, and return in the early hours of the following day to resume his duties with SOE.

Hesketh-Prichard had, for an amateur, an exceptional knowledge of radio, and he played a significant part, though an unorthodox one, in the exploitation by SOE of two important devices. One of these, known as Eureka, was, by the standards of the early 1940s, a relatively small piece of equipment which enabled agents in the field to direct aircraft towards the chosen dropping grounds. The other was the S-phone, with which airman and agent could talk over a distance of about thirty miles with no danger of their conversation being intercepted more than a mile from the agent's position. But the most valuable contribution to SOE's communications which Hesketh-Prichard made was in enabling a number of Polish radio engineers to exercise their considerable skills.

SOE was at first dependent on SIS for the radio transmitters and receivers which were used by agents in the field. The first set which was considered acceptable for dropping by parachute weighed about 50 lbs. It was carried in the rigging of the parachute with which the agent dropped and was as likely as not to hit him on the head when he landed. The first SOE officer infiltrated into occupied Yugoslavia, D. T. (Bill) Hudson, who came by sea, was equipped with a set encased in a heavy oak box of the kind used in the Northern Territories of Australia. It had to be transported mostly by mule.

SOE made commendable progress in developing smaller sets. As evidence of its success was the decision made in 1947 by Knut Haugland, a leading member of the Norwegian resistance, to take with him on Thor Heyerdahl's *Kon Tiki* expedition a radio set built by SOE. It was the only set aboard *Kon Tiki* to survive a voyage of 101 days. The Poles also made progress, not least because Hesketh-Prichard had the ear of SOE's chief finance officer, John Venner, who respected his judgment.

Venner was a chartered accountant with an attractive dead-pan form of humour, who came from the firm of Edward Moore & Son to SOE via the RAF. A Member of Parliament, Godfrey Nicholson, aptly described him as one who 'in his profession was of the calibre of a statesman'. He led a team of finance officers who were exceptional in a number of respects. The general inclination of most of them was to be helpful, and the kind of activity by which their merits were judged was obtaining, by devious means, large quantities of used notes in scarce foreign currencies.

On Hesketh-Prichard's recommendation Venner arranged for a factory to be established at Stanmore for the production, according to Polish designs, of small and easily portable radio transmitters and receivers. Some 700 sets of different kinds were dropped into Poland alone from 1941 to 1944. Hesketh-Prichard, who had the considerable advantage, when he went into the field himself, of being able to act as his own radio operator, insisted on taking a Polish set with him. He considered it appreciably superior to any other.

Throughout 1941, 1942 and 1943 SOE activities were gravely

hampered by shortage of aircraft. The Air Ministry's policy of making as few bomber aircraft available for SOE's purposes as possible, except when under pressure from Prime Ministerial decree, was understandable at the time. It was based on a belief in the accuracy and effectiveness of aerial bombing which, though subsequently proved to be largely fallacious, was held with both conviction and tenacity.

To those concerned with dropping agents and supplies into such distant countries as Poland and Czechoslovakia the aircraft shortage was particularly frustrating, and in introducing Squadron-Leader Jacko Allerton into SOE Hesketh-Prichard almost certainly hoped that his charm and influence would serve to divert one or two more aircraft to the support of SOE. This hope was not fulfilled, but, acting in concert, the two men did bring about some improvements in the aircraft which the Air Ministry decided it could spare.

Together they visited Handley Page, the designer of the Halifax bomber, and pointed out that the aircraft used for flying to Poland and Czechoslovakia in the winter were fitted with tropical cooling and sand extractors for the engines. Most of the talking was done, not by the squadron-leader, but by Hesketh-Prichard, the captain in Army uniform. They found Handley Page very receptive to their ideas, and as a result modifications were carried out which increased the payload, the range and the safety of the Halifaxes.

The operational mission on which Hesketh-Prichard was eventually sent was planned by Peter Wilkinson, whose normal mental stance was two or three moves ahead of most people with whom he had to deal. The purpose of the mission was infiltration into Austria in support of a resistance movement if one could be found.

With hindsight it is known that there was the potential for an Austrian resistance movement, unco-ordinated though it was, and in the last months of the war Allen Dulles, the head of OSS in Switzerland, was in touch with elements of it. But by the end of 1943 SOE had achieved virtually nothing on Austrian soil. Wilkinson decided that the best prospects for infiltration were from Yugoslavia, and he and Hesketh-Prichard were therefore landed in a part of Bosnia controlled by Tito's Partisans.

Their first tasks were diplomatic rather than military. Tito greeted them frostily, but Wilkinson improved the atmosphere somewhat by making him laugh. When Tito complained of a shortage of weapons Wilkinson asked him why he did not emulate the Poles and buy weapons from the Germans. Tito thought this a huge joke and laughed loudly. He called in his Chief of Staff, who also thought it a huge joke and also laughed loudly. Wilkinson was then given a signed photograph of Tito as a *laissez-passer*. Tito, he thought, was probably influenced by the belief that the presence of British officers among the Slovenian-speaking minority might be useful when frontier adjustments came to be considered.

Once the mission was firmly established Wilkinson was recalled, but Hesketh-Prichard remained. He fought in a number of engagements alongside the partisans, who greatly respected both his courage and his endurance, which for a man declared unfit for military service of any kind was considerable. In one day he was reported to have killed forty-five Germans with a rifle. Here at last he was able to challenge his father's achievements as a sniper.

In the late summer of 1944 the possibility that Allied armies advancing from the south and west might reach Vienna by Christmas was being seriously considered. To facilitate the advance SOE was instructed by Allied headquarters in Caserta to do all it could to mobilize resistance in Austria. Hesketh-Prichard therefore persuaded a somewhat reluctant Slovene Partisan command to send in a fighting patrol to secure a base in the Saualpen, to which Slovenes living in Austria might rally.

The operation, which Hesketh-Prichard had planned for some time, involved crossing the River Drava. A specially designed folding boat, provided by SOE, was dropped by parachute, and in October some eighty men joined Hesketh-Prichard in a successful crossing. A week later he reported reaching the highest point in the Saualpen.

Then the weather turned against him. Supply drops could not be made. The Germans retained effective control of most of the countryside, little food could be procured, and the cold was intense. On 3 December Hesketh-Prichard sent a radio report that survival now depended on immediate supplies by air of food and reinforcements. He included a personal message for Wilkinson, which read: 'Give my love to all at White's. This is no place for a gentleman.' After that there was silence.

What happened to Hesketh-Prichard is a matter for conjecture. Investigations were made after the war by British officers in Austria and Yugoslavia, and Wilkinson instituted a detailed search of the relevant German files. Hesketh-Prichard had disappeared, and although a report was received from Yugoslav sources that he had been severely wounded and probably killed by Germans on 3 December, no evidence was discovered to substantiate this. The investigators found local people reluctant to talk, but they did learn that Hesketh-Prichard's attempts to enlist the help of Austrians and not merely Slovenes had not been popular. The conclusion reached by the investigators was that the Partisans almost certainly killed him.

The activities of SOE having included, as they did, so many individual exploits performed in unusual settings with unusual methods, it is not surprising that a literature has grown up presenting a series of success stories imbued with romance and glamour. Such episodes did occur, but in the work of SOE, as in other forms of warfare, action had to be preceded by reconnaissance; even in the reconnaissance which proved negative casualties occurred; and the lives of the ablest were not spared. Alfgar Hesketh-Prichard was a victim of this requisite of war.

Wilkinson believed that, had he survived, Hesketh-Prichard would have made an outstanding contribution to British industry. He was probably right. Of the other members of their operational group Wilkinson, who left the Army after the war, became British Ambassador in Vienna; Edward Renton was an orchestral conductor of standing; Charles Villiers became Chairman of British Steel. Hesketh-Prichard, dead before he was thirty, had already given more than a hint of greatness.

When he began to visit our office in February 1942 Gus March-Phillipps had recently returned from an exploit which combining, as it did, the qualities of piracy and panache gave noticeable pleasure to Winston Churchill. It would also have given pleasure to a British public starved of news of success had the Government thought it politic to reveal what had happened. In fact, for good reasons, the details were kept secret.

With a crew of five, including himself, March-Phillipps had taken a Brixham trawler named *Maid Honor* under sail to Lagos. One reason why he chose a wooden-hulled sailing vessel was that it was less likely than most to attract magnetic mines. In Lagos he was joined by other members of his operational party, who had arrived there by more orthodox forms of transport.

In the territorial waters of the Spanish-controlled, and therefore neutral, island of Fernando Po two enemy vessels were berthed. One was a large Italian liner, *Duchessa d'Aosta*, the other a German tanker, *Likomba*. Between them they were making a useful contribution to the enemy war effort by enabling German submarines to refuel. The SOE mission in West Africa had kept these vessels under observation, and one of its members, Leonard Guise, made detailed preparations for an attack to be launched on them. His plans included arranging for the ships' officers to be on shore attending a party given by a Spanish doctor on the night chosen for the attack.

March-Phillipps was in charge of the assault party, which consisted of men whom he had selected in England and some volunteers from the Nigerian civil service. The journey from Lagos to Fernando Po took more than four days, *Maid Honor* being left behind in Lagos and the assault party being transported in two tugs, *Vulcan* and *Nuneaton*.

The tugs reached the scene an hour before the agreed rendezvous and found the harbour lights still blazing. March-Phillipps indicated that he would like to attack immediately, shooting his way in if necessary, but he was dissuaded from doing so. As Leonard Guise expressed it many years later, they were engaged on a burglars' mission and 'burglars don't go in shooting'.

In fact the attack when it came was an unqualified success. The Italian liner, the German tanker and another vessel which happened to be secured to the tanker were all captured without a shot being fired. They were then towed out to sea, where they were taken over by the Royal Navy. The *Duchessa d'Aosta* was reputed to have been the richest maritime prize of the war to date.

When he returned to Baker Street to report on his West African mission March-Phillipps, who had a certain sense of theatre, appeared in an African bush hat, breeches and riding boots. It was in this guise that he met Marjorie Stewart in a lift. When he asked her what she did in the organization she replied that she was the lift-girl. That evening they met again, at a party to celebrate the West African venture. Two months later they were married.

March-Phillipps had been a regular soldier and was commissioned in the Royal Artillery. He served in India, but in 1931 at the age of twenty-three he resigned his commission and returned to England, earning his living as a sporting journalist. He also published a number of novels, largely concerned with sailing or riding, activities in which he excelled.

One reason why he left the Army was to seek a cure for his stammer, which he found a major affliction. He had also acquired a distaste for certain aspects of regimental soldiering. In one of his novels, *Ace High*, he wrote of the central character, who also served in India and also resigned his commission: 'He had drained that life of all it had to give him: shooting, pigsticking, polo. He had made himself a first-class soldier, trained a first-class section, only to find himself wedded to a routine.'

March-Phillipps's physical appearance commanded immediate respect. Like Alfgar Hesketh-Prichard he had broken his nose falling from a horse, and his wife was later to say of him: 'He looked

29

frightfully conventionally good-looking if you got him at the right three-quarters, and very beaky if you got him at the wrong one.' She also referred to 'a scarred, beautiful mouth'. He always dressed immaculately.

He was profoundly religious and wedded to beliefs in traditional values and traditional crafts. His father, who wrote a number of books on architecture, was a convert to Roman Catholicism. He himself professed the same faith and looked to an Elizabethan past for inspiration and guidance. Indeed as patriot and pirate, soldier and occasional poet, he sought consistently to emulate the greatest of the Elizabethans. His choice of a sailing vessel for the voyage to West Africa was made not only because of the danger of magnetic mines. Emotionally he preferred sail to steam, and, while he was far ahead of most contemporary military thought in devising training schemes, he believed that serious consideration should be given to the use of bow and arrow as a method of silent killing.

As a commander March-Phillipps combined in an unusual way the handicap of a violent and sometimes uncontrollable temper and a capacity to inspire devotion in those who served under him. Peter Kemp, who was later to appear in a variety of operational theatres in which SOE was engaged, described him as 'the gallant idealist and strange, quixotic genius who had been our commander and our inspiration'. Professor M. R. D. Foot, the distinguished historian of SOE, wrote that March-Phillipps's 'fiery, disdainful, self-assured manner left an unforgettable impression of force, and men who worked under him came near to worshipping him'.

In 1940 on a beach at Dunkirk March-Phillipps had found himself next to a young officer in the Royal Army Service Corps named Geoffrey Appleyard. Crouching in a sandhole as German aircraft dive-bombed at will, March-Phillipps said he felt 'a b-b-bloody coward'. The two men took to each other at once, and later the same year, when March-Phillipps was put in charge of a Commando troop, he arranged for Appleyard to serve under him.

Appleyard had a background of a school run by the Society of Friends and a family engineering business in Yorkshire. At Cambridge he gained first-class honours in engineering and ski-ed for the university. In Norway he caused something of a stir by competing, as an Englishman, in ski-racing at the very highest level. He and his sister gave what they believed to be the first demonstration of water-skiing off Scarborough and Bridlington.

The letters which Appleyard wrote to his parents while serving under March-Phillipps combined a boyish enthusiasm with some shrewd general observations and a consuming interest in ornithology. March-Phillipps clearly impressed him deeply, not least because he was the first officer he had met who regularly knelt for ten minutes in prayer before going to bed.

Appleyard was fascinated too by the role which March-Phillipps envisaged for Commando units, and in one of his letters to his parents he expressed the belief that through the influence of these units a new spirit could and would be created in the Army. As an expression of this spirit the members of March-Phillipps's unit, while stationed on the west coast of Scotland in the latter part of 1940, clubbed together and bought a 32-foot boat from a fisherman for £35. This they used for training themselves to become a water-borne raiding force. March-Phillipps also set the unit the task of writing essays on how to win the war. One member, Jan Nasmyth, produced what was in effect a blueprint for the future Small Scale Raiding Forces. This came to the notice of Colin Gubbins and the unit was incorporated within SOE.

One of its earlier tasks was the landing of Appleyard, now established as March-Phillipps's second-in-command, and a Frenchman named André Desgrange, from submarine and canoe south of the Loire estuary to pick up two agents. Although no recognition signal was seen from the shore, Appleyard felt an instinctive certainty that the agents were where they were supposed to be, and, abandoning caution, he walked up and down the beach flashing his torch and shouting. After a time the agents appeared. They had not given any signals, they explained, because they believed themselves to be under observation by the Germans. They were both brought safely to England.

Among those who were recruited to March-Phillipps's unit was a Dane named Anders Lassen. Well over six feet tall, with exceptionally good looks, blue eyes and fair hair, he was commonly and, as it happened, quite appropriately described as a modern Viking. His mother was a successful writer of children's books, but he himself, lacking academic qualifications and being able to claim no real distinction when young, other than exceptional skill in shooting, decided in 1939 to go to sea as a cabin-boy. After war broke out in Europe, while serving in a tanker, he became the ring-leader of a mutiny which caused the master of the tanker to disregard his instructions to sail for a German or neutral port and to make instead for Bahrein, where a British crew were taken on.

Lassen continued to serve at sea for some eighteen months until he came into contact with one of a group of Danes who were determined to return clandestinely to Denmark. He was sent to one of the SOE training schools at Arisaig in the western Highlands. There it was thought that his particular skills were better suited to the kind of operation in which March-Phillipps was engaged than to undercover work in Denmark. Among his many likeable qualities was a readiness to accept a reprimand gracefully. Donald Hamilton-Hill, who played a major part in the development of SOE training, later recalled an occasion on which Lassen, fully accepting the reasons for a reprimand and showing at least a semblance of contrition, said: 'I have told all the men: in future verk before vimmin.'

Lassen, like Appleyard, took part in the Fernando Po operation, and both became fully involved in March-Phillipps's next major enterprise, the staging of raids across the English Channel to attack enemy outposts. It was of this activity that Winston Churchill said: 'There comes out of the sea from time to time a hand of steel which plucks the German sentries from their posts with growing efficiency.' In a manner which was characteristic of SOE, and which was among the reasons why the organization did not endear itself to some of the more orthodox officers of the other armed services, the men who operated the boats, as well as those who formed the raiding parties, were, normally, Army and not naval officers.

March-Phillipps, Appleyard and other members of the unit were at times operating in the Channel on three or four nights a week with a degree of risk which increased steadily as German forces became more and more aware of their presence. Peter Kemp, comparing a cross-Channel raid, in which the final paddle-in had to be conducted in complete silence and growing tension, with other forms of SOE action, said that a raid was 'frightening because either you pulled it off, probably without any loss to yourselves, or you were inclined to lose the whole party because if the enemy spotted you coming you were a sitting duck'.

Among the raids carried out was one on Les Casquets in the Channel Islands, when a German signals station was put out of action and the Germans operating this and the lighthouse were all taken prisoner without a shot being fired. Kemp was accidentally wounded in this action by another member of the unit and so was prevented from taking part in another raid on Port-en-Bessin, which was launched on the night of 12–13 September 1942. Appleyard had broken a bone in his foot, and though he was adjudged fit to act as navigating officer on the Port-en-Bessin operation he was not allowed to be a member of the landing party. To these injuries Kemp and

32

Appleyard owed their lives. The raiding party led by March-Phillipps came under heavy German fire, and he and ten others were killed.

While Gus March-Phillipps was conducting cross-Channel raids his wife Marjorie was trained for operational duties. Her plan was to become a conducting officer for agents sent to France, with a view to being later parachuted in herself, but when she had completed her parachute training she discovered that she was pregnant. She was certainly SOE's first pregnant parachutist. Her daughter Henrietta, when she grew up, engaged in a quest to recreate the character of the father she had never known. This she did in a radio programme with the help of survivors from the raiding parties and others. Of her father and Appleyard she herself said: 'Sometimes I wondered whether Gus and Apple were real. . . . They were so very idealistic.'

After March-Phillipps's death Appleyard took charge of the unit which was their joint creation. Among the operations carried out under his command was one on the island of Sark, when two Germans were taken prisoner. As a precaution against the danger of escape their hands were tied behind their backs. In spite of this, one did escape and was duly disposed of by Anders Lassen. When his dead body was found the Germans declared the tying of his hands to be an offence against the Geneva Convention. This was to serve as the pretext for Hitler, the following year, to order the chaining of prisoners taken in the major raid on Dieppe which was carried out largely by Canadians.

Before long the survivors of the March-Phillipps–Appleyard unit were transferred to other formations which had recently come into being and which took over from SOE some of the tasks which the unit had pioneered. Lassen became a member of the Special Boat Service under Earl Jellicoe and engaged in raids on a variety of Mediterranean islands. He also became more and more irregular in his appearance, frequently disdaining to wear the insignia of an officer or his decorations, which included the MC with two bars. Although plentifully engaged with both 'verk and vimmin' he expressed from time to time a desire to be involved in what he called 'the big war'. This was to be granted, and for his part in an action at Lake Comacchio in April 1945, in which he was killed, he was posthumously awarded the Victoria Cross.

Appleyard also served in the Mediterranean, at first with a Commando unit, which later became No. 1 Small Scale Raiding Force, and afterwards in command of a squadron of what was to become the 2nd Special Air Service Regiment. An aircraft in which he was being flown to Sicily crashed, and his body was never found. The Rev. Leslie Weatherhead, the well known Minister of the City Temple in London, who had known Appleyard as a member of his church in Leeds, said of him: 'If a visitor dropped down from Mars and visited each country to find out what earth's inhabitants were like, and if I had a chance to suggest whom such a visitor should meet in England, I should suggest Geoffrey Appleyard.'

Chapter 3

Polish Tragedies

In 1940 Jan Karski, a courier from occupied Poland, reached France and was received by General Sikorski, the Prime Minister of the Polish government in exile, which was then established at Angers. Sikorski gave him instructions that the underground movement must not confine itself to resistance but must maintain, at no matter what cost, all the apparatus of an underground state. During the years of occupation which followed this ideal was never lost sight of. Similar attempts to establish an underground state in the Polish territories occupied by Soviet forces during 1940 and much of 1941 were less successful. Karski himself, on visiting a professor under whom he had studied at Lwów University, was told that the Gestapo and the GPU, as the Soviet security apparatus was then called, were very different organizations, the Soviet secret policemen being for the most part more intelligent, better trained, more systematic and less crude.

In the pursuit of their various tasks, political as well as military, the Polish resistance organizations remained independent of SOE to a degree experienced in none of the western European countries occupied by the Germans. Wherever Poles did have dealings with SOE personal relations tended to be cordial. Indeed of certain members of SOE a number of Poles retained the fondest memories. These were the girls of the FANY (First Aid Nursing Yeomanry) who staffed some of the training schools and the houses in which Poles who were about to be parachuted back to their own country were kept until the moment came for their departure.

One Polish parachutist wrote of these girls that 'you couldn't have found a finer type of Englishwoman anywhere. Cultured and friendly, hard-working and smiling, they created the relaxed, happy atmosphere so necessary before the coming adventure.' In the daytime they would cook or sweep or drive cars, and in the evening 'in exquisite long dresses' they would join the parachutists in dancing tangoes and waltzes and kujawiaks. 'Though they were young and attractive, not to say beautiful, we had no heart-pangs over them.'

Nevertheless, no matter how friendly their relations were with Harold Perkins and his staff or with FANY girls, those concerned with Polish resistance maintained as high a degree of secrecy about their operational and political activities as they could within the limitations imposed by exile and financial dependence. One reason for this was a long tradition of conspiracy and resistance, which bred a fear of penetration by outsiders. Another was a distrust, at first perhaps instinctive, of British foreign policy, a distrust which in the event was to be fully justified. As a result the involvement of members of SOE in Polish resistance tended for the most part to be indirect rather than direct.

Although the Polish underground state apparatus included such features as an elaborate educational system, with provision for the taking of university degrees, it was understandably shaped for the most part to promote resistance. Some 200 of the principal resistance leaders were paid small salaries from central funds to enable them to operate as full-time professionals. After the arrest of his two predecessors the chief of these was General Bór-Komorowski, who slept briefly in a different place nearly every night, continually changed his name and documents, and always carried with him a phial of potassium cyanide. It was after nearly five years of this existence that he had to exercise the functions of a supreme commander when the people of Warsaw rose against the Germans in the summer of 1944.

Training courses lasting five months were instituted for other leaders, and from 1941 until shortly before the Warsaw rising some 8,500 men and women went through the officer-training schools. Radio contact between Britain and Poland was continued without interruption, and to ensure an adequate supply of operators a transmitter in Britain sent lessons in radio procedure and morse code to classes organized by the Home Army in Poland.

The standard reprisal rate established by the German command was the taking of a hundred Polish lives for every German killed. The greatest single act of genocide in the war took place in Poland with the destruction of virtually the entire population of the Warsaw ghetto in addition to the extermination of millions of other Jews. Yet the resistance organization, slowly reinforced by Poles sent from Britain, who after a few weeks of acclimatization were considered fit for operational duties, remained intact. After the war Colin Gubbins was to write: 'If an operation was decided upon in Britain you could be absolutely certain that it would be carried out in Poland at the first available opportunity after the date given.' For obvious military reasons many of the operations he referred to were in direct support of the Red Army.

To Britain the Polish resistance looked mainly for money and arms. Money was provided quite plentifully, although the Joint Chiefs of Staff did at one stage defer, for purely political reasons, the sending of 10 million dollars allocated by the United States to the Polish underground. Supplies of weapons and explosives, on the other hand, were never adequate. The total tonnage of supplies dropped to Poland during the war was little more than a tenth of that dropped to Greece and about one-sixteenth of the amount dropped to both Yugoslavia and France.

In attempts to make good the deficiencies the Poles manufactured their own arms in secret factories, diverted supplies intended for the German armies, and stole or bought what they could from German soldiers. Whenever a German was found to be venal he was ruthlessly exploited by the underground organization, being continually threatened with exposure unless he continued to do as he was instructed. As a result of the various methods employed about two-thirds of the weapons available to the Polish Home Army when the Warsaw rising began were provided by their own efforts. The remaining third was dropped from aircraft operating from the bases established at first in Britain and later in southern Italy. The total volume was to prove pitifully small.

In 1943 and 1944 Stalin's plans for the post-war role of Poland and the kind of government the country should have became increasingly evident. They were particularly clearly illuminated after the German discovery of graves in the Katyn Forest containing the corpses of some 14,000 Poles, nearly all of them officers, and the evidence, which proved to be incontrovertible, that this act of genocide was a Soviet and not a German one. The Polish government in exile asked for an independent enquiry to be conducted by the Red Cross. The Soviet Union replied by breaking off diplomatic relations and refusing from then onwards to recognize the Polish government. To replace it a number of communists, some of whom had spent many years in the Soviet Union, were already being groomed.

As the prospects of a post-war settlement of the kind hoped for by the Polish government diminished, the underground movement in Poland became politically increasingly isolated. In an attempt to improve direct communications Stanisław Mikołajczyk, who had become Polish Prime Minister after the death of Sikorski in an air crash off Gibraltar, wrote a personal letter to Winston Churchill in

February 1944 asking for a team of British observers to be sent to the Polish Home Army. He received a chilling rebuff. As Foreign Secretary Anthony Eden would not agree to the sending of such a mission without Soviet approval, and it was not until October that Gubbins was able to persuade the British Cabinet that a mission of SOE officers, which was standing by in readiness, should be sent whether the Soviet government agreed or not. By then the Warsaw rising had failed, Bór-Komorowski was a prisoner of war, and the mission was unable to achieve anything of value.

Whether an SOE mission arriving in Poland several months earlier could have had any serious influence on events is a matter for speculation. Peter Wilkinson, exceptionally well qualified to judge, expressed the opinion long after the war that it could not. He may well have been right, but there is abundant evidence that the Polish government in exile and the Polish Home Army had become less and less aware of what the other was doing and thinking, and Bór-Komorowski was deplorably ignorant of the capacity and intentions of the western Allies. The timing of the order to the people of Warsaw to rise against the Germans took the Polish government by surprise. In his strategic planning Bór-Komorowski thought seriously in terms of intervention from Britain by the Polish parachute brigade, whereas any competent British liaison officer could have explained to him that this would not happen. Of the intention of the western Allies to agree to the cession of large areas of pre-war Poland to the Soviet Union he first learnt from a German newspaper which he read in a prison camp.

In western Europe, once a resistance movement had come into being and proved itself capable of striking effective blows, SOE's main concern was to ensure that the actions of the resistance conformed so far as possible with the requirements of the Supreme Allied Commander. This meant in practice that widespread sabotage and mass risings had to be timed to give maximum support to the invading force. In Poland such co-ordination was tragically lacking.

There were individual actions in which the Polish underground co-operated directly and successfully with the western Allies in Poland itself. One such followed reports that the Germans were manufacturing a new kind of rocket. One of these had landed accidentally on Swedish territory and its description confirmed information received from Polish intelligence. The rockets were in fact prototypes of the V2 which was to be used to bombard London. When it was learnt that the Red Army, advancing through Poland, had overrun an experi-

mental launching site at Blizna, the British government understandably asked to be allowed to send an expert mission to inspect it. This
was agreed in principle.

The members of the mission were held up for some time in
Teheran before visas to enter Soviet territory were granted. Later they
were told that though the Russians had indeed captured parts of an
experimental rocket they had somehow lost them. Finally the
mission left with a promise that the rocket parts would be despatched
later. The package which was eventually received contained pieces of
an old aircraft.

Clearly other efforts had to be made, and a new opportunity
presented itself when another experimental rocket landed in Poland
in May 1944. It buried itself in a bank of the River Bug and did not
explode. For some time there had in effect been races between the
German occupying forces and the Polish Home Army to recover
pieces of rockets which had landed, and this time the Poles won.
Photographs were taken of the rocket, and essential components,
including a radio transmitter and receiver, were put into sacks and
transported by bicycle on a 200-mile journey, the cyclists having to
cross the lines of the retreating German Army.

The Polish Home Army then undertook to prepare and defend a
landing ground so that the rocket parts could be flown to Britain. A
Dakota aircraft piloted by a New Zealander named Guy Culliford with
Flight-Lieutenant Szrajer of the Polish Air Force as navigator landed
successfully. A member of the Polish Home Army, Jerzy Chmielewski,
who had been deputed to accompany the rocket parts, climbed on
board with his load. Another passenger was carried on board. This
was a very gallant Pole named Józef Retinger, who was something of
an *éminence grise* in the Polish government. He had been a close
friend of Sikorski and was also on very friendly terms with Gubbins.
At the age of fifty-six and in poor health he had been dropped by
parachute a month earlier and had injured his leg badly on landing.
He was now returning to make a political report.

Although the aircraft had been landed without great difficulty,
taking off was far less easy. Indeed for a time it seemed that it was
irretrievably bogged down. The passengers were told to get out while
new, gently sloping trenches were dug in front of the aircraft. Again
the attempted take-off failed, and twice more the passengers climbed
out and new trenches were dug. Finally after an hour and a half,
during all of which time there were German troops within hailing
distance, the Dakota took off. After it had landed at Hendon airfield
Chmieleski sat on the packages containing the V2 parts and refused to

hand them over to anyone except a suitably accredited Polish officer. Anyone else who approached him was threatened with a knife.

That the Polish underground movement was capable of such organization and such improvization indicated, as did a hundred other less dramatic incidents, what might have been achieved had its efforts been co-ordinated with those of an invading army, as, for example, were the actions of the French resistance with the strategy of General Eisenhower's command. But the invading army in Poland was the Red Army, with which the Polish Home Army had only intermittent contact. The Home Army had received no supplies from the Soviet Union, and unlike the Balkan countries, or indeed France and Italy, there was no large-scale communist resistance movement which the Soviet Government might have been willing to supply. It was in these circumstances, and with the prospect of co-operation with the Red Army no more than a barely formulated hope, that the Warsaw rising was ordered.

For a week or two some degree of co-operation between the Red Army and the Warsaw insurgents seemed not impossible. Even before the rising began at the end of July 1944 the Soviet-controlled Radio Kościuszko called upon the people of Warsaw to take up arms and to fight the Germans in streets and houses and factories. A week after the beginning of the rising a Soviet officer named Konstantin Kalugin made his way to the headquarters of the Polish Home Army and expressed the opinion that the Red Army would enter Warsaw within two or three days.

Whether these actions concealed Stalin's real intentions or whether he changed his mind is not clear, but on 13 August a communiqué was issued by Tass condemning the rising, and before long the Polish commanders were being described as 'criminals'. Then came the refusal by the Soviet government to allow Allied aircraft, after dropping arms to the insurgents, to land on Soviet territory. Professor Hugh Seton-Watson, the brilliant historian of eastern Europe, who himself served for a number of years in SOE, has advanced the interesting theory that one reason for the Soviet rulers' refusal may have been their fear of allowing Allied airmen, particularly Americans, to see the primitive conditions in which Soviet troops lived. Whatever the reasons were, the denial of landing rights to Allied aircraft effectively destroyed what little chance of success the Warsaw insurgents may have had.

To reach Warsaw from an airfield near Brindisi crews had to fly between 800 and 900 miles with virtually no meteorological information or radio aids. Sir John Slessor, Commander-in-Chief of the RAF in the Mediterranean theatre, doubted from the outset whether aircraft could make the flight to Warsaw, circle over a comparatively small area of the city, drop their loads, and return to southern Italy without an unacceptable proportion of losses. After five aircraft had been lost on a night on which only two succeeded in dropping containers on Warsaw, half of which fell into German hands, Slessor imposed a ban on all further flights.

In the face of intense political pressure and demands from the Polish air crews under his command that the flights should continue Slessor rescinded his ban. Polish, British and South African crews went into action again, losses mounted, and although the loads which were dropped successfully were a welcome stimulus to the Warsaw insurgents, they were far too few to affect the final issue. About a fortnight after the rising broke out all attempts to supply Warsaw by aircraft returning to southern Italy were abandoned.

Churchill then proposed to Roosevelt that they should inform the Soviet government that their aircraft would land on Soviet territory unless Stalin directly forbade it, but Roosevelt, confident of his capacity to make deals with the man he referred to as 'Uncle Joe', would not agree. When permission for landings was finally given more than a hundred US Flying Fortresses made daylight drops on Warsaw, but by then it was mid-September and the outcome of the battle of Warsaw was already decided.

While the street fighting in Warsaw continued the Red Army remained immobilized on the east bank of the River Vistula, which divides the main city of Warsaw from the suburb of Praga. There were in fact sound military as well as political reasons why the Red Army did not launch an attack when the Warsaw rising began, and that the Polish Home Army was not aware of these was a further example of the disastrous consequences of the lack of co-ordination of action. But on 25 August Marshal Rokossovsky did inform Stalin that he was ready to attack Warsaw. The order for the attack was not given. The Polish insurgents, of whom only about 5 per cent possessed arms when the rising began, were left to fight alone against well equipped German troops whom Hitler had ordered to defend Warsaw at all costs.

As more and more areas came under German control the Polish Home Army was increasingly dependent for its lines of communication on the city's sewers. At one stage a procession of 1,500 fighting men, 2,000 walking wounded, some hundreds of stretcher cases and 500 civilians, including nurses, made a four-kilometre journey through sewers under intensive dive-bombing. A building in which an important meeting of Home Army commanders was being held was guarded by a sixteen-year-old boy armed with a scythe, with which he fought until he was killed. There was a fighting platoon of deaf-mutes, including a woman, for whom an elderly priest acted as interpreter. The supply of anaesthetics ran out. Dysentery was rife. Horses, cats and dogs were all eaten for food.

To such a conflict there could only be one outcome. After sixty-three days of intensive street fighting what remained of the Home Army surrendered. Its members had by then been granted combatant status by the Germans. No such status was accorded them by their Soviet allies. All that was gained by the struggle was summed up by a recent historian of the Warsaw rising, J. H. Zawodny, when he entitled his book *Nothing but Honour*. Of that there was an abundance.

Before they finally retreated the Germans destroyed nearly every building in Warsaw which still remained. In this ruin a Polish government was established, whose President, Bolesław Bierut, was a professional NKVD agent.

For SOE there was the humiliation of knowing that for the country which had produced the first effective resistance movement with which it had had the privilege of collaborating the outcome had been disaster. In the final stages SOE officers, apart from helping to load some supplies at Brindisi airfield, most of which fell into German hands, were able to do virtually nothing.

Although the national dedication to the struggle inside Poland was perhaps as total as that of any other people in any comparable conflict, there were also Poles, no less patriotic in their motives, who took part in underground warfare independently of the highly disciplined Polish official organizations and in association with Poland's allies. Some of them were people of unusual distinction who sooner or later found themselves within the ranks of SOE. Among these were the ex-Polish Consul in Addis Ababa, Jerzy (George) Giżycki, and his wife Christine, formerly Krystyna Skarbek.

George Giżycki was a man who seems to have been as untameable as he was uncompromising. A. G. G. de Chastelain, who for a number of years was in charge of the SOE mission in Istanbul and who therefore had the opportunity of meeting, at least *en passant*, many of SOE's more resourceful operators, said of Giżycki that he was both the most difficult and the most capable man he had ever met.

Giżycki had travelled widely and written much about Africa. He had worked as a cowboy in the United States and as a trapper in Canada and could use a knife and a lasso with the skill of a professional. In appearance he was described as like an eagle with chilly grey eyes in which a smile never appeared. He dominated his wife Christine, whom he first met when he saved her from possible disaster on a dangerous ski slope, as no man ever dominated her before or after. She even described him as her Svengali.

Christine's own family background was of land-owning aristocracy on her father's side, the Skarbeks having been powerful nobles in the fifteenth century, and Jewish middle class on her mother's, the Goldfeders being prominent in banking circles. Christine was known as a girl of rare beauty, with exceptional skill as a horsewoman, a strong spirit of independence and a bubbling sense of fun.

When Skarbek largesse and financial incompetence had disposed of the Goldfeder fortune Christine found herself, at a rather early age for one of her background, obliged to earn a living. For a time she worked in an agency for Fiat cars. Her office was above a garage, and when she became seriously ill X-rays revealed scars on her lungs, believed to have been caused by petrol fumes. These scars were to be of importance to her during her service with SOE.

She also worked as a journalist in Paris. For holidays she had a particular liking for the Polish skiing resort of Zakopane. When skiing did not provide her with enough excitement she would indulge, probably only for kicks, in a certain amount of amateur smuggling. In this way she came to know a number of the mountain people of the Polish frontier areas, a knowledge which was also to be of importance in her wartime career.

When Germany invaded Poland in 1939 Giżycki and his wife were in East Africa. They immediately set off for London and moved in circles where Christine was already not unknown. Among those whom she met soon after her arrival were F. A. Voigt, the wise and far-seeing editor of *The Nineteenth Century and After*; Sir Robert Vansittart, the uncompromising opponent of the appeasement of Hitler, who already within the Foreign Office had been edged on to a side-track of diminishing responsibility; and George Taylor, the Australian who played such an important part in the early development of SOE. With Taylor Christine established the kind of immediate *rapport* she often had with people of rare and not publicly recognized distinction.

Giżycki was determined to make his way to Finland to fight against the invading Soviet Army, but Christine had other plans. Taylor arranged for her to be sent to Budapest, ostensibly as a journalist, but with an under-cover mission whose terms she in effect drew up herself. Once established in Hungary, her intention was to make her way into Poland with propaganda material which, she hoped, would convince her compatriots that, contrary to nearly all the evidence, Britain had not abandoned Poland and would continue to prosecute the war vigorously.

In Budapest Christine came into contact with a Pole whom she had met a couple of times before, named Andrzej Kowerski. Their social paths had naturally crossed, for Kowerski too belonged to the *szlachta*, the name given to the Polish land-owning upper class, whose members exhibited as their most determining characteristics complete social ease, an excellent command of French and an apparently inexhaustible supply of people whom they referred to as their cousins.

Kowerski was a man of powerful physique and had been a gifted athlete in his youth, but had had the misfortune to be shot in the foot by a guest at a shooting party. Several amputations of the leg had followed. In spite of this handicap he had served in Poland's only mechanized brigade in the campaign against Germany and had received the highest Polish award for gallantry, *Virtute Militari*. In Hungary he too was engaged in a mission of his own choosing for which he drew up his own rules. This consisted of removing, by various clandestine means, members of the Polish armed forces from the camps where they had been interned and transporting them across the frontier into Yugoslavia.

When she arrived in Budapest Christine's marriage had already effectively foundered. She and Kowerski became lovers, so beginning a relationship which never turned into marriage but which survived, essentially unimpaired, until death, even though both were to be driven from time to time to other people and indeed to different continents.

When Christine told Kowerski of her plan to cross the Tatra mountains into Poland in mid-winter he was horrified. So too was Jan Marusarz, an experienced ski instructor from Zakopane, who had an intimate knowledge of the conditions which would have to be faced. But Marusarz, as many others were to do later, succumbed to Christine's power of persuasion and agreed to take her with him. When they did make their crossing the snow for much of the way was four to five metres deep and thirty people lost their lives in a blizzard which swept across the Tatras.

Christine spent five weeks in Poland on this occasion, staying for much of the time in Warsaw and visiting her mother and other Jewish relations. She learnt that a number of her friends belonged to an

44

underground organization known as the Musketeers, the creation of Stanisław Witkowski, an eccentric inventor and engineer. Witkowski had had his own direct links with the British SIS and was not responsible to the official Polish underground authorities. Through the contacts she made and the information she was able to assemble Christine now became, in effect, not so much a propagandist as an intelligence agent and courier.

Christine made a second trip to Poland in June 1940. Again she returned with much information, but she failed in one of her self-imposed tasks. This was to persuade her mother to leave Poland. The mother's refusal was, inevitably, to prove fatal.

On her third trip Christine had her first experience of being arrested. She was with a new travelling companion named Władysław Ledóchowski, and the contents of their rucksacks included the equivalent of about a thousand dollars in various currencies and some compromising documents. The arrest was made by Slovak frontier guards. In a combined operation, in which Christine's part was to distract the guards' attention, they succeeded in disposing of the documents in a swiftly flowing river. But the money had still to be explained, and the Slovak guards had no doubt that their prisoners were couriers intending to enter Poland illegally. Christine now took charge. The guards, she pointed out, were faced with two alternatives. One was to take the money and let their prisoners go. The other was to hand over both prisoners and money to higher authority. The guards accepted her reasoning and they were set free.

As her lines of communication were strengthened Christine became more involved with facilitating the escape from Poland not only of Poles of fighting age, but of British prisoners of war who had been captured in France and sent to camps in Poland. Indeed it was on receipt of information that a number of British prisoners of war were being held in an establishment for deaf-mutes in Warsaw that she made her fourth and final trip across the mountains.

In their efforts to help prisoners to escape Christine and Kowerski received the direct encouragement of the British Ambassador in Budapest, Sir Owen O'Malley, who had had the assurance of the British government that for this particular purpose plenty of money was available. To Kowerski it was made clear that his primary task must be to facilitate the escape of Polish pilots, who were badly needed in Britain.

Kowerski's activities and, to a lesser extent, Christine's were of course known to various Germans in Budapest, who put increasing pressure on the authorities of a still neutral Hungary to find grounds for arresting them and handing them over to German jurisdiction. Kowerski had established excellent relations with some influential Hungarians, including a colonel, whose family he helped to escape from the Soviet-occupied part of Poland, and from them he received several warnings that the time had come for him and Christine to leave Hungary.

They were reluctant to abandon their work, but the warnings had not been given lightly, and at four o'clock one morning came the knock on the door of their flat which they had half come to expect. In the separate interrogations which followed Christine and Kowerski, who had of course rehearsed what they would say and who had the advantage of a very real telepathic communication, maintained the same cover-story consistently. Christine had another strategem. This was to bite fiercely into her tongue until blood flowed freely. She then coughed the blood into a handkerchief convincingly enough to persuade a Hungarian doctor that X-rays must be made of her lungs. These showed the scars which had been revealed after she had been working above the garage in Warsaw, and the doctor pronounced her to be in an advanced stage of tuberculosis. It seems unlikely that the doctor was really deceived, but the scars shown in the photographs and the fact that Christine was related, albeit rather remotely, to the Hungarian Regent, Admiral Horthy, were enough to secure both her release and Kowerski's.

O'Malley was certain that the Germans in Hungary would not be satisfied with what had happened, and he insisted that Christine and Kowerski leave the country at once. Christine was hidden in the boot of the Ambassador's car, which an Embassy official drove across the Yugoslav frontier. Kowerski preferred to leave in a small Opel car which he had acquired and which was to remain his own private form of transport through much of the rest of the war. He felt he knew the frontier guards well enough to make his own arrangements. Before they left O'Malley furnished them both with British passports and asked them to choose their own names. The names they chose were Christine Granville and Andrew Kennedy.

The Opel transported them to Belgrade, Sofia and then Istanbul. In Sofia they handed to Aidan Crawley, who was then Assistant Air Attaché, a microfilm which Christine had just received from Poland showing German armour massing near the frontier with the Soviet Union and confirming reports Christine had had that the Germans would attack before long. This seemed startling information at the time, though the German intentions were of course known to a limited few through the breaking of the German codes.

In Istanbul Christine arranged for her husband to take over the task of maintaining the lines of communication which she had established with Poland, and she and Andrew Kennedy, as he had become, both of them now on the payroll of SOE, made their way by Opel to Cairo to report for further duty.

By the time Christine and Kennedy reached Cairo they had shown themselves to be people of exceptional initiative and resource who had served well both their native country and the country in whose service they were now engaged. In Cairo they were to face new tests of character.

SOE had made an arrangement with the Polish government in exile that all secret communications with Poland would be through official Polish channels. It could therefore be plausibly argued that by employing Christine SOE was failing to honour this agreement. The counter-espionage section of the Polish Second Bureau, whose staff contained some markedly unattractive types of secret policemen, had a subtler plan. In its view the offence of Christine and, to a lesser extent, Kennedy was not so much being in the service of SOE, though this was certainly frowned upon, as having connections with the independent organization of Witkowski's Musketeers. Stories were therefore circulated that Christine and Kennedy were suspected of being secretly in contact with the Germans.

In retrospect it may seem strange that such suspicions could be seriously entertained, but the information was skilfully conveyed, and in the world of secret warfare allegations of dual loyalty made by official organizations against individuals who are operating virtually in a freelance capacity can never be taken lightly. Moreover by their very presence Christine and Kennedy had become something of an embarrassment to those who had made pledges to the Polish government about the control of communications. In a brief interview during a short visit to Cairo Peter Wilkinson informed Christine and Kennedy that their services were no longer needed by SOE, though the small salaries they received were not stopped.

George Giżycki's reaction to this was one of disgust. He decided he wanted nothing more to do with British secret services and made his way, as soon as he could, to Canada, where he was reported to have taken a job as a lighthouse keeper. Andrew Kennedy's reaction was one of indignation. Christine's was one of patience.

I remember vividly my first meeting with Christine. It took place in the Gezira Sporting Club in Cairo. Guy Tamplin, who had been for some time the representative in Cairo of SOE's Polish and Czech sections, and who may well have been unique among British officers at that time in speaking Polish and Russian perfectly and French and German very nearly as well, told Christine an office job had been found for her in some other secret organization. Christine declined the offer. When I asked her, after Tamplin had left, why she had done so, she replied: 'J'ai tant d'endurance physique mais pas intellectuelle.'

The true reason for her refusal was, I believe, to be found in a quality which served to explain a number of Christine's future actions. This was a quiet determination never to accept the second-rate. In issues which were important to her she wanted the best or nothing.

Christine set her own standards, which were high, but she was not intolerant of failure or inadequacy. Indeed she had a tendency to collect lame ducks and social misfits. The pretentious she would dismiss tersely with such comments as 'bloody fool' or 'quel poltron'. Her friendship, once given, was unshakeable.

In wartime it is not easy for anyone to be totally impervious to rank. Most people accept the structure as it is. Some try aggressively to turn it upside down. Christine was simply indifferent. She would treat a general or a sergeant with exactly the same courtesy and, if she thought their human qualities merited it, the same degree of attention. She had an aristocratic disdain of difference of race and colour, and she even had a good-humoured tolerance of the mild anti-semitism which was prevalent among many of the people whom she met in Cairo.

Although she spurned the offer of an office job Christine was certainly not pining for adventure during the years she spent in Cairo. Indeed she rather enjoyed the salamander existence of basking in the sun at the Gezira Club. Being largely undomesticated, she found it easier to live in a hotel or a boarding-house than in a flat. Socially she liked café life, which allowed her to arrive and leave when she pleased. Being thoroughly feminine, she was certainly conscious of her appearance, though she frequently dressed in a manner which attracted little or no attention. This, I believe, derived from a certain chameleon quality which helped her to be so supremely successful as a secret agent.

After the war descriptions appeared in a number of publications of Christine as a gun-toting female who would happily toss hand-grenades whenever the occasion demanded. The origin of these was almost certainly to be found in the mischievous streak which had been so noticeable in her childhood, and which led her from time to time to indulge in the most outrageous fantasies when talking to people whom she was not disposed to take seriously.

In reality she was a peculiarly gentle being who disliked noise in general and firearms in particular. When she was being taught how to use a pistol she shut her eyes every time she fired and announced that she could never bring herself to shoot anyone. Nor did she. In emergencies she employed other weapons, including her formidable power of persuasion. This derived partly from feminine charm, partly from a controlled indignation which, it was easy to believe, might suddenly erupt into fury, and partly from an ability to persuade any man on whom she was working that he was unusual in being perceptive enough, not only to understand the arguments she was advancing, but to agree with them.

The allegations made against her by the Polish Second Bureau were treated by Christine with contempt, and during her period of inaction in the Middle East she continued to meet her Polish friends as and when she chose. One of these was Michał Gradowski, a shortish man with great strength and solidity of frame and a zest for living, for friendship and for anecdote.

Gradowski, whose family came from what used to be known as the Polish Ukraine, was educated largely outside Poland. He graduated in agricultural science at Louvain University, did his military service in Poland and returned there in 1939 expecting to fight against the Germans.

The opportunity to do so was for the time being denied him. He was taken prisoner, but, as he afterwards put it, not having the soul of a prisoner, he escaped with a small group by jumping from a train in the middle of the night. He made his way to occupied Warsaw, where he met an old friend, Prince George Czetwertyński, who put him in touch with Stanisław Witkowski, the head of the Musketeers. Witkowski told Gradowski he was working closely with the British, and Gradowski volunteered to serve as a courier taking information out via Budapest. This was agreed. Witkowski also gave Gradowski a password which, he said, would bring him directly into the presence of General Sikorski.

Early in his clandestine career Gradowski came to the conclusion that for a single journey bluff and first-class travel could provide a better safe-conduct than the more orthodox and laborious methods such as Christine Granville had to use for her repeated crossings of mountains. On his journey to Budapest he was accompanied by a nineteen-year-old girl named Ziozia Bronikowska, whose family came from the Poznań area and who spoke perfect German. They travelled across Czechoslovakia in a first-class railway compartment, wearing various Nazi party insignia. To a party official Gradowski began by apologising for his indifferent German, explaining that he was an Alsatian whose family had made the mistake of giving him a French education, a shortcoming he was now trying to rectify. Cordial relations were maintained throughout, Gradowski concealing micro-films on his person and the girl concealing guns in her handbag.

In Budapest Gradowski handed over his microfilms and other infor-mation to Father Laski, a gallant Polish priest who provided a reception point for couriers coming from Poland and who later died in a concentration camp. A few days before Gradowski's arrival in Budapest the German Army had invaded Yugoslavia. Nevertheless he agreed to try to make his way through Yugoslavia to bring informa-tion to Istanbul. In attempting to cross the Hungarian-Yugoslav border he was arrested. He was handcuffed and put in the charge of a Hungarian escort, whose instructions were to return him to Budapest.

After repeated requests Gradowski was given permission to go to the lavatory. He succeeded in freeing one of his hands and then jumped from the train. Whereas in Poland when jumping from a train he had landed, as planned, on an embankment, this time he landed in a cutting. He crashed against a wall, broke his kneecap and rolled over, his head coming to rest a few inches from the line along which the train was still passing.

After a certain amount of desultory shooting the hunt for Gradowski was evidently called off. He hid for a day in bushes and then began to walk by night, dragging his injured leg and navigating by the Pole star. For food he had one bread-roll which he divided into four parts, one part to be eaten each day.

This was the country of the legend of Count Dracula. Gradowski saw marshlights, had hallucinations, conversed with ghosts and avoided human beings until early one morning he met a priest who was on his way to church. He addressed the priest in German, but the manner in which the priest indicated that he did not speak German suggested he had no wish to do so. The priest took Gradowski to his home, where they found they could communicate in Latin, fed him and helped to arrange transport for him to Budapest.

After he had received treatment for his knee from a friendly doctor, who was in fact a gynaecologist, Gradowski was again ready to under-take the journey to Istanbul, but this time he decided to resort once more to the method of bluff and first-class travel. He assumed the identity of Baron Ostrog, a German Balt of Estonian nationality, who had been educated in France and who had a mission to enlist Estonian exiles in the German cause. To support this role he was provided with an excellent forged document, ostensibly signed by Dr Goebbels, commending his mission.

In Budapest Gradowski made the acquaintance of the girl-friend of the German commandant of the local military airport and later, through her, of the commandant himself. The commandant treated him with evident respect, and their relationship was given added piquancy by the fact that they were now sharing the same girl-friend. When Gradowski said he wanted to visit Sofia the commandant told him this would present no difficulty, but in the end the aircraft in which he offered Gradowski a seat was scheduled to land first at Belgrade. Although Belgrade was then in German hands Gradowski felt he could not refuse the offer.

On the journey to Belgrade all went well. Once again Gradowski engaged in conversation with a high-ranking party official, and with each drink they took from each other's hip-flasks they duly said 'Heil Hitler'. At Belgrade Gradowski remained in the aircraft awaiting take-off for Sofia. Then a German NCO came aboard and announced that Baron Ostrog was required to leave the aircraft.

To Gradowski, who had microfilms and other incriminating evidence on him, it now seemed clear that the Germans had known all along who he was and had set this trap to lure him to Belgrade. He had already been issued with a cyanide tablet to enable him to commit immediate suicide. He placed this in his mouth so that he could bite it if the need arose. In fact he learnt that he was to be transferred to another aircraft. Until it was ready to leave he was entertained in the officers' mess from whose windows he was able to observe all the aircraft on the airfield. The final stage of his journey to Istanbul was made in a taxi which he shared with the German consul.

Although he had arrived in Istanbul apparently under German protection Gradowski was given security clearance with gratifying speed and was invited to work for SIS. He declined the offer and asked to be allowed to rejoin the Polish Army.

As an emissary from the Witkowski organization Gradowski was not very warmly received by the Polish Army authorities, but he did at least avoid the beating-up which another of Witkowski's couriers, a dedicated Polish patriot, received at the hands of the Polish Second Bureau. Gradowski's rank was only that of second-lieutenant, but in spite of this the password he had been given by Witkowski carried sufficient weight for him to be granted a personal interview by Sikorski, who was then not only Prime Minister but Commander-in-

Chief of the Polish Armed Forces. Gradowski told Sikorski of the regret felt inside Poland that there were rifts between the Poles in exile. He found Sikorski disappointingly ready to shuffle the blame for all this on to his subordinates.

The rifts between the Poles in the Middle East, which were among those to which Gradowski referred, were partly a natural consequence of lack of action by fighting forces and were partly deliberately fomented. One Polish officer, who had links with the Soviet Union, was even the instigator of a plot to have Sikorski assassinated when he was visiting the Middle East, a plot of which I had cognizance several months before Sikorski was killed in an air crash. Whether the plot succeeded or whether the crash was altogether an accident may never be known beyond doubt. What is certain is that the British government and the crew of Sikorski's aircraft neither planned nor were responsible for his death and had nothing to gain from it. Nor is there any evidence of German complicity.

While Gradowski was engaged for the most part in routine duties in the Polish Army information was received by SOE in Cairo that in all the occupied Balkan countries Poles were to be found who had been sent there by the Germans to do forced labour. These seemed likely to provide good recruits for mutiny or subversion. Polish officers were parachuted to both Yugoslavia and Greece with this end in view, and a search was made for an Albanian-speaking Pole. None could be found.

Gradowski had renewed his acquaintance with Andrew Kennedy, whom he had known before the war, and with Christine, whom he had met briefly. It was Christine who recommended him as a possible choice for operational duties in Albania in the absence of an Albanian speaker. He was interviewed, selected, given the basic SOE training and parachuted in as a British officer with the name of Michael Lis.

Michael Lis had no opportunity to contact any Poles doing forced labour. Instead he was assigned the normal duties of a British liaison officer. These he fulfilled with some distinction. In November 1943 the Germans launched a major attack against the Albanian Partisans at Dibra. Lis was the only British liaison officer who was with the forward position of the Partisans throughout the action. Afterwards the Albanians spoke in the warmest terms of his gallantry under fire. The citation for the MC, which he was awarded, called attention not only to his endurance and bravery, but to his 'unfailing cheerfulness'.

After the war Lis became increasingly friendly with General Gubbins. It is an indication of the esteem in which he held him that Gubbins, shortly before he died, presented Lis with the service revolver he had had in the First World War, saying he could think of no one to whom he would rather give it.

The rehabilitation of Christine and Andrew Kennedy as people deemed worthy of employment in SOE was a comparatively slow process, which was made possible by their own exemplary conduct under a cloud of suspicion and by an injection of common sense into areas of SOE where it was needed. Kennedy became SOE's first trained one-legged parachutist and was then sent to Italy to help with the training of Poles who were to be parachuted back to their own country. Christine learnt, slowly and with some difficulty, to become a radio operator.

One day a signal was received at the SOE base near Algiers from southern France asking for a woman to be sent in who could serve as a courier. Conscription of labour had been introduced by the Germans, and as a result it had become easier for women than for men, particularly young men, to move across the countryside with some degree of freedom.

The request had come from a man who was outstanding among the many remarkable agents whom SOE despatched to occupied France. This was Francis Cammaerts, whose father was a distinguished Belgian man of letters, whose mother was a Shakespearean actress, and one of whose grandmothers was a Bayreuth opera singer. Early in the war Cammaerts, who had been a master at Beckenham and Penge County School for Boys, had registered as a conscientious objector and had been directed to agricultural work. The death of his brother in the RAF, marriage and the birth of his first child had served gradually to modify his opinions. A meeting with Harry Ree, a friend from Cambridge days, who had taught at the same school as he had, made him aware of the existence of SOE.

Selwyn Jepson, the popular novelist, who was the chief recruiting agent or, as he might be better described, talent-spotter for one of SOE's two French sections, soon decided that Cammaerts was a man of the calibre required. Maurice Buckmaster, head of that section, was of the same opinion. A report from one of the SOE training schools in Beaulieu, by contrast, described Cammaerts as 'rather lacking in dash' and 'not suitable as a leader'. Buckmaster and Jepson were to be proved right and the training school wrong.

Cammaerts reached occupied France for the first time by Lysander aircraft, which landed him near Compiègne towards the end of March 1943. He made his way to Paris, spent one night there, and learnt the next day that the man in whose flat he had stayed had been arrested.

For a young man in his mid-twenties on his first mission it was an unnerving start. He then set off for St Jorioz near Annecy, where he was disturbed by the evident lack of security within the organization which he had been instructed to join. His suspicions were proved right when it was learnt that the St Jorioz group had been effectively penetrated by Hugo Bleicher of the Abwehr, the professional and therefore pro-Nazi German counter-espionage organization.

From such false starts as these, and indeed from another one in Cannes, where again he found the security alarmingly lax, Cammaerts, whose original cover-story was that of a schoolmaster recuperating after jaundice, gradually built up an organization. He did so by adhering strictly to the lessons he had been taught during his SOE training. Over a period of fifteen months he never spent more than three or four nights in the same house. He insisted that all those with whom he worked must at all times have a satisfactory explanation of their actions which they could produce if they were suddenly arrested. He made sure that whereas he could contact a large number of resistance workers very few knew how to reach him.

By the late summer of 1944 Cammaerts had carried out his mission so successfully that Maurice Buckmaster could later write of him that 'in his capacity as an envoy of the Inter-Allied General Staff' he 'had under his orders 10,000 men, of whom at least half had been armed by his efforts'. His area of operations extended from Lyons to the Mediterranean coast and to the Italian and Swiss frontiers. All this had been achieved in spite of the disadvantage of a French accent which was not perfect, a bearing and gait which were noticeably English and a height which made him so conspicuous that he was widely and affectionately known as 'le grand diable anglais'.

When visiting the scenes of Cammaerts's operations soon after the Germans had been driven out Buckmaster was impressed by the evident admiration felt for Cammaerts. Much of this was due to the relentlessly conscientious manner in which Cammaerts undertook his duties. It was necessary for him to establish relationships of mutual trust and respect with a wide variety of people, and to achieve this he spared himself nothing. On one occasion, although he was so tired he found it difficult to keep his eyes open, he spent four hours with a French country stationmaster discussing Proust. Xan Fielding, whose principal exploits for SOE were performed in Crete and who joined Cammaerts in southern France in the summer of 1944, later described him as 'a smiling young giant' for whom resistance was 'tantamount to a new religion'.

To meet Cammaerts's demand for a courier SOE in Algiers chose Christine. For her new role she took the name Pauline Armand. On 8 July 1944 she was dropped by parachute, landing several miles off target with such an impact that the butt of her revolver was smashed and she herself was injured. When she reached the waiting reception committee her language shocked several of its more conventional members.

The area where Christine dropped was the high, wooded plateau of the Vercors. Here, contrary to the precepts which Gubbins had put forward in his pamphlets on guerrilla warfare, the French Forces of the Interior had decided to establish a fortress, to which members of *maquis* came *en masse*. The FFI's plans for action in the region were based largely on a belief, which was obstinately held, that Allied forces would land in southern France in July. In fact the southern invasion had long been planned to take place in mid-August.

On 14 July more than seventy United States aircraft dropped supplies to the Vercors in a spectacular operation for which the date seemed at the time well chosen. A full-scale German assault, preceded by aerial and artillery bombardment, followed. For countering this the arms received by the *maquis* were altogether inadequate. The result was slaughter, and the French commander in the Vercors found himself demanding intervention by a parachute regiment, much as General Bór-Komorowski was to do in Warsaw a month later, and with little more prospect that his demands would be met. When the battle was effectively lost Cammaerts, whose own plans for the Vercors had envisaged operations by self-contained groups of fifteen to twenty men, with Christine and a few others had to make a journey of seventy miles in twenty-four hours in order to regroup and resume action elsewhere.

As had happened in her earlier missions Christine had her own self-imposed tasks in addition to those which Cammaerts gave her. In Cairo she had had a number of discussions about the possibilities of effecting large-scale desertions of troops of different nationalities who had been conscripted by the Germans and also of the troops of Germany's less than enthusiastic allies. To test what could be done she crossed the Alps into Italy, made contact with both Italian and Russian troops, and brought about the desertion of several hundred. She then achieved a similar result with a number of Polish conscripts whom she addressed by loud-hailer in their own language. During her trip to Italy she was twice arrested by Germans and twice persuaded her captors to let her go by convincing them that she was, as she claimed, a local peasant girl.

It was in the course of one of her trips that news was brought to Christine that Cammaerts and Fielding had both been arrested. For some time Cammaerts had been travelling as an official of the Highways and Bridges Department, and he had all the necessary papers to support his cover-story. When he was held up at a road-block near Digne in the company of Fielding and a French officer named Major Sorensen for what appeared to be a routine check he was not therefore greatly concerned.

Fielding had not been in France long, and although as a child he had learnt to speak French perfectly he was out of practice, not least because of a long period of operational activity in the Cretan mountains. One of the documents with which he had been furnished in Algiers was out of date, and a German security official, who had been watching the proceedings, became suspicious. He asked Fielding who Cammaerts and Sorensen were, and Fielding disclaimed any knowledge of them. A search of their pockets then revealed that the three men between them had a large number of banknotes, all with consecutive numbers. It was a piece of carelessness arising from the ease with which they had recently been travelling around the country. All three were taken to Digne prison, from which, they could reasonably assume, there was no way out other than execution or transfer to a concentration camp.

When Christine heard of the arrest she set off for Digne prison immediately. An elderly and kindly gendarme, whom she had approached with a request that she might be allowed to bring some necessities to her husband in prison, put her in touch with an Alsatian named Albert Schenck, who served as a kind of liaison officer between the French prefecture and the German Sicherheitsdienst. To Schenck Christine announced that she was not only a British agent but Cammaert's wife and, for good measure, General Montgomery's niece. The lesson she had learnt from her relationship with Admiral Horthy had not been forgotten. She also made the point that as Allied forces had now landed in southern France it would be very much in Schenck's interests to secure the release of Cammaerts and his fellow-prisoners.

Schenck told Christine that he himself could do nothing but that there was a Belgian named Max Waem who had more authority and might be willing to help. He did not think that Waem would be interested in any transaction which brought him less than two million francs.

To Waem Christine talked for three hours. At one stage she produced some crystals which, though broken and useless, added verisimilitude to her claim that she was in direct radio contact with the Supreme Allied Command. At the end of the three hours Waem agreed to her terms. His own conditions included that of an assurance of protection from the *maquisards*, an offer which had also to be extended to Schenck. The price remained two million francs.

With commendable speed SOE in Algiers arranged for the money to be parachuted in. Cammaerts, Fielding and Sorensen were ordered out of prison, not, as they supposed, to go to their place of execution, but to find a car waiting for them with Christine in the passenger seat in front. The resistance groups with which Cammaerts was associated, and which he had done so much to build up, maintained their momentum, and as the Allied armies began to advance they held open the whole of the *route Napoléon* from Cannes through Digne to Grenoble.

In the latter part of 1944 Christine and Kennedy were both selected as members of missions to be sent to Poland if conditions allowed. But the first SOE mission to Poland having been able to achieve virtually nothing, it was decided, quite reasonably, to send no more. The Poland which was beginning to emerge from 1944 onwards was not a country in which either of them wanted to live, and so, when the war came to an end, they, like thousands of other Poles, had to start a new life in a new environment.

For Michael Lis, with his cosmopolitan upbringing, the problem was not a grave one. He began by forming a small plastics company and later joined a leading firm producing agricultural chemicals, becoming their European manager and later president of two of their European subsidiary companies.

Kennedy was cushioned for a time by a job in the Allied military government of Germany, but before long he was thrown on his own resources. Gradually he succeeded in building up a number of business interests in Germany.

Christine was less fortunate. She found post-war Britain a drab place, which in many respects it was. She had a variety of temporary jobs. These included operating the telephone switchboard in India House and selling dresses in Harrods. Later she made a number of voyages to Australia as a stewardess in a liner.

On the first of these voyages she met a steward named Dennis Muldowney, who was of Lancashire Irish background and who became one of a long list of men whose relationship to Christine was part that of passionate admirer and part that of lame duck. An undersized man of unprepossessing appearance, he was also a schizo-phrenic.

Between voyages Christine lived in a small hotel in Kensington. Muldowney, largely in order to be on hand when she returned to England, took a job as a kitchen porter in the Reform Club. He became more and more persistent, and Christine repeatedly begged him to leave her alone.

On the evening of 15 June 1952 Christine returned to her hotel and found Muldowney waiting in the foyer. He had brought a knife with him. With this he stabbed her to death.

A number of people were to say later that Christine, who had succeeded spectacularly in time of war, had proved incapable of adapting herself to conditions of peace. This I do not accept. It was only seven years after the war that she died, and those years were not easy for many people in circumstances similar to hers.

In searching for a new way of life she was of course constrained by her adamant determination never to accept the second-rate, though she might at times have to make do with the fourth- or fifth-rate. She was still journeying in the spirit, as well as rather restlessly in the flesh, when she met her death. Where that journeying might have led her can only be surmised, but I believe it would have been to something of exquisite quality. She had an indomitable spirit; she had great patience, as she had shown during the years in Cairo; and all those who served with her operationally, and many hundreds who did not, considered her to be in certain respects unique.

Some years after the war I was playing a party game, in which those present were asked to nominate the three people of their personal acquaintance to whom they would most readily apply the epithet 'great'. After some deliberation I put forward as my nominees Siegfried Sassoon, C. S. Lewis and Christine Granville. I do not think I have since had cause to change my judgment.

If I had to choose one person of my acquaintance as a symbol of perfect moral integrity I think I might well choose Francis Cammaerts.

Chapter 4

Assignments in Albania

A few days after his twenty-first birthday Julian Amery found himself entrusted with the task of preparing plans for a revolt in Albania and maintaining communications with potential leaders of Albanian resistance. Family background and early acquaintances helped to some extent to explain how at such an age he came to be given such an assignment. His own character and inclinations explained rather more.

His father, Leopold Amery, of whom Winston Churchill once said that he seemed to think the British Empire was his private property, had a better claim than anyone else to have been the author of the Balfour Declaration on the future of Palestine. When Leopold Amery was in occupation of Admiralty House as First Lord of the Admiralty Julian, from his nursery, regularly exchanged salutes with Admiral of the Fleet Lord Beattie. As a boy he received a golden dagger and a golden scimitar from King Feisal, the leader of the Arab revolt against the Turks. A little later the great Zionist, Chaim Weizmann, whom he and his father happened to meet on the Orient Express, gave him a box of Austrian toy soldiers.

From his schooldays at Eton he acquired, he later claimed, self-reliance and the habit of forming his own judgments. This he attributed largely to the practice of allowing every Eton boy from the moment he entered the school to have a room of his own, where he could think what he liked, read what he liked and, to his intimates, say what he liked. 'The room', he wrote, 'is a seed bed of individualists.'

After lunching in Austria with Franz von Papen, the German professional politician who was in effect hired to confer a spurious respectability on the creators of national socialism, Julian Amery decided that the prospect of a new world war must be taken seriously. After lunching with the Duke of Alba, General Franco's representative in London, he went to Spain to learn something at first hand of the Spanish Civil War.

His first visit to Spain was cut short to enable him to return for the next Oxford term, but in the long vacation he was back in Spain as a correspondent for the *Daily Express*. He came under fire, met an English combatant officer, Peter Kemp, whom he was to encounter later in SOE, and, through moving about a country at war and experiencing front-line conditions, gained greatly in self-confidence.

From his father, who was an expert mountaineer, he learnt other skills which could be of value in SOE, including skiing. Like Geoffrey Appleyard he was an early addict of water-skiing, but Amery's choice of practice area was the Mediterranean rather than the North Sea. He was, he believed, the first person to water-ski from Cap Ferrat to Monte Carlo.

The long vacation of 1939 was to have been Amery's last before taking his finals, and he decided to spend August and September on the Dalmatian coast reading books on economics. When Germany invaded Poland he made his way to Belgrade, presented a letter of introduction from his father to the British Minister, Sir Ronald Campbell, and was appointed Assistant Press Attaché. One of his earlier actions after acquiring diplomatic status was to steal a briefcase which belonged to a German and whose contents the British Naval Attaché found interesting.

Much of the early activity of Section D revolved round the British Legation in Belgrade. Amery, having given indications that he might be suited to its work, was duly enrolled, at first under the guidance of a former Arctic explorer, Lieutenant-Commander Alexander (Sandy) Glen, who appeared on the diplomatic list as Assistant Naval Attaché. In the absence of anyone better equipped Amery was asked to prepare a report on the possibilities of action in Albania. He wisely sought the guidance of a knowledgeable *Times* correspondent, Ralph Parker, who put him in touch with two Albanian brothers named Gani and Said Kryeziu.

Albania differed at that time from other countries in south-eastern Europe in that it was already occupied by an alien power, namely Italy, which was not yet at war with Britain. Plans for resistance had therefore to be made for a future contingency but with access to the country already restricted. The Kryezius recommended Section D to enlist the help of the one Albanian commander who had successfully resisted the invading Italian forces by his defence of Durazzo and who was something of a national hero. This was Abas Kupi, a mountain warrior who could neither read nor write. Abas Kupi came to Yugoslavia from Turkey, agreed to co-operate with the Kryezius, and broadened the incipient organization by bringing in Mustafa Jinishi, a member of the Albanian Communist party. In this way an embryo resistance organization in direct contact with the British was created, and waggonloads of corn concealing propaganda material and, later, rifles and ammunition were smuggled across the Yugoslav-Albanian border.

Amery's participation in Albanian affairs was to be interrupted for a number of years, during which he was engaged on other duties. Having become aware of plots to overthrow Prince Paul of Yugoslavia and King Boris of Bulgaria, both of whom, in conditions of uneasy neutrality, were pursuing pro-German policies, he recommended that Section D should give serious attention to the possibility of supporting the plots.

The Yugoslav conspirator whom Amery favoured was a Montenegrin named Jovan Dzonović. In Bulgaria he discussed plans with leaders of the Peasant party, in particular Gheorghi Dimitrov, who, confusingly, had both the same Christian name and the same surname as the better known Bulgarian communist, who was then in the Soviet Union. The British Foreign Office viewed with disfavour the idea of supporting *coups d'état* in either Yugoslavia or Bulgaria, and Sir Ronald Campbell made it clear that he did not want Amery in Belgrade.

When a *coup d'état* did take place in Yugoslavia in 1941 and a government came into power which was determined to resist invasion the carefully planned German time-table of aggression was upset. Some military strategists have even claimed that but for the delays which occurred in Yugoslavia in 1941 the German armies would have reached Moscow before being halted in mid-winter.

The extent of SOE's involvement in the 1941 *coup d'état* is still debated, though it is known that at least one of the principal Yugoslav conspirators was regularly in touch with SOE representatives. After the war Amery was still of the opinion that much more could have been achieved if Dzonović had been supported in his plans to overthrow Prince Paul a year earlier. In Bulgaria no *coup d'état* took place in either 1940 or 1941, and Dimitrov – that is to say the Peasant party Dimitrov – had to be brought out of Bulgaria in a packing case purporting to contain British Legation archives. He must have been a discreet conspirator, for I later shared a sleeping-car compartment on the Taurus Express with him for three days and three nights, during which I discovered nothing about him other than his name.

Amery served for some time in the Middle East, where he established friendly relations with officials of the Jewish Agency, which was in effect the precursor of the future Israeli government. The British government had reservations about allowing Jews in Palestine to enlist in the Allied armed forces, other than in restricted roles and in small numbers, for fear of offending Arabs. Because of the undercover nature of its operations and its limited requirements in manpower SOE was not included in any such ban, and Dr Weizmann, who was the Jewish Agency's President, personally entered into an agreement for the use of Jews in special operations.

When Amery was asked to produce a number of young men who could pass as Arabs for a secret mission he therefore approached Moshe Shertok, the Jewish Agency's *de facto* Foreign Minister, and the men were duly produced. In fact only one of them spoke Arabic, but this lack of expertise was compensated for by the quality of the volunteers and, particularly, by the personality of their leader. He was Moshe Dayan, later to become Israel's most famous soldier.

Dayan's unit was to be infiltrated, together with a small group of Australians, ahead of regular troops who were about to mount an invasion. The territory to be invaded, Syria, was still under the control of an administration which had declared itself loyal to the Vichy government. One of the tasks assigned to the combined Jewish-Australian group was to seize a bridge and save it from demolition.

Although the numbers involved amounted to less than a platoon Dayan appreciated the considerable political importance of the operation. If it succeeded the British would, he knew, be much readier than they had been to use Jewish troops in combatant roles. As none of his own men knew the area they had to cross Dayan chose as a guide an Arab, who performed his duties admirably, possibly spurred on by knowing that his wife and children were being held by Jews until the operation was completed.

There are conflicting accounts of the action which followed, Australian reports giving most of the credit to two Australians and Jewish reports giving most of the credit to two Jews. There is, however, no doubt that Dayan and a colleague advanced under covering fire on a French frontier post. Dayan tossed in a grenade, and the post was captured. The bridge was also held.

In the course of the action Dayan acquired a pair of field-glasses, which had belonged to a French officer who was killed. He was looking through these when they were hit by a bullet. Fragments of the shattered glass penetrated his eye, and in extreme pain he followed the subsequent progress of the battle, as he afterwards wrote, through his ears. He was taken to hospital, but his eye could not be saved. It was then that he began to wear the black eye-patch which was to become familiar to millions through press photographs and television.

SOE suffered from a shortage of Albanian speakers. For a time Section D's plans for fomenting unrest in Albania were the responsibility of Colonel Frank Stirling, who, after a close association with T. E. Lawrence, had been a personal adviser to King Zog of Albania and had supervised the training of Zog's gendarmerie. After Stirling was transferred in 1941 to other duties SOE's Albanian section consisted for well over a year of one woman. This was an anthropologist and student of folklore named Mrs Hasluck, commonly known as Fanny.

Fanny Hasluck was one of those intrepid female travellers who in the years before 1939 were to be found enjoying positions of authority in the most surprising places. She had visited Albania for the first time in 1919 and had been expelled twenty years later by the Italians, who had accused her, rightly or wrongly, of being a spy. She was the author of a work on Albanian grammar and had a deep affection for the Albanian people. Much of this she later extended to the British liaison officers who were sent to the country. She even had the endearing habit, when she learnt of their exact whereabouts in the field, of calling their attention to pleasant spots for picnicking.

Through the close contacts she maintained with Albanian exiles, and with the few Albanians who came out to Istanbul and beyond, Fanny Hasluck was certain that there were rebel bands operating in Albania. There were good grounds for her belief. Italian rule in Albania was neither popular nor particularly efficient. Over large areas of the mountains the clan system prevailed and fighting was common, particularly for the settlement of blood feuds. Men habitually went about armed, and houses had been constructed largely to serve as fortresses. The Communist party had a certain following, particularly among students and the landless, and its military potential was steadily developed by some veterans from the Spanish Civil War and by contact with the Yugoslav Partisans.

A decision was therefore taken to send a British military mission to Albania, and in the absence of suitable operational officers who spoke the language the mission was chosen on the basis of recent military achievement. Its leader, Neil (Billy) Maclean, was a regular officer, who was commissioned in the Scots Greys in 1939. He had served as a subaltern in Palestine and early in the Second World War had commanded a battalion of Amhara irregulars in the Abyssinian campaign. He was tall, fair-haired and exceptionally handsome. Julian Amery, who had known him at school, when he had been impressed by the knowledgeable way in which Maclean had talked about collecting silver, wrote of the toughness which he concealed 'beneath an elegant and lackadaisical manner'. He was, Amery added, at ease in extremes of violent action or 'dream-nurtured sloth'. Maclean was twenty-four when he was given command of the mission to Albania.

The second-in-command, David Smiley, was also a regular soldier, who had been commissioned in the Household Cavalry. He too had served in Abyssinia as well as in Syria and the Western Desert. He was an expert in demolition. Peter Kemp was to write of Smiley's ability to make up his mind quickly and speak it with a directness 'that compelled attention without giving offence'. He could talk knowledgeably on subjects ranging from the fall of the Mongol Empire to the cultivation of cacti. In Albania Smiley developed a strong affection for a mule, whom he named Fanny, and when the progress of guerrilla war was more than usually frustrating he could sometimes be seen with an arm around the mule's neck whispering into her ear.

Maclean and Smiley were parachuted to one of the British military missions in Greece and then made their way over the frontier. In Albania they were treated at first with suspicion. This was understandable. Rather more surprising was the belief that, in spite of the unmistakably British appearance of both of them, they must be Greek spies.

By the quality of their personalities, their evident military skills and the careful distribution of some of the gold sovereigns which they brought with them, and which were to become common currency in Albania, Maclean and Smiley gradually built up a position of some authority. Maclean's brief had been to give help and promises of arms to groups which could confidently be expected to fight Italians and Germans. His mission was not deemed to be a political one.

In accordance with their instructions therefore he and Smiley devoted much of their energies to training the guerrillas whom they found most active. These were the forces controlled by the National Liberation Committee. This body was in effect a front for the Communist party. Its directing spirit was its chief political commissar, Enver Hoxha.

So well did Maclean and Smiley carry out the tasks assigned to them on their first mission that it was found both possible and expedient to send in more missions. Whether the missions were sent to the right places and the right groups must be a matter of opinion. What is certain is that from 1943 onwards, among the staffs of the various Allied organizations concerned with resistance in the Balkans, of which, after a time, SOE was only one, problems of supply tended increasingly to take precedence over other problems. The expertise of people such as Fanny Hasluck was thought to be needed less rather than more. There was also a widespread inclination to treat Albania as simply a smaller replica of Yugoslavia. Some of the consequences of all this were to be unfortunate.

In 1943 a decision was taken to send two senior British officers to Yugoslavia, one to Tito's Partisans, the other to the forces of Draza Mihailović. One of those chosen was Brigadier E. T. Davies, who had acquired the nickname 'Trotsky' because a Sandhurst instructor had written of him that he had 'a kind of disciplined bolshevism'. This may well have been among the reasons why the War Office selected him for a somewhat irregular assignment. Davies himself later recorded that it seemed to him 'a fantastic thing' to ask a regular battalion commander, who knew nothing of the territory – he was referring to Yugoslavia – who had never parachuted and was forty-three to undertake such a mission, but he duly accepted.

When he reached Cairo Davies discovered that Winston Churchill had his own views on the right man to send to Marshal Tito, and he himself was assigned to Albania. The reasoning which prompted this decision seems to have been that, if Yugoslavia merited the presence of two British brigadiers, Albania surely merited the presence of one.

Maclean and Smiley had quickly adapted themselves to the requirements of guerrilla warfare, particularly the need to travel light. Davies was a gallant and well liked officer, but it seems improbable that he had ever studied Gubbins's pamphlets on guerrilla warfare, and after two decades as a regular officer he had decided views on how a headquarters should be staffed.

In his mission to Albania Davies included a chief clerk, who was in charge of reams of paper. An officers' mess and a sergeants' mess were established, with two huts for visiting officers. A cook, a baker and a barber were also appointed, all of them Italian prisoners. Special importance was attached to the barber because Davies, as he afterwards recorded, gave orders that 'particular attention was to be paid to personal appearance'. He had never, he added, been able to understand why 'a soldier needs to look like a brigand when he is on special operations'. The whole mission stood to at sunrise and sunset.

All this was as puzzling to Albanians generally as, to Enver Hoxha, was Davies's refusal to give a review of the world political situation on the grounds that he was a soldier, not a politician. Hoxha commented, reasonably enough from his point of view, that military situations depended on political situations.

It was one of the principal weaknesses of Davies's system that about a hundred mules were needed to transport his mission's stores. It was not easy to feed such a number and impossible to hide them for long. The outcome was to be foreseen. The Germans had set a high price on Davies's mission. Albanian collaborators were duly found, and the mission was ambushed. Davies was shot several times in the stomach and taken prisoner.

Although he was in uniform he might have expected to be shot or sent to a concentration camp as one engaged in what the Germans considered bandit warfare. In fact he was humanely treated and survived the war, but died while still in his early fifties. Some of the other members of the mission escaped to join British liaison officers elsewhere, but the second-in-command, Arthur Nicholls, after a terrible journey in which he suffered from frostbite and gangrene, died in the mountains.

The whole episode was a tragic example of what could happen in an operation which was ill-conceived in the first instance, and which was planned and carried out in defiance or contradiction or, most probably, simple ignorance of the principles of guerrilla warfare which had been defined for SOE some years before the organization came formally into being.

Billy Maclean had made his own observations during his first tour of duty in Albania and had formed a fairly clear picture of what was likely to happen unless effective action, part military, part political, were taken. After being brought out by sea to report he asked to be allowed to return with the specific task of trying to effect a reconciliation between the National Liberation Committee and the followers of Abas Kupi, who had remained persistently loyal to the British. This was agreed. He was authorized to promise arms to all those who would fight the Germans but to make it clear that no arms would be sent to any guerrilla leader unless he had already taken the field.

To accompany him Maclean chose David Smiley and, as a political adviser, Julian Amery. The party was parachuted into Albania on 19 April 1944. It was already late for the task which Maclean had set himself.

It was not to the credit of someone concerned with mounting the operation that the parachutes with which Maclean and Amery were dropped were not the standard silk ones but the cotton variety sometimes used for dropping stores. Fortunately they landed safely.

Some of the tasks which the mission performed could be classified as military. Smiley had the satisfaction of destroying a bridge which was regularly used for German transports and of knowing that it was six weeks before even temporary repairs could be effected. The mission also attracted a group of Turkoman deserters from the German forces, whom they organized into three fighting squadrons. In *Sons of the Eagle*, one of two absorbing books in which he depicted wartime Albania, Amery described how one of his boyhood dreams came true and he found himself riding at the head of a Turkoman horde. 'It was', he wrote, '*Prince Igor* with the Kruya mountains for a backcloth and lit only by the camp fires and the moon.'

Most of what the mission did and said was, however, affected by political considerations. Abas Kupi still hoped that the British would recognize Zog, who was then living in England, as King, but, realizing that they were unlikely to do so, agreed to the mission's suggestion that he should meet Enver Hoxha to discuss the formation of a common front. His only condition was that if the meeting did take place a British officer should be present.

Abas Kupi would have preferred to adopt the policy enjoined on a number of resistance movements in western Europe. This was to build up forces for a time of decisive action while continuing with particular acts of sabotage. He was understandably distressed by the reprisals which followed overt action against the Germans. For a number of British liaison officers it was indeed a sickening experience to see the consequences of the policies they had come to implement, the burnt villages, the homeless women and children. But this was war, and they had their orders.

After long discussions Abas Kupi accepted the terms of the Maclean mission. He even said that if the mission could impose friendship between him and the NLC he would be glad, though he added that he understood the intentions of the NLC too well to have any confidence in the outcome. He also agreed to call for action.

The first Partisan division of the NLC thereupon launched a major attack on Abas Kupi's followers. There can be little doubt that the immediate reason for the attack was the information brought to Enver Hoxha of the agreement reached between Abas Kupi and the Maclean mission.

Abas Kupi was declared an 'enemy of the people' by the NLC, a statement tantamount to a declaration of civil war. The British government was committed to support of the NLC, and it was logical that the Maclean mission should now be withdrawn. It was also indicative of what was happening in certain quarters concerned with resistance in the Balkans that the mission was forbidden to bring Abas Kupi out for fear of offending Enver Hoxha.

Abas Kupi had a rather shrewder appreciation of what might or might not influence Enver Hoxha's actions. He also had his own standards of conduct, from which he did not intend to depart. He made a twenty-seven-hour journey, during which he fought two actions against the Germans, in order to rejoin the Maclean mission and to say that it was his duty to escort its members safely to the coast.

Shortly after their return to Italy Maclean and Amery were received by Harold Macmillan, who was then British Resident Minister in the Mediterranean area. Such was the confusion by that time in British policy towards the Balkan countries that they found Macmillan, the principal British political figure in the whole theatre of war, un-equivocally in favour of doing what Maclean had been expressly forbidden to do, namely bringing Abas Kupi out of Albania. As it happened, Abas Kupi was wise enough to make his own way out. He died in exile many years later.

In retrospect it is difficult to pronounce SOE's involvement in Albania as other than an ultimate failure, which had auspicious beginnings.

The decision to transfer support in Yugoslavia from Mihailović to Tito was made from military considerations, in particular an assess-ment of the damage Tito's Partisans could inflict on the Germans. As such it was fully defensible. The same considerations did not apply in Albania.

German forces were, it is true, tied down in Albania in considerable numbers. A German parachute regiment was sent in as soon as it was realized that the Italians were suing for an armistice. Captured documents showed that the Germans attached importance to the British missions and exaggerated the power they wielded. Important individual acts of sabotage were carried out on SOE's initiative, including the destruction of chrome mines. Nevertheless the principal reason why German troops remained as long as they did was not to deal with Albanian guerrillas but to try to prevent an Allied invasion. After a time the German policy was to control the towns, the main lines of communication and the airfields, and to involve themselves as little as possible in what was happening elsewhere.

Once this was known to be German policy the NLC devoted most of its energies to eliminating its political rivals. When, belatedly, enough RAF aircraft were made available to drop supplies in sub-stantial quantities, most of these supplies were used for that purpose.

Perhaps not surprisingly a Muslim follower of Abas Kupi told Julian Amery that, while he quite understood that there were three parties in Albania, the agents of the Germans, the agents of the British and the agents of the Russians, what puzzled him was that the agents of the Russians were financed by British gold.

This indeed they were. The outcome of resistance was the complete triumph of the NLC. Albania became a police state, effectively sealed off from the outside world, and it was a telling commentary on British wartime involvement that, when an important conference was held in Oxford in 1962 to consider all aspects of resistance in Europe in the Second World War, the only country invited to send delegates which declined to do so was Albania.

Albania was, in short, one of the European countries in which the final balance-sheet of SOE's activities was not a very favourable one. (The Netherlands, for wholly different reasons, was another.) Yet the quality of men sent by SOE to Albania was as high as that to be found in any sphere of SOE's activities.

One of them was an explorer who, like others of his kind, gravitated towards SOE, feeling, no doubt, that it could provide him with the kind of activity for which he was already physically and mentally well equipped. This was Sandy Glen, Julian Amery's first mentor in subversive activities in Belgrade, who was to be a future Chairman of the British Tourist Authority and holder of a variety of other public offices.

Glen was the son of a Glasgow ship-owner. Before going up to Oxford he made a journey to Spitsbergen with seven other young men in a Peterhead fishing boat. Immediately after taking his finals at Oxford he became a member of an expedition to the little known territory called North-East Land. The leader of the expedition, Andrew Croft, was later to serve for a number of years in SOE. In a foreword to Glen's autobiographical work, *Footholds Against a Whirlwind*, Edward Crankshaw described him as belonging to a generation of young explorers who decided that 'the snow and the ice and the winter darkness of the Arctic (for others the desert and the jungle) should be seen as friends instead of enemies'.

During the North-East Land expedition, which lasted fourteen months, Glen discovered that with a temperature outside of −40 degrees Fahrenheit it was possible beneath the icecap to enjoy conditions comparable, as he put it, with those of a warm June day at Henley. Among other discoveries he made, which he found applicable both to Arctic conditions and to the life of a British liaison officer in the Balkans, was that good manners were even more important in such circumstances than at home, and that physical adaptability becomes a habit of mind which need never leave those who have once known it. In fourteen months in North-East Land he never, he later recalled, had to order anyone to do anything.

Glen's wartime activities included a certain amount of gun-running in Yugoslavia, revisiting Spitsbergen, serving in SOE's Norwegian section, operating a supply base on the Albanian coast and parachuting into Yugoslavia, where he was present at the first meetings between Tito's Partisans and the Red Army. He did not rate his contribution to the war effort in Albania very highly, but while he was there he had the opportunity of meeting a man whom he described as 'a first-class officer' and a delightful companion.

This was the future Director of the Shakespeare Memorial Theatre, Anthony Quayle, who was to combine the roles of actor, producer and theatre administrator, both in his own country and abroad, with, arguably, as much distinction as any other Englishman of his generation.

Quayle left Rugby School earlier than he would have wished because of family financial difficulties. Faced, as he saw it, with a choice between working in the theatre or in journalism, he decided in favour of the theatre because, as he afterwards explained, the girls were prettier. He began as a stooge to a music-hall comedian and had graduated to the point of being an established Old Vic actor when war broke out in 1939. There followed for him six years of real, as opposed to celluloid, war, including a period as an SOE liaison officer in Albania.

Unlike so many who described their experiences in SOE in memoirs, Quayle described his in a novel entitled *Eight Hours from England*. The disguise is fairly transparent and was not really intended to deceive. Quayle even gave the central character, Major Overton, his mother's family name.

The book evokes memorably the atmosphere of operations in Albania: the lice and the thefts, the feuds and the frustrations, the isolation and the companionship. The initial briefing given to Overton is all too authentic. 'Know anything about Albania? No? All the better: you won't have a political bias. It's the least developed of all the Balkan countries, and so possibly the best fun.' There was no Fanny Hasluck around to brief Overton.

First-hand experience of life in enemy-occupied territory was needed to evoke one observation in Quayle's *Eight Hours from England*: 'In this strange existence every man encountered had a special significance, for on the correct assessment of his character might at any moment depend life itself.'

Another British liaison officer to operate in Albania was one for the exercise of whose talents SOE might almost seem to have been designed. This was Peter Kemp.

At Cambridge Peter Kemp was elected secretary of the university's Conservative Association. He was a somewhat unorthodox Conservative, so much so that his father once said that he thought God must have made him for a bet. When he came down from Cambridge, being determined to take an active part in the Spanish Civil War, he enlisted in the force which appealed most strongly to him politically and romantically. This was the army of the Requeté, a movement which had originated in the Carlist war in the 1830s. It was aligned militarily, although not ideologically, with the main forces of General Franco.

Kemp rose from the rank of private to that of sergeant and was later commissioned. In a deliberate search for experience of serious warfare, which he did not believe he would find with the courageous, idealistic, but rather loosely disciplined and technically ill qualified troops of the Requeté, he obtained a transfer to the Foreign Legion. He was sent to the Guadalajara front, where he was severely wounded in jaw, forearm and hand. At one stage he was engaged, although he did not know it, in an action against a British battalion of the International Brigade.

He also became familiar with some of the other concomitants of the kind of war which he would later experience with SOE. These included lice, jaundice and seeing prisoners shot. They also included encounters with a wide range of rich and not readily forgotten characters. One whom he met in Spain was a White Russian colonel, who was so disgusted by the way the British, as he put it, had let the Tsar down that he had decided to abstain from drinking Scotch whisky. Another, who was to become a close friend and who also served in SOE, was Archibald Lyall, wit, *bon viveur*, linguist and travel-writer. He was the author of *Lyall's Twenty-five Languages of Europe,* a work of erudition which, Kemp later discovered, enabled one of its devotees to complete the seduction of a Lithuanian chambermaid in less than fifteen minutes.

Because of the wounds he had received in Spain Kemp, like Alfgar Hesketh-Prichard, began the Second World War classified as unfit for military service. Also like Hesketh-Prichard he found ways of overcoming this restriction. A chance meeting with Douglas Dodds-Parker brought him into contact with MI(R), and he was directed to the cavalry Officer Cadet Training Unit at Weedon. Here what to many seemed the archaic discipline of the riding school proved to be by far the most useful training he received for the kind of war in which he was to be engaged. He also met Harold Perkins, who was later to send him to occupied Poland.

The first operational mission for which Kemp was selected was planned to take place in Norway in 1940. It was to have involved a journey by submarine, the blowing-up of the Bergen–Oslo railway, reconnaissance of a lake as a possible landing place for seaplanes, and escape to Sweden. Because of damage to the submarine the operation, fortunately perhaps, was never launched. There followed the series of raids under the command of Gus March-Phillipps and Geoffrey Appleyard, from which Kemp emerged as one of the comparatively small number of survivors, and selection as a liaison officer to be parachuted into Albania.

In his briefing before being dropped Kemp was told more than once that he was to ignore politics and consider himself purely a soldier. He was already sophisticated enough to doubt whether such a briefing could have any real meaning. During the ten months during which he traversed the length of Albania from the Greek frontier to Montenegro his doubts were to be amply confirmed.

In the course of his journeyings he was twice completely surrounded by enemy forces, once shooting his way out, the other time escaping disguised as a woman. He was prostrate for a time with malaria, when long passages of Boswell flashed through his mind and he would awake to find himself making pronouncements in the manner of the great doctor. He made a reconnaissance of an area which had been incorporated by the Axis powers into Albania and which had formerly been partly Montenegrin and partly Macedonian. His presence there was considered unwelcome by Tito's Partisans. He also paid a visit to the Albanian capital, Tirana, in order to prepare a political report. Julian Amery paid a similar visit, but, being comparatively short and dark, he at least could pass as a Mediterranean type. Kemp was tall and fair and unmistakably Nordic.

Before his final departure from the Balkans Kemp came into contact with Bill Hudson, the first man to be sent by SOE to occupied Yugoslavia. They were to serve together on a mission to Poland, which has been referred to before and will be referred to again. The culmination of their mission was a month's detention by the NKVD in a Soviet prison.

After the NKVD had released him Kemp spent a week or two on leave in Ireland, and the contrast between Russian and Irish hospitality caused him some anxiety when he had to face a medical examination before being accepted for service in the Far East. To his relief the doctor who examined him gave him a piece of paper, which was apparently a prescription and on which were written the words: 'Say no thank you three times a day.'

The new operational sphere for which Kemp was chosen was Japanese-occupied Thailand or, as it was then called, Siam, with which Britain was formally at war. That there was a Free Siamese Movement was known in 1943, but when SOE received information that the effective leader of the movement was Nai Pridi, the man whom the Japanese had accepted as Regent, doubts were understandably expressed.

Two parties of Siamese, who had been trained by SOE and on whom exceptionally good reports had been received from the training schools, were parachuted in, but both were captured. The leader of one of the parties, who was known as Khem, was smuggled out of prison by a warder, himself a member of the Free Siamese Movement, and taken to the chief of the Siamese police, whom the warder believed to be sympathetic to the FSM's aims. Khem told the police chief he was an emissary of the British, and on the Regent's instructions he was given secret access to his radio set and ciphers and allowed to communicate with SOE.

To SOE it was not at first clear whether Khem was operating with the approval of the Regent or under the control of the Japanese. The disastrous experience in the Netherlands, where for a long time all communications with SOE were controlled by the Germans, naturally influenced thinking. Andrew Gilchrist, a future British Ambassador in Dublin, who had joined SOE after serving in the British Legation in Bangkok and who knew the Regent personally, therefore proposed a test question. This was to ask the Regent to name Gilchrist's home in the Scottish Highlands. A Siamese girl was believed to be the only person in Siam who knew the name, and the Regent knew that Gilchrist and the girl had been on friendly terms.

The Regent passed the test and, with the supporting evidence it now had, SOE decided it was in touch with a genuine resistance movement. The decision proved to be correct. A senior SOE officer, Victor Jacques, a lawyer by profession, was able, in spite of his height of 6 feet 4 inches and his unmistakably European appearance, to spend five days with the Regent, come out to report, and then return as Lord Louis Mountbatten's personal representative. A number of other operational missions were also sent in, including one led by David Smiley.

Shortly after dropping into north-east Siam Smiley was severely injured by an incendiary device in a briefcase which burst into flames accidentally. He suffered first, second and third degree burns, was unable to sleep and was continually assailed by maggots. One rather gruesome signal from an officer accompanying him reported the removal of seventy-three maggots from Smiley's neck.

Smiley was brought out by Dakota, and when Kemp reached the SOE operational base he found him, as he put it, 'nearly well enough to return to the field'. Kemp himself was suffering from a recurrence of malaria and from bacillary dysentery, but with the help of yet another sympathetic doctor, who dosed him heavily, he decided he was fit for operational duty.

Kemp was accompanied into Siam by an officer who had also been involved in Albanian resistance. This was Rowland Winn, who had broken his leg in a parachute landing and had spent a painful month in a shepherd's hut in the Albanian mountains. He and Kemp had first met when Winn had been a newspaper correspondent in the Spanish Civil War.

Winn, a stocky figure with a thick moustache and a monocle, had original ideas on soldiering. Finding life in a holding camp in Virginia Water excessively boring, he had left a note for his brigadier to say he had gone to London and, if required for operational duty, could be found at the Cavalry Club. When the aircraft which was to drop him and Kemp west of the Mekong River began to circle over the dropping zone he was to be seen mumbling or intoning. He was not, Kemp discovered, praying, as might have been expected, but reciting appropriate verses of Noël Coward's *Mad Dogs and Englishmen*.

Kemp spent five months in Siam, which in the latter days of occupation offered certain compensations for hardships endured. To celebrate his thirtieth birthday a party was held, at which the food on offer included sucking pigs, ducks, water buffalo, eels, frogs, barking deer, bamboo shoots and a variety of tropical fruits, all served by pretty, smiling girls. Kemp's radio was then out of action. To many people in these circumstances the temptation, after nearly six years of war, to lapse into a condition of total hedonism would have been considerable.

The temptation was resisted, and even after the Japanese surrender Kemp and Winn found themselves supplying smuggled arms to their French and Laotian allies to enable them to defend themselves against attacks by the Viet-Minh. In one of three admirable books of memoirs which he wrote, and which must rank high in the literature of SOE, Kemp described how service in the organization had caused him at different times to play the parts of journalist, commercial traveller, politician, brigand, gigolo and, finally, smuggler.

Smiley and Winn returned to England earlier than Kemp, who took over Smiley's command. After an interlude in Java Kemp's final phase of service in the Far East was on the island of Bali. There he assumed command both of the Japanese naval and military garrison and of the civil administration until the Dutch authorities returned.

By then Julian Amery and Billy Maclean had jointly stood as Conservative candidates for the parliamentary constituency of Preston, which at that time returned two members, Amery being returned by a small majority and Maclean losing by fourteen votes. Maclean was later to serve as MP for Inverness. Amery became Secretary of State for Air and held other ministerial offices concerned with civil aviation and housing. Rowland Winn, as Lord St Oswald, was also active politically. David Smiley continued soldiering, among the posts he was to fill being that of commander of the armies of the Sultan of Oman.

Peter Kemp remained a lone operator, writing his books, turning up as a newspaper correspondent in a variety of places where people fought for ideals which they held dear, including Budapest in 1956, undeterred by his wounds and his gout and other physical afflictions.

There may be braver men than Peter Kemp, but I am not certain that I have met any of them. He, no doubt, would dispute the implied verdict. In one of his books of memoirs, *No Colours or Crest*, he described how, when he came under shellfire in Albania, he threw himself to the ground, as experience had taught him to. David Smiley, by contrast, in Kemp's words, 'showed an irritating indifference and walked on, his head held high, as though he were being pelted by urchins with snowballs while mounting guard'.

Chapter 5

Yugoslav Conflicts

Of the SOE officers sent to occupied Yugoslavia two may be said to have made major contributions to an understanding of what was happening inside the country and to the determination of the policy of the western Allies. One of these was a South African mining engineer. The other was a young Oxford don.

The mining engineer, Bill Hudson, was a tall, good-looking man of magnificent physique, who had been an amateur boxer of distinction. He came to Yugoslavia in 1937 and worked for a French company, for whom he managed a gold mine. He also did a good deal of prospecting and so became familiar with extensive areas of Yugoslavia as well as acquiring a good knowledge of Serbo-Croat.

Hudson was introduced to clandestine warfare by S. W. (Bill) Bailey, a metallurgist, who was one of those men of foresight whom Chester Beatty had made available to Section D. Bailey was a gifted linguist, had a good understanding of Yugoslav politics and politicians, and moved explosives around the country with calm assurance. He became mentor to Hudson, Julian Amery and a number of other members of SOE on a variety of subjects.

Hudson was appointed Assistant Naval Attaché in the British Legation in Belgrade, although he knew virtually nothing about ships except how to blow them up. Sandy Glen later recorded that 'Bill Hudson sank at least one German-going ship loading manganese ore on the Dalmatian coast.' Whether this is true or not, a number of enemy ships did come to grief off the Yugoslav coast at that time in circumstances which have not yet been fully explained. When a violent explosion occurred in Split aboard an Italian ship an enquiry was held. At the enquiry several of Split's prostitutes testified that they had heard Italian sailors say they intended to scuttle the ship because they did not relish the prospect of having to fight against the Royal Navy. Their explanation, surprisingly perhaps, was accepted.

Hudson left Belgrade and reached Istanbul, where he learnt that an attempt was to be made to sail a tanker, which the Germans were known to be watching closely, to Egypt. As it seemed unlikely that the vessel could pass the Dodecanese without being captured Hudson was instructed to prepare her for demolition. He then took passage in the tanker with full authority to put the demolition drill into effect as soon as he received the order to do so. Against expectations the tanker came safely through, first to Cyprus, and then to Egypt.

On 28 August 1941 Winston Churchill informed Hugh Dalton that he had heard from General Simović, who was then Prime Minister of the Yugoslav government in exile, that there was widespread guerrilla activity in Yugoslavia. This, he wrote, needed 'cohesion, support and direction from outside'. Dalton replied that plans had already been made to achieve what Churchill wanted.

It was generally assumed that the guerrilla activity was being carried out by the so-called Četniks, a body whose name had formerly been given to Serbian irregular detachments which had fought against the Turkish occupation forces. The most prominent of the Četniks was Colonel Draza Mihailović, a regular officer in the Royal Yugoslav Army. Bill Bailey was personally acquainted with Mihailović and was aware of his strongly pro-British and anti-German sentiments. Glen and Amery had invited Mihailović to dinner during their tour of duty in Belgrade, and both had come to the conclusion that he was too much of a regular soldier in his habits of thought to be suited to clandestine activity, although Mihailović had in fact lectured on guerrilla warfare at the Yugoslav military academy.

After the defeat of the Yugoslav Army in the summer of 1941 Milhailović with a small band of followers made his way to Ravna Gora. There he reached an accommodation with local officials, in the first instance by handing over a number of escaped convicts, who were plundering the countryside, to the police. Gradually he was able to build up his forces, with recruits coming to him from Belgrade. Mihailović's following was exclusively Serbian and Montenegrin, and his control over the various Četnik bands which grew up was looser than was generally supposed outside Yugoslavia. Several of the commanders of small detachments were Orthodox priests or village elders, whose concern was almost wholly with local rather than national affairs.

It was to this resistance movement that it was decided to send a mission consisting of two officers of the Royal Yugoslav Army and Bill Hudson. By then Hudson had the rank of captain in the British Army, although, as he afterwards pointed out, he had not even learnt how to salute. The mission was despatched by submarine, Julian Amery taking passage as briefing officer. He gave Hudson his ciphers and brought a message of good wishes from Winston Churchill but was able to offer little else which was likely to be of value.

The commander of the submarine, Wilfrid (Sam) Woods, was a tall, impressive figure who later became Commander-in-Chief, Home Fleet, and, after his retirement from the Royal Navy, Chairman of the Royal National Life-boat Institution. Noticing that Hudson and his companions were rather ill-equipped, he provided them with various items from his ship's stores, including a pair of binoculars. With these it was possible to see that the coast of Montenegro, where the party was to be landed, was fairly well guarded.

Hudson and the two Yugoslav officers went ashore on 20 September 1941. They had to cross a good deal of open ground, consisting of scrub and limestone, in the early morning, but had the good fortune to meet a Franciscan friar, who was looking for his goats. The friar acted as their guide, and they were able to make contact with a resistance group of about a hundred men. These men were followers not of Mihailović, but of the Croatian revolutionary Josip Broz, who chose to be known as Tito.

One of them was Milovan Djilas, an independent-minded Montenegrin intellectual and author, subsequently, of a number of political works. He was soon to be dismissed by Tito from the Montenegrin command for so-called errors and after the war was to have a long stretch in prison for even more errors. Another was Arso Jovanović, whose adherence to Stalinism after the break between Tito and the Soviet Union in 1948 was to cost him his life. Jovanović agreed to accompany Hudson and the Yugoslav members of his mission to Serbia, where Hudson was to have his first meeting with Tito.

Tito was a Moscow-trained revolutionary, who had been imprisoned for subversive activities in pre-war Yugoslavia. The Yugoslav Communist party had been declared illegal, and at the beginning of the Second World War it had only about 8,000 members. Of these Tito, as Secretary-General, was by far the most influential. Among his tasks had been to find recruits for the Spanish Civil War, and as a result he was provided with a trained élite of guerrilla fighters for his later campaigns.

Tito regarded himself as being wholly under Stalin's orders, and when Germany invaded the Soviet Union in 1941 he waited for instructions. 'For once,' as Djilas was to write later, 'Moscow did not delay,' and Tito began to build up, with exemplary speed and efficiency, a guerrilla force. This force was at all times under communist control, but it was wisely described at first, largely for recruiting purposes, as the National Liberation Partisan Detachments, to be foreshortened after a time to the single word 'Partisans'.

From the outset the strategy of the Partisans and that of the Četniks differed fundamentally. Mihailović wished to conserve his forces and bring them into effective action when, as he assumed they would, Allied armies landed in the Balkans. This belief in future Allied landings was widespread among the Četniks. Jasper Rootham, an SOE liaison officer with the Četnik forces, who described his experiences in a book entitled *Missfire*, was repeatedly told that when the Allies landed every bridge and every railway line in Yugoslavia would be destroyed. Mihailović was concerned with the effects of reprisals and wished where possible to prevent the destruction of property.

As a revolutionary Tito had no interest in preserving property or the existing social order. His policy was to bring recruits out of the towns, enable them to live off the countryside, and achieve maximum mobility. This mobility was maintained to a remarkable degree even when the strength of the Partisan forces began to be measured in divisions. In so far as they served to arouse the anger of the population against the occupying forces Tito rather welcomed enemy reprisals.

Tito and Mihailović met for the first time the day before Hudson landed in Yugoslavia. The meeting was a limited success, for Mihailović was under the impression that Tito was a Russian. Nevertheless in the autumn of 1941 there was still a possibility that a temporary wartime alliance could be forged and a common front presented. On Hudson, as the sole representative of the Allied world outside, was placed the considerable burden of doing what he could to bring this about.

Tito was favourably impressed by Hudson and treated him with some frankness. Djilas, for his part, was struck by the fact that Hudson made no attempt to conceal his knowledge of the Serbo-Croat language. He expected something much more subtle in a representative of the British secret service. Djilas also described Hudson as 'sparing in humour', but that the same kind of humour should appeal to a South African mining engineer and a Montenegrin marxist was not perhaps to be expected.

Djilas gave orders that the radio set which Hudson had brought with him should be hidden and told Hudson that the Partisans were looking for it. Tito thereupon countermanded these orders, saying Hudson should be treated as an ally. Hudson, for his part, used the set to report favourably on the fighting potential of the Partisan forces he had encountered. Tito also protected Hudson from verbal attacks by other Partisan leaders for the way in which Britain had treated Czechoslovakia in 1938. But when Hudson suggested establishing radio communication with a British base, offering to arrange ciphers, wavelengths and schedules if the Partisans could capture a suitable radio set from the Germans, Tito expressed no interest. At that stage he felt that the only link with the outside world he needed was the link with Moscow.

While he was with Tito Hudson received instructions by radio from SOE to make his way as soon as possible to the headquarters of Mihailović. One reason why he was required to move quickly was that Mihailović had established radio communications with the British via Malta, using a set which had been built for him by an amateur. He was sending his messages *en clair*, and it was obviously desirable for him to be able to communicate in cipher. Hudson told Tito openly that he intended to visit Mihailović, and Tito responded by providing him with suitable documents.

For a man who had stumbled unexpectedly on a resistance organization of which he had no prior knowledge; whose mission was greeted by the peasants, as Djilas noted, 'with hope and joy' but was regarded by men under the direct orders of Moscow with unconcealed distrust; whose travelling companions were, understandably, considered politically undesirable; and who brought with him nothing of material help to the Partisan movement, Hudson, by the force of his own personality, had achieved not a little. With Mihailović he was to be less successful, largely because of the presence of the two Yugoslav majors who accompanied him and who ought never to have been sent.

The two Yugoslav majors, Ostojić and Lalatović, carried out their instructions to the letter and were in no way guilty of dereliction of duty. They were however emissaries, not of the Allied High Command, but of the Royal Yugoslav Government, which, because of its narrow and almost exclusively Serbian outlook and the petty bickering between its ministers, was in many respects the least satisfactory of all the exiled governments which found their way to Britain.

The presence of these two officers in the company of Hudson and the messages they brought from the government in exile convinced Mihailović that he had the unqualified support of Britain. He believed, rightly, that the western world knew nothing of the activities of the Partisans. Accounts of his own military engagements, usually exaggerated, were being broadcast via Malta, and he saw no reason to compromise.

Sensing that civil war could soon come about, Hudson sent

warnings to SOE not to provide military support for Mihailović until the outcome of further negotiations with the Partisans was known, and until Mihailović had given satisfactory assurances that he could and would fight against the Germans. These warnings were to be disregarded.

When Hudson informed Mihailović that he intended to revisit Tito, a Četnik council of war was held in order to decide whether or not Hudson should be killed, because of the danger of what might happen if he fell into the hands of the Germans. The purpose of this meeting and its outcome were communicated to Hudson by Mihailović himself. Though Hudson's life was spared Mihailović stated emphatically that he was not willing to have him present when he next met Tito, as he considered the meeting to be an internal Yugoslav affair. Tito by contrast stated that Hudson's presence would be welcome.

The second and final meeting in time of war between Mihailović and Tito was wholly nugatory. Tito proposed joint operations against the Germans and against General Nedić's collaborationist forces, common provisioning of Partisans and Četniks, and the setting up of provisional administrations in liberated areas. Mihailović turned all these proposals down.

Shortly after the meeting Mihailović launched an attack against the Partisan headquarters in Uzice, in which he lost about a thousand men. A little more than a month after this the young King Peter in exile appointed Mihailović Commander-in-Chief of the Yugoslav Army.

After he had launched his attack against the Partisans Mihailović refused to see Hudson or to allow him the use of his radio. Before long Mihailović was forced to retreat, with a comparatively small force, into east Bosnia, and at this point he abandoned Hudson altogether.

Hudson had already had his money, his compass and his ring stolen when he had been stopped by followers of General Nedić. Now he had to face a winter in the mountains alone, with no resources, no radio and no other means of communication with the outside world. His living conditions were appalling, and such nourishment as he had came largely from potatoes. Only a man of exceptional moral and physical fibre could have survived. Hudson did survive, and after some months he came on the air again and was able to provide various British authorities with information about conditions in Yugoslavia, of which they were dangerously ignorant.

What might have happened if Hudson had arrived without Majors Ostojić and Lalatović and been able to reason with Mihailović alone; if

SOE had accepted Hudson's advice on how and when to furnish Mihailović with material support; and if transport had been made available for sending in more officers to provide second and third opinions on Hudson's assessments are questions which will never be answered.

Throughout 1942 Mihailović's fame spread widely. This was not surprising. During most of that year the war news was, from the British point of view, almost wholly bad, and the thought of a guerrilla leader operating in mountains within the confines of *Festung Europa* brought cheer and comfort. The BBC made much of Mihailović's movement in broadcasts to a variety of countries, and it even seemed likely that, just as the name of the Norwegian Quisling had become the popular symbol of collaboration, so the name of Mihailović might come to stand for resistance.

There were however a few people outside Yugoslavia who had doubts. One of these was Hugh Seton-Watson, son of the man who had done so much to ensure Czechoslovakia's independence after the First World War, himself a Winchester and New College scholar and a future Professor of Russian History at London University's School of Slavonic and East European Studies. In SOE's offices in Cairo Hugh Seton-Watson applied his considerable mind to an examination of all the information available on happenings inside Yugoslavia. This led him to the conclusion that the great bulk of the German forces there had been sent to areas in which Partisan rather than Četnik forces were operating.

Seton-Watson's findings were confirmed from an impeccable source. This was the process known as Ultra, whereby the contents of German messages in cipher were known to the British. The Ultra findings were communicated to only a few people, but they tipped the scales in favour of a decision to send some exploratory missions to the Partisans. The help of the organization in the United States known as British Security Co-ordination, headed by Sir William Stephenson, was invoked, and several Serbo-Croat-speaking Canadians were made available.

One mission to Slovenia was led by Major William Jones, a one-eyed Canadian veteran of the First World War and a man of great gallantry, great goodwill and great gullibility. Another mission had an unfortunate end. This was led by Major Terence Atherton, who had worked for many years as a journalist in Belgrade and who, like Hudson, tried to move between Partisan and Četnik forces. Somewhere along the way he and his radio operator, whose set was not functioning, were murdered. It is generally believed that they were killed for the gold they were carrying, and the political allegiance, if any, of their murderers has never been definitely established.

Towards the end of May 1943 a mission was dropped near Tito's headquarters which included two officers of the rank of captain. One of them, Bill Stuart, was a Canadian engineer in his early forties, who was born in Zagreb, where his father had served as consul, and who spoke excellent Serbo-Croat. The other, F. W. D. (Bill) Deakin, was a young Oxford historian whom Winston Churchill had engaged as a research assistant when he was working on the life of his ancestor, the first Duke of Marlborough.

This association with Churchill gave rise to a belief among the Partisans that the British Prime Minister had paid them the compliment of sending his secretary to join them. In fact Deakin was chosen for the mission entirely without Churchill's knowledge. He had come into SOE through one of the more orthodox channels, the War Office having passed on its records of his command of languages, which included French, German and Italian. He served for a time under Stephenson in the United States and was sent to Cairo largely through insisting that he should be allowed to go into the field.

The Deakin-Stuart mission arrived to find the Partisans engaged in battle. In a bombing attack which took place soon after they reached Tito's headquarters Stuart was killed. Tito and Deakin were both wounded, Deakin having his left boot blown off when his leg was hit. A German order, which was captured later and which was written two days after the mission's arrival, stated that, the Partisans having been encircled, no man capable of bearing arms was to leave the circle alive.

In fact Tito extricated some 10,000 Partisans from the circle. It was done by night in silence in such a way that the Germans seemed unaware of the Partisans' presence. In his book, *The Embattled Mountain*, in which he described his experiences in Yugoslavia, Deakin wrote: 'We moved as the blind, and survival depended on keeping touch. Fear was latent and subtle: its most conscious and pervading image in the mind was the thought of being lost and left behind alone.' He quenched his thirst with dew from fir cones and for food followed the Partisan example of boiling wild spinach and clover in a mess tin.

Deakin did not have Hudson's physique. He was of stocky build, and his legs might have been thought too short for his body. He was a city dweller suddenly transported into conditions of mountain warfare. But his equanimity and the conduct of the other members of his mission, another Canadian of Croatian origin, a British radio operator, a Northern Irish NCO in the Royal Marines and a Palestinian Jew, aroused the admiration of the Partisans, as the diaries of Vladimir Dedijer, a close associate of Tito's, who was appointed interpreter to the British mission, make clear.

Milovan Djilas described Deakin as 'outstandingly intelligent'. Fitzroy Maclean, who was to become Deakin's commanding officer in Yugoslavia, wrote that 'his friendly nature endeared him to all who came in contact with him' and did much to overcome Partisan suspicions. Basil Davidson, another British liaison officer with the Partisans, who spent a short time with Deakin after being parachuted in, found him not only in good spirits but capable of describing the setting as 'pure Robin Hood'.

Deakin was aware that Tito attached great importance to the presence of the British mission, not at first as a source of material aid, but as witness that the Partisans were fighting the Germans and fighting them effectively. They were doing so at that stage almost exclusively with arms captured from the enemy, and Deakin was much impressed by their fighting qualities.

Bickham Sweet-Escott, the staff officer, who in his book *Baker Street Irregular* gave a good picture of SOE's activities as seen from the centre, singled out Deakin's radioed reports from the field as being of exceptional quality. Largely for this reason it was decided to bring him out so that he could report fully in person. This gave him an unexpected opportunity to renew his acquaintance with Winston Churchill, who was on a visit to Cairo. He also met Jan Christiaan Smuts, enemy of the British in the South African war and close adviser of Churchill's in the Second World War. As they were about to go into dinner together Smuts asked Deakin who he was. Deakin replied that he supposed he was some sort of bandit. Smuts commented: 'So was I once.'

Of Deakin's discussion with Churchill there seems, surprisingly, to be no written record, in spite of the fact that the British Ambassador to the Royal Yugoslav Government was present. The conclusion Churchill later reached was that Britain needed what he called 'a daring ambassador-leader with these hardy and hunted guerrillas'. He also expressed the opinion that help to the Partisans must be increased, if necessary at the expense of the bombing of Germany. This was not the only occasion on which Churchill's personal intervention was needed to augment the meagre supply of aircraft made available to SOE.

For his daring ambassador-leader Churchill chose, not 'Trotsky' Davies, who had been proposed, but a man who had found the only escape route which nobody could deny to a member of the Foreign Office staff who wanted to join the armed forces, namely to stand for Parliament. This was Fitzroy Maclean, who had served in the British embassies in Paris and Moscow, and who in 1941 became both MP for Lancaster and a private in the Cameron Highlanders. In September 1943 he was parachuted to Tito with the rank of brigadier. He was joined by a capable, intelligent and sensitive regular soldier named Vyvyan Street. His mission was later to be augmented by the presence of Randolph Churchill and Evelyn Waugh.

Meanwhile SOE had sent a number of missions to the Četniks. The chief of these was headed by the man who came to know Mihailović better than any other Englishman. This was Bill Bailey, sophisticated and lively-minded metallurgist, now a somewhat portly officer with the rank of colonel. Bailey made contact with Hudson and having at last a radio set at his disposal, Hudson sent a series of more than two hundred messages summarizing the information he had acquired about conditions in Yugoslavia.

The British liaison officers found the Četniks for the most part friendly, hospitable and conscious of being surrounded by a disturbing number of enemies. Mihailović even told Bailey that his enemies were first Tito, then the Croats and Muslims, and then the Germans and the Italians. With a list as formidable as this it was not surprising that the Četniks chose, where possible, to husband their resources. Nor was it surprising that they sometimes greatly exaggerated their military achievements. Unfortunately for them the effect of this was, as Jasper Rootham stated, to undermine the confidence of the British officers who were 'the sole impartial interpreters of their cause to the outside world'.

Basing his judgment on first-hand observation, Rootham commented: 'Mihailović's movement was, in spite of all its shortcomings, hindering and not helping the Axis.' This was the prevailing view among the British liaison officers with the Četniks, but the scale of hindrance was so small, particularly in relation to what the Partisans were achieving, that the possibility of withdrawing support from Mihailović began to be considered seriously.

As an interim measure it was decided to send in a senior military observer, another brigadier, and to specify certain targets which Mihailović should attack as evidence of good faith. Unwisely Mihailović declined to take up the challenge, probably because he did not believe the British meant their threats seriously. The process of evacuating all British missions from Četnik-controlled territory was therefore begun. In making this evacuation possible Mihailović and the other Četnik commanders behaved with impeccable loyalty towards their former British allies. One Četnik leader even asked Rootham's permission to kiss the small Union Jack he had with him.

An officer of the United States Office of Strategic Services (OSS), Robert H. McDowell, a professor of Balkan history, remained for a time with Mihailović after the British had abandoned him. The reason given for his continued presence was that he could help American airmen, who had been shot down in the Balkans, to escape. The Partisans did not of course believe this explanation.

Mihailović's followers dwindled steadily in numbers until he himself became a lone and hunted fugitive. He was caught, brought to trial, and executed for high treason in July 1946.

With Fitzroy Maclean appointed as Churchill's personal nominee, and able to bypass SOE in consequence, the part played by SOE in 1944 in determining British policy towards Yugoslavia was less and less important. There were other reasons too why its role became a secondary one.

After the withdrawal of the British missions from the Četniks a policy of full support for the Partisans was decided upon, and the principal need was now the supply of conventional military stores. The Chiefs of Staff therefore came to the reasonable conclusion that the control of operations to Yugoslavia should be vested in the service which provided the transport, namely the RAF. A new body came into existence named the Balkan Air Force under the command of Air-Vice-Marshal William Elliot. It was, Sir John Slessor recorded with justifiable pride, 'the first occasion, other than in the air defence of the United Kingdom, that the predominant partner was to be the airman.'

The Balkan Air Force carried out its task admirably. Supply problems seemed suddenly to disappear. One of the major tasks was the evacuation of wounded Partisans, of whom nearly 1,000 were airlifted from Montenegro in a single day.

SOE had long had to depend on four Liberator aircraft for supplying all the resistance movements in the Balkans. Of these one was almost permanently grounded and two were frequently undergoing engine repairs. That anything at all was achieved with such resources may seem remarkable. It was also a sad illustration of the rigidity of inter-service compartmentalism that when aircraft were needed for another service, namely SOE, scarcely any were available, whereas once the RAF assumed command there was a sudden abundance.

British liaison officers were frequently asked whether it was really true that the British Empire had virtually no aircraft to spare to support resistance in the Balkans. Whatever answers these liaison officers chose to give, those they spoke to continued to believe that it was by an act of deliberate choice that the aircraft were not available.

Their beliefs were confirmed when a huge force of bombers attacked Belgrade on, of all days, the Orthodox Easter Sunday, causing minimal damage to military installations and reminding the inhabitants vividly of what the Germans had done in 1941. British liaison officers themselves learnt something of the true picture when a pilot, who had been instructed to transport some American nurses to the Italian mainland, somehow managed to land them in Albania. An airlift operation was planned for which a Wellington and two Dakotas, with thirteen Lightning fighters as escort, were suddenly available. In fact they were not needed, as a single British liaison officer shepherded the nurses to the coast, where they were picked up.

It has sometimes been suggested that the decisions to abandon Mihailović and to give full support to Tito were made largely because of communist influence in certain quarters of SOE. Having known fairly well all those members of SOE whose advice on this issue was taken most seriously – I exclude Fitzroy Maclean, who never regarded himself as part of SOE – I do not give much credence to the conspiracy theory. Nevertheless it merits examination.

Within SOE it had been decided from the outset not to engage people who were known to be fascists or communists. In a secret organization, whose members could have ready access to representatives of foreign powers, including those of the enemy, this was a wise restriction. Fascists could be expected to sympathize with the regimes of countries with which Britain was at war. Communists could be expected to sympathize with the regime of a country which, until it was attacked, had, both by pronouncement and by action, shown itself more favourably disposed to Hitler's Germany than to Churchill's Britain, and which at no stage shared any of the British government's war aims other than the defeat of the common enemy.

In Baker Street the screening process designed to exclude fascists and communists worked fairly well. It was not of course perfect. During a brief visit to London I found myself sharing one of SOE's hideout flats with a young officer with the rank of captain. The next day he was placed under arrest. I learnt later that for some months he had been communicating all the secret knowledge he had acquired to a Soviet contact. Nevertheless in London the Soviet Union's penetration of SOE was much less effective than its penetration of SIS or the Foreign Office, or indeed of MI5. German penetration was nil.

In Cairo security precautions were applied much less vigilantly. Indeed it was a standing joke among SOE officers that a request to a taxi-driver to be taken to Rustum Buildings, SOE's head office in Cairo, elicited, more often than not, the comment: 'Secret house?' The very atmosphere of Cairo, a rest centre for servicemen returned from the desert, with its fleshpots and its sunshine, encouraged a certain laxity. The general administration of SOE in Cairo suffered from the frequency with which the head of the mission was removed. Security was also weakened by the tendency to regard MO 4, as Cairo's SOE mission was publicly called, as an adjunct of GHQ, Middle East, with the result that there were frequent postings to it of men and women from units which had little or no screening procedures.

It was not therefore surprising that a few people with advanced left-wing views found their way into SOE in Cairo, but a clear distinction has to be made between the adherent of the advanced left and the agent of a foreign power. Outstanding among those with left-wing sympathies in SOE was Basil Davidson, a tall, handsome man and an able and prolific writer, who, as a genuine journalist, had been associated with Section D in Budapest. Davidson made no attempt to conceal his political opinions. Indeed much of his working life seems to have taken the form of a search for some kind of equation between communist regimes in the Stalinist and post-Stalinist worlds and his own high standards of personal decency, a search conducted with something of the tenacity of Christian when journeying through the Valley of the Shadow of Death.

Had Davidson wanted to stay in the SOE office in order to influence policy, he could no doubt have done so. In fact he opted for an operational role and in August 1943 was parachuted into Yugoslavia. There he conducted himself with outstanding gallantry, even crossing the Danube in hazardous conditions and with the handicap of dysentery, in order to assess the possibilities of promoting resistance in Hungarian-occupied territory. In doing so he was carrying out ably and conscientiously his duties as a British liaison officer. If the fervour with which the Partisans fought and their devotion to their cause strengthened his sympathy with their regime, this was not surprising. Other British liaison officers, less predisposed in favour of the Partisans, were no less impressed.

The least critical admirer of the Yugoslav Partisans was the Canadian William Jones, who seems to have found the movement

1 *above left*
Tom Barnes

2 *above right*
Andrew Kennedy

3 *right*
Christine Granville

4 *right*
Patrick Leigh-Fermor

5 *above left*
G. A. Holdsworth

6 *above right*
F. F. E. Yeo-Thomas

7 *left*
Gus March-Phillipps

8 *left*
William Stephenson

9 *right*
Inder Gill and Themi Marinos
10 *right*
Marjorie Stewart

11 *right*
Freddie Spencer Chapman

12 *above*
Gorgopotamos Bridge Operational
Party

13 *left*
Hon. C. M. Woodhouse (*left*) and
Gerald K. Wines

14 *left*
Maurice Buckmaster

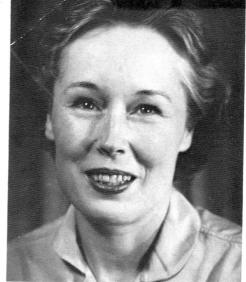

15 *right*
Mary Holdsworth

16 *right*
Michael Lis

17 *right*
Patricia Jackson

18 *left*
Alfgar Hesketh-Prichard
19 *left*
Peter Wilkinson

20 *below*
Earl of Selborne and Patricia
Hornsby-Smith

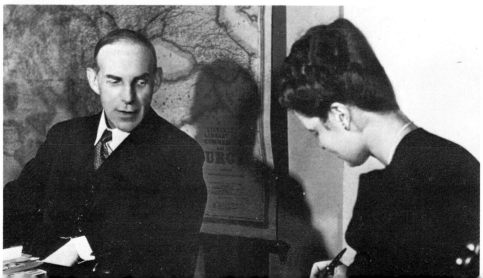

21 *right*
Peter Kemp

22 *right*
Anthony Quayle

23 *right*
Peter Fleming

24 *above*
(*left to right*) Claude Fenner, John Davis, Richard Broome, Basil Goodfellow

25 *left*
David Smiley (*left*) and Billy Maclean

barely distinguishable, in several respects, from a religious revivalist meeting.

Jones was one of the first liaison officers in the Balkans to bring out a book on his experiences, his *Twelve Months with Tito's Partisans* being published in 1946. In this, after likening the relationship between a Partisan commander and his men to that prevailing in a well organized sports team, he stated that the spirit which permeated Partisan life was 'essentially and fundamentally religious zeal'. The Partisans' knowledge of 'the principles of Jesus Christ was', he declared, 'profound'. 'Swearing and cussing', he pointed out, 'were never heard', and there was a general understanding that 'sexual matters should be postponed until after the war'. He even recorded, as an example of devotion to duty, an occasion on which 'a strapping big chap' was so distressed at making his commanding officer late for an appointment that 'he completely lost his appetite for supper'. No doubt he did.

Jones's reports from the field were spirited, colourful and inordinately long, but they were never taken very seriously by the policy-makers. He himself was both hurt and puzzled when he received a signal from Cairo instructing him to keep both feet firmly on the ground. This, he freely admitted, he would have found difficult.

A more influential figure than Jones was James Klugmann, who had been Secretary of the Cambridge University Communist party. Peter Kemp, who had known Klugmann at Cambridge, was startled, on arriving in Cairo, to find him installed in the SOE office. He was also surprised when he was asked, though not by Klugmann, to sign a document stating that he had been subjected in Baker Street to indoctrination on behalf of Mihailović. This, understandably, he refused to do.

Klugmann had a first-class mind, as his academic record showed. He had a somewhat owl-like appearance, which was redeemed by a warm smile and a gentle manner. He was a meticulous worker, and within SOE's Yugoslav section in Cairo he rose from the rank of sergeant to that of major with startling rapidity and without, seemingly, much change in the nature of his duties. After the war he maintained his dedication to the communist cause, sometimes engaging in that form of mental acrobatics known as christian-marxist dialogue.

As might have been expected, Klugmann did nothing to discourage communists from being enrolled in SOE as operational officers. One such whom he befriended in Cairo was Frank Thompson, who, coming from a literary background at Boars Hill near Oxford and inspired by the poets of the 1930s, had maintained an undergraduate enthusiasm for the communist cause. He was one of two British officers sent by SOE to the Bulgarian Partisans.

The Partisans found Thompson's enthusiasm slightly embarrassing. He made lavish promises of arms and then sent furious signals to SOE when these were not fulfilled. He even proposed an airlift operation to move Partisans to the interior of Bulgaria.

As a gesture of solidarity Thompson divested himself of his officer's insignia. His faith remained unimpaired when the numbers of the Partisan group with which he was associated dwindled concurrently with the exhaustion of his supply of gold sovereigns. In the end he was captured and executed. He died giving the clenched fist salute.

Thompson seems to have been an attractive young idealist, but it was clearly absurd to send him on what was planned, or should have been planned, as a rigorous fact-finding mission. For this Klugmann must share at least some of the blame, but for all his unwavering allegiance to communism there was never, so far as I am aware, any evidence to suggest that Klugmann was an agent of a foreign power.

Klugmann's voice was not without importance in the shaping of policy, but there were others in SOE, or associated with SOE, whose counsel was much more decisive than his. Of these none was a communist. The most influential was certainly Fitzroy Maclean, Scottish landowner and Conservative Member of Parliament. Bill Deakin, research assistant to Winston Churchill and at no time a communist, also carried considerable weight. So too did Hugh Seton-Watson, whose historical writings in the tradition of humane liberalism are a massive indictment of communism in eastern Europe in practice. Then there was Brigadier C. M. Keble, a regular soldier and head of the SOE mission in Cairo during the period when the most crucial decisions concerning Yugoslavia were made.

Keble was a peppery little man with a marked physical resemblance to a beetroot. He behaved at times both outrageously and maliciously. His treatment of Fitzroy Maclean, for instance, fully justified Maclean in his wish to have as little to do with SOE as possible. But Keble's general unpopularity and lust for power masked an ability to go straight to the heart of problems. To him the issues in Yugoslavia were essentially military. The Partisans were clearly doing more damage to the Germans than the Četniks were, and for this reason the Partisans should, he considered, be supported.

Finally there was the opinion of the officers who had served with Mihailović. Churchill invited Hudson to visit him at Chequers and asked whether he considered the decision to transfer support from Mihailović to Tito had been correct. Hudson replied that he did and that further support of Mihailović would have served only to increase bloodshed. Bailey, with an even deeper knowledge of Yugoslav affairs, was of the same opinion.

To what extent, if any, Tito's decision to refuse to bow to the demands of the Soviet Union in 1948 was influenced by his encounters with representatives of SOE and with the Maclean mission, and by the consequences of these encounters, is a question not easily answered.

As trained communists the Partisan leaders regarded these first emissaries from the west with hostile suspicion, seeing them as representatives, not only of British imperialism, but of a sinister, powerful and all-pervasive intelligence service. Milovan Djilas is particularly revealing about this. Early in the war he found that a Montenegrin professor of his acquaintance had an English mistress. 'I looked upon her,' he wrote, 'with distrust. How could an Englishwoman in Montenegro be anything but an agent of some intelligence service?' In fact the woman broke with the professor, joined the Partisans, and was killed in action. But the ingrained suspicion felt by all the Partisan leaders towards any British subject operating in Yugoslavia in any capacity was not easily allayed.

Tito came to respect both Hudson and Deakin, not least for their conduct under fire. Fitzroy Maclean maintained their tradition, and Djilas generously admitted the astonishment he felt during a German air raid on Drvar in February 1944 at the sight of Maclean's 'tall, bony figure moving about on the road as if nothing were happening'. Maclean's practice of wearing the kilt on ceremonial occasions also aroused the Partisan leaders' respectful curiosity.

Doctors sent by SOE to the Partisans made a particularly good impression. One of the greatest of the Partisans' achievements was the manner in which they cared for and transported their sick and wounded, whose numbers presented, in conditions of guerrilla warfare, massive human and administrative problems. Of the help given by a skilled surgeon named Ian Mackenzie, who was parachuted to the Partisans and performed numerous operations under fire, Deakin wrote that it 'reflected a moral credit on the British mission beyond the bounds of conventional tribute'.

Not all the members of the Maclean mission attained the standards of its leader. Although his personal courage was respected by all, the drinking habits of Randolph Churchill, for instance, aroused some criticism from the more uncompromising Partisans, as did his apparent lack of interest in Partisan affairs. But even these were compensated for by his very presence, confirming, as it did, the Partisans' belief that Winston Churchill had sent them first his secretary and then his son. In general the conduct displayed and the effects of dangers shared were such that Djilas was able to comment that 'the perfidy of the sons of Albion grew in proportion to their distance from us'.

The number of men and the quantity of material sent by the British to the Yugoslav Partisans at the time of their most intense struggle against the Germans was small. It is unlikely therefore that this form of help would have had much influence on the political thinking of the Partisan leaders but for the contrast it afforded with what the Soviet Union had to offer.

In 1942 and 1943 Tito and his principal advisers found Soviet policy towards Yugoslavia increasingly puzzling. Night after night radio contact was established in the hope of hearing news of Soviet supplies to be dropped by air. Instead there came lengthy political directives. These were to be expected, but some of their contents were surprising. The Soviet Union continued to recognize the Royal Yugoslav government in exile, raising its legation in Moscow to the status of an embassy and even attributing Partisan military successes to the forces of Mihailović. Tito for his part was instructed not to make any mention of a Yugoslav republic and not to raise the question of the abolition of the monarchy. He was even asked why it had been thought necessary to form a proletarian brigade.

The explanation was that Stalin, having accepted the concept of Soviet and western spheres of interest, within which Yugoslavia remained somewhat indeterminate ground, did not wish to provke a confrontation over Yugoslav affairs while he had more pressing concerns. By adopting this policy he intended to sacrifice nothing, for he was fully confident that Tito would deliver Yugoslavia into the communist camp when called upon to do so. But the Yugoslav leaders began to have their doubts, particularly when they were told, as they repeatedly were, that the Soviet Union's failure to supply them with arms was due solely to technical difficulties.

An expression of these doubts occurred after the Partisans had conducted certain secret and independent negotiations with the German authorities in March 1943. These were entrusted largely to Vlatko Velebit, the son of a former general in the Royal Yugoslav Army and the Partisans' principal unofficial diplomat. The main purpose of the negotiations was to effect an exchange of prisoners, but other possibilities were considered. As Djilas, who was himself one of the negotiators, put it, 'we did not shrink from declaring that we would fight the British if they landed'.

The negotiations were brought to an end on the orders of the German Foreign Minister, Joachim von Ribbentrop, but some prisoners were exchanged, including Tito's wife. Later a discussion took place about the negotiations among Tito's immediate advisers in which he was asked what the Russian reaction was likely to be. He replied that the Russians also thought first of their own people and their own army. It was an expression of independence which, to some of those present, seemed almost Lutheran in its daring.

It was nearly a year after this pronouncement by Tito that the first Soviet military mission reached his headquarters. Whereas Maclean and other British officers were dropped by parachute, the Soviet mission arrived in RAF gliders accompanied by a fighter escort. The contrast was noted by the Partisans, although it was later explained that the choice of transport had been determined by the fact that the leader of the mission, Lieut.-General Korneyev, had lost a leg at Stalingrad.

The Soviet mission did little to endear itself to the Partisan leaders. According to Fitzroy Maclean, it came as surprise to Korneyev and his second-in-command, Major-General Gorshkov, that they were not expected to take command of the Partisan forces, and once they learnt this their interest declined. Korneyev made it clear that he would rather have been appointed Military Attaché in Washington. He also became very disagreeable when drunk. Gorshkov even went so far as to make disparaging comparisons between Yugoslav and Soviet Partisans.

By the spring of 1944 Tito had been campaigning long enough not to feel in need of the military advice which the Soviet mission was prepared to offer. But he did need arms, and the Soviet mission brought with it about a dozen sub-machine guns and large quantities of vodka and caviare. The gap between Tito's first request to the Soviet Union for arms and the arrival of the first supplies from that quarter was approximately two years.

Tito's act of defiance which led to the break with the Soviet Union in 1948 resulted mainly from his appreciation of Yugoslavia's capacity to resist invasion from any quarter. He did not look to the west for help of any kind. Nevertheless it was during those years spent in the mountains from 1941 onwards that he and his closest followers came to understand that the Soviet Union was not so much a source of doctrinal truth as a country which pursued its own interests. They also learnt that it was possible to co-operate with so-called imperialist powers and to establish relationships with representatives of those powers on a basis of mutual respect. In making this second form of enlightenment possible the pioneering missions of Hudson and Deakin played a significant part.

Deakin, himself an historian of distinction, is among those who have expressed the opinion that Tito's wartime contact with the British did influence his judgment and actions in 1948 to no small extent. Julian Amery is another. The full truth is likely to be known in the west only when an authoritative biography of Tito appears by someone with full access to the relevant documents and no obligation to subscribe to a party line. For this we shall no doubt have to wait a very long time.

Before being brought out of Yugoslavia for the last time in 1943 Bill Hudson met Peter Kemp, who was in the process of being brought out of Albania. Their meeting took place in Berane, which in the course of the internal and other conflicts in Yugoslavia from 1941 onwards had the remarkable distinction of changing hands forty-one times. Their meeting was to be the beginning of a new operational association.

Hudson was appointed to lead the one belated SOE mission which was sent to Poland. Kemp was chosen as a member of the mission. Their instructions were to observe and report and to avoid battle unless it became necessary to fight a way out of a trap.

From the outset the mission was dependent on the protection of the Polish Home Army. So impressive was its organization that Kemp, as he later recorded, felt a sense of security such as he had never known before in enemy-occupied territory. His confidence in the Home Army was confirmed during an encounter with Germans, when the British mission's crossing of a stretch of open ground was successfully covered, at considerable personal risk, by a Pole with a Bren gun.

Unfortunately during the action the mission's radio set was lost, and from then on communications had to be through Home Army channels. Not surprisingly, at least to those with knowledge of Polish politics and security in exile, the co-operation in the field did not extend to the home base, and none of the messages sent through the Home Army reached SOE in London.

The Hudson mission duly contacted a corps headquarters of the Red Army at Żytno, and all its members were promptly placed under arrest. As negotiations concerning the future of Poland were still being conducted between the Soviet Union, the United States and Britain, it was clearly undesirable from the Soviet point of view that the voices of British liaison officers with first-hand knowledge of conditions in Poland should be heard.

When any danger that they might influence decisions was deemed to have passed the members of the mission were released and given the standard alternative treatment: comfortable accommodation, attractive, well rehearsed girl companions, and nightly tickets for the Bolshoi ballet. They came back to England via Baku and Teheran with a sense of nothing accomplished.

After the war Hudson returned for a time to South Africa and continued prospecting. He found some valuable deposits of zinc, which in South Africa, in contrast with the general mineral wealth, is something of a rarity, and staked a claim. The South African government wanted the zinc and offered him a price for the property which he found unacceptable. Gradually the price was raised, and Hudson, with something of the patience and determination he had shown when abandoned in Yugoslavia, still held out. He was in the position of hardly being able to afford the cost of a meal when he finally got the price he wanted.

Deakin, after serving as political adviser to the Balkan Air Force and as Head of Chancery in the British Embassy in Belgrade in 1945 and 1946, returned to the academic life. In 1950 he was appointed to the much coveted and sought-after post of head of a new Oxford college when he was made the first Warden of St Antony's.

It was at St Antony's that he organized in 1962 the impressive conference on European resistance, which was attended by distinguished historians and by people who had themselves played prominent parts in resistance movements. A few of the delegates, including Deakin himself, were qualified to attend in both capacities.

Hudson was one of the delegates. Characteristically maintaining his independence of judgment on Yugoslav affairs, he offered, as his principal contribution, evidence, supported by photographs which he had brought back from the field, of acts of destruction carried out by Mihailović's Četniks against the Germans. Perhaps not surprisingly he was told after the war by the Yugoslav Minister of the Interior that he would not be welcome in the new Yugoslavia.

Chapter 6

The Byron
Tradition

Greece entered the Second World War when she was attacked by
Italian forces from Albania. The Greeks fought back with evident
success and at one stage nearly a quarter of Albania was in Greek
hands. Then in April 1941 German forces, which had moved through
Yugoslavia and Bulgaria, invaded Greece, exploiting once again with
success the already familiar technique of the *blitzkrieg*.

In fulfilment of a pledge given to the Greek government and with
little or no hope of military victory, a force under British command,
including a sizeable New Zealand contingent, went to the help of the
Greek Army. It was driven off the mainland of Greece by the end of
April 1941 and off Crete a month later. With the successful German
airborne invasion of Crete the British war effort seemed to have
reached its nadir of disaster.

One consequnce of the speed of the German advance was that considerable numbers of officers and other ranks, both British and New
Zealand, were left behind on the Greek mainland and Crete. Some
were content to settle down to village life, some escaped to rejoin
their units, a few were later to play significant parts in resistance.

In the summer of 1941 SOE in Cairo prepared plans for sending
officers into Crete, mainly in order to contact the British and New
Zealanders, whose numbers may well at that stage have run into four
figures. One of the first men chosen was a twenty-four-year-old officer
in the Royal Artillery, the Hon. C. M. (Monty) Woodhouse.

A Winchester and New College, Oxford, scholar, with firsts in
mods and greats, Woodhouse came down from Oxford in the summer
of 1939. He pictured his future career as that of an Oxford don and was
working as an archaeological student in Athens when war broke out
in September. He returned to England, joined the Army, quickly
received a commission, and, when a British military mission was sent
to Greece after the Italian invasion, was appointed one of its members.
In the short and disastrous Greek campaign he served on the staff of
Major-General, later Field-Marshal, Henry Maitland Wilson, widely
known as Jumbo. He escaped from Crete in June 1941 and was

brought into contact with SOE through one of his acquaintances in the military mission to Greece.

Woodhouse was tall, fair, pink-cheeked and, both at twenty-four and subsequently, much younger than his years in appearance. His height and his colouring might have been considered crippling disadvantages in anyone trying to pass as a civilian in any part of Greece. To compensate for them he had prodigious powers of physical endurance and a good command of modern Greek. He was to acquire, perhaps unprecedentedly quickly, a formidable grasp of the complexities of Greek politics. This was made possible by unusual mental powers and, to some extent at least, by the nature of his academic discipline.

Woodhouse returned to Crete by caique in November 1941. The main task which he had to perform, the rounding-up of servicemen and bringing them off the island, was normally the concern of the escape organization, MI9, and not that of SOE. However, Germans and Italians were still to be found in the villages in large numbers, and resistance of the kind which later came into being was still hardly contemplated. Nevertheless initial contacts were made.

After five months Woodhouse was withdrawn from Crete, the caique which took him out having first brought in the man who may be considered the principal architect of SOE's involvement in Cretan resistance. This was another Oxford first-class classical scholar and archaeologist, an Australian named T. J. (Tom) Dunbabin. Woodhouse's greatest contribution to Greek resistance lay ahead of him. It was to be made on the Greek mainland.

In the summer of 1942 SOE in Cairo was asked by GHQ, Middle East, whether it could mount an operation on the Greek mainland to destroy one of the principal railway bridges in the mountains. If the bridge could be put wholly out of action movements of German troops would be seriously disrupted and the arrival of reinforcements in the Western Desert delayed. To have its full strategic effect the demolition would have to be carried out almost immediately, and the operational party had therefore to be assembled hurriedly.

Brigadier E. C. W. (Eddie) Myers, who was then on the GHQ staff, was approached by a fellow staff officer and asked whether he would take command of the operation. Myers, who had been commissioned in the Royal Engineers and who was one of the comparatively few Jews at that time to reach high rank in the British Army, was a respected staff officer whose engineering skills were considerable. He was also a trained parachutist. He did not speak any Greek, but as the operational party was not expected to stay in Greece for long, this was not held to be a disqualification.

Myers hesitated before accepting. As a regular soldier he wanted to be involved in the second front in Europe and was not particularly interested in a Greek sideshow. He also felt he had had enough of the Middle East theatre of war. He agreed to take on the job if no one else suitable could be found but said he would do nothing to seek it. The next day he was summoned to the SOE office in Rustum Buildings and learnt that the operational party which he was to lead would be dropped into Greece in four days' time.

The party numbered twelve. It was to be transported by three Liberators, four men being dropped in uniform from each aircraft. To serve as Myers's second-in-command SOE had chosen Monty Woodhouse. His mission was to be somewhat different from that of Myers in that he was to stay in Greece with a British radio operator and a young Greek officer named Themi Marinos, who had been decorated for gallantry in Crete. All the other members of the party were to be withdrawn from Greece once the bridge had been destroyed. They were therefore chosen for the most part for their skill in demolitions.

One of the Sapper officers, Denys Hamson, who had a Smyrna banking background, was a man of considerable parts. He was bilingual in English and French and was later to serve with the French *maquis*. He spoke fluent Greek and while on his operational mission in Greece was delighted to find himself near the birthplace of one of his favourite Greek poets, some of whose verses he had himself set to music.

Another Sapper officer was a forthright New Zealander named Tom Barnes, who had travelled widely in Australia and in little-explored parts of New Guinea. A third, a very young officer named Inder Gill, who had a Sikh father and a Scottish mother, gave an appearance of extreme shyness. In action, Hamson was to note, he always appeared to be 'cool and without nerves'. After India gained her independence Gill was to rise in the Indian Army to the rank of lieutenant-general.

The briefing which Myers, Woodhouse and the others received from SOE in Cairo was extremely cursory. Agents of the British were operating at that time in Greece and information was coming out from a variety of sources, but, whether because of compartmentalism, jealousy, lethargy or other reasons, little of it was made available to those who were about to be sent into the field. They were told of a resistance figure named Zervas but were misled about his whereabouts. They were also given the names or pseudonyms of one or two men who were believed to command a certain following not far from the site of one of the principal targets, the Gorgopotamos railway viaduct in the mountains of Roumeli. On the current political situation in Greece they received no instruction whatever.

Denys Hamson in his book *We Fell Among Greeks* gave a vivid picture of the reactions of the operational party when about to board the three aircraft which were to drop them into Greece. Themi Marinos, the Greek, sang an erotic tango song. Tom Barnes, the New Zealander, was silent. Somebody else described his exploits in bed. Monty Woodhouse told shaggy-dog stories. The tension was followed by anti-climax, as the ground signals could not be spotted and the aircraft returned to base.

At the second attempt Myers and Woodhouse both decided that their parties should be dropped even if no signals were seen, and this was what happened. The only damage suffered was by Denys Hamson, who had a number of cracked ribs.

After wandering about in the dark and meeting peasants here and there the members of the operational party gradually made contact with one another. They were also put in touch with a man named Karalivanos, whose name had been given to them during their briefing in Cairo, and learnt that he had five followers. Their next important discovery was that Zervas was several days' march away. The news that visitors from England had dropped from the sky soon spread so widely that it was rumoured that a whole enemy division had been deployed to round them up.

Woodhouse volunteered to go in search of Zervas. He set off with a guide, a revolver and a water-bottle, a khaki handkerchief concealing the colour of his hair. Over much of the way there was no sort of organization to guide him on the whereabouts of enemy troops, and several times he was about to enter a village when he learnt that the Italians were in full occupation. In all, he covered more than 200 miles, including a number of crossings of trackless mountains, before arriving at Zervas's headquarters.

Zervas greeted him with astonishment and delight. When he learnt of the plan to attack a bridge he agreed to meet Myers as soon as possible. He also arranged for seventy of his best men to accompany him and Woodhouse.

Myers invited Zervas to take command of a joint attack on the Gorgopotamos railway viaduct, which was the target he had chosen, and offered to serve as his chief of staff. Zervas thought it would be wiser to set up a tripartite command, consisting of the two of them and a Greek named Aris, who was the superior of Karalivanos. Although it offended his soldierly instincts, Myers accepted this arrangement. He did not at that stage fully appreciate its political significance.

Zervas's followers were supplemented by some eighty men provided by Aris. This combined force was divided into groups, for there were three main operational tasks. One was to ambush any reinforcements sent by the enemy by road or rail. One was to attack the Italian garrison guarding the bridge. The third was demolition.

The first heavy snows of winter had fallen shortly before the operation was mounted. The operational groups had to climb a 4,000-feet mountain on their way to the bridge, the explosives being transported by mule.

The attacks on the Italian garrison at each end of the bridge succeeded, and the signal was given to Tom Barnes and Denys Hamson, who led the demolition party, to lay the charges. Preliminary reconnaissance had suggested that the girders to be destroyed were L-shaped and charges had been prepared accordingly.

Close examination now showed that the girders were U-shaped, and the carefully assembled bars of plastic explosive and timber had to be taken to pieces and new charges prepared. This upset the whole timetable of the operation. Some of the waiting men became restive, and Myers had some difficulty in preventing an order from being issued instructing the Greeks present to withdraw. He succeeded in doing so, the fuses were lit, and suddenly two hundredweight of high explosive brought the bridge toppling and then crashing down.

The demolition was an unqualified success, and not one member of the combined force was killed. What nobody knew at the time was that this was to be the only engagement in the Second World War in which the communist-controlled forces known as ELAS and the moderate republican EDES, which was led by Zervas, co-operated fully and successfully.

As the members of the Myers Mission were about to leave for an agreed point on the coast, from which they were to signal to the submarine which would bring them back to Egypt, a message was received through a radio set, which had recently been dropped to Woodhouse, that the submarine would not be coming. New instructions, it was added, would be brought by a liaison officer who would be parachuted in shortly.

The essence of the new instructions was that the mission was to remain in Greece. This was greeted by some with bitterness, by others with equanimity. For all of them it meant that they would face new tasks in which one of their principal preoccupations was to be Greek politics.

When Greece was invaded by Italy in 1940 her form of government had for some years been a dictatorship under a monarchy. The effective ruler was General Ioannis Metaxas, who governed by decree and whose regime was relatively efficient and not widely unpopular. Metaxas died in 1941. In the same year King George II of the Hellenes left Greece to form a government in exile.

The royalist cause had a limited following in Greece, not least because George II represented only the third generation of a ruling family which had never become wholly Greek and which was referred to disparagingly as the Glucksburg dynasty. A rather obstinate man of limited outlook, the King was a firm anglophile and related by blood to the British royal family. His decision to continue the war against Germany contrasted with the wishes of a number of his monarchist supporters. He enjoyed the loyal support of Winston Churchill and the personal friendship of Field-Marshal Smuts, whose influence on British wartime foreign policy it was dangerous to underestimate. The government formed in exile by the King under Emmanouil Tsouderos exercised virtually no authority in Greece.

Those who effectively resisted the Germans and Italians in Greece were nearly all republican in sympathy. The leader to whom SOE looked with the greatest hope, and with whom it had established early contact, Colonel Napoleon Zervas, had had a colourful and slightly disreputable career. He had been involved in a *coup d'état* as long ago as 1926, had been cashiered from the Army and had become a professional gambler. He was widely read and a good *raconteur*. Denys Hamson described him as 'a comfortable, portly man with wise, quiet, understanding eyes'. His fighting forces, the National Republican Greek League, known by its Greek initials, EDES, operated almost exclusively in north-western Greece and numbered in 1943 about 5,000 men. Zervas had a good understanding of guerrilla warfare and was prepared to work with the British almost unreservedly. He lacked ruthlessness, and Woodhouse knew of occasions on which he allowed German prisoners to escape rather than condemn them to slaughter.

The other main fighting force, the National People's Liberation Army, or ELAS, was communist-controlled, though for a long time a number of its leaders, when dealing with the British, concealed their political affiliations. ELAS grew steadily in numbers from about 5,000 in the spring of 1943 to between 35,000 and 40,000 six months later. The area in which it operated was much larger than that of EDES.

ELAS had the familiar communist tripartite command, with a political adviser, a military leader and a popular leader or *kapetanios*. Aris Veloukhiotis or, as he was originally called, Athanasios Klaros, the *kapetanios*, took his name Aris from the war god. A former school-master who claimed to have been trained in Moscow, he was usually surrounded by a bodyguard of handsome young men and was generally assumed to be homosexual. Hamson, who had very strong likes and dislikes, which he made little attempt to conceal, described Aris as 'the most ruthless, the most cold-blooded, the cruellest' man he had ever met.

Aris was an individualist who was prepared to back his own judgment. His decision to take part in the attack on the Gorgopotamos viaduct was made against the advice, and possibly against the direct orders, of the central committee of the Communist party. He deemed it unwise to allow Zervas unqualified credit for the action.

Aris's decision to join in the attack was in part a reflection of a division of opinion in the inner circle of the Greek Communist party. Within this circle there were some who believed that the main effort should be concentrated on winning the minds of the people in the cities. The success of the Communist party in resisting conscription of labour by the Germans in the winter of 1942–3 offered, even when considered simply as a contribution to the war effort, some justification for this policy. The opposing faction believed that the leadership should, like Tito, take to the hills where the main fighting was to be found.

By the end of 1942 there were already indications that this fighting might before long take the form of civil war, for only a month after their successful co-operation in destroying the Gorgopotamos bridge Aris launched an offensive against the forces of Zervas. The events which followed inevitably increased both the dimensions and the complexity of the tasks which Myers and his mission faced. As Myers himself put it in the account he wrote of his experiences entitled *Greek Entanglement*, 'British officers had to hurry hither and thither, keeping the peace; sometimes, as they did so, suffering rebuke, and even insults, from the political advisers of ELAS. For high-spirited officers, who had volunteered for hazardous sabotage work, the tasks which I had given to many of them called for the greatest efforts in patience and tact.' In addition to ELAS and EDES there were other resistance groups, and in certain areas problems arose from the conflicting claims of Greece and neighbouring countries to Macedonian territory.

The complexities of politics inside Greece were supplemented by political differences outside the country. Unlike other governments which made their way to London, the Greek government in exile established itself in Cairo. This meant that the British Ambassador to the government, Reginald (Rex) Leeper, had to be in Cairo too, and unfortunately for the development of British policy in Greece Leeper's relations with SOE's Cairo office were predominantly bad.

For this SOE must in the first instance bear most of the blame. The British Foreign Office was not informed in advance of either the Gorgopotamos operation or the decision to retain Myers's mission in Greece. Similarly in its dealings with the Greek government SOE was disinclined to divulge any more than it had to. In as cosmopolitan a city as Cairo such attention to security was understandable, but it was to prove costly in terms of diplomatic relations.

For the first four months after the arrival of Myers's mission the British Foreign Office exhibited little interest in what was happening in Greece. Then Leeper became aware that the Myers mission was becoming as much political as military in character. This he resented, and unfortunately his resentment increasingly took the form of a personal antagonism towards Myers, an antagonism sometimes expressed with a petulance to be excused only on the grounds that he periodically suffered from ill health.

Leeper's task was not an easy one. The British government was committed to supporting a king who had little following in Greece. Myers's radio reports repeatedly pointed out how small this following was. Leeper, understandably, was mainly concerned with Britain's long-term interests. The military command in Cairo, equally understandably, wanted immediate military results. When in April 1943 SOE in London sent its Cairo office a directive instructing it to be 'guided' by the Foreign Office the Joint Planning Staff of the Commanders-in-Chief in Cairo commented on this document that 'operational rather than political considerations are at present paramount'. In practice therefore SOE staff officers in Cairo and, more demandingly, Myers and Woodhouse in Greece, found themselves saddled with the task of trying to reconcile conflicting British military and diplomatic policies.

From November 1942 until August 1943 Myers's almost exclusive concern was with events in Greece. Inexperienced though he was politically and tangled though the political scene remained, he was to achieve, with Woodhouse's guidance, an encouraging measure of success. Politics concerning Greece pursued outside the country were to prove, by contrast, a maze from which he himself could find no satisfactory way out.

The most important military task assigned to SOE officers in Greece in 1943 was the destruction of transport and communications in such a way that the Germans would be led to believe that Allied armies were about to invade the mainland of Greece. This had to be achieved by both example and persuasion.

One of the targets chosen was the Asopos railway viaduct, whose importance was comparable with that of Gorgopotamos. On this occasion the forces of ELAS, which were well established in the area, refused to co-operate, and Myers decided that the action would be carried out exclusively by British Commonwealth forces, including three officers in the Royal Engineers who were parachuted in specially for the operation.

The viaduct was guarded by some forty Germans with six heavy machine guns and a number of light automatics. The members of the demolition party had to carry their explosives down a narrow gorge, which in places was only two or three feet wide, and then over waterfalls. At times they advanced by aerial ropeways, at others they waded through icy water carrying their explosive packs above their heads.

A German guard who approached was silently coshed, the sound of his body falling being drowned by that of the torrent below. There was a bad moment when someone knocked against a loose bolt, which fell with a loud clang on to the girders. But the operation was completed successfully, and the main railway line to Athens was put out of action for four months. A young New Zealand officer, Donald Stott, displayed such outstanding gallantry that Myers recommended him for the VC. As no shot was fired – in itself evidence of the success of the operation – the award could not be made.

The first Allied landings in Sicily took place on 10 July 1943, and it was in the three or four weeks immediately before this that maximum efforts were required in Greece in order to divert German troops and attention. During this period Tom Barnes personally supervised attacks on three bridges, each separated by most of a day's march, in the course of five nights.

Winston Churchill later recorded that two German divisions were diverted by the actions in Greece. Some historians have subsequently disputed this claim, pointing to discrepancies between what Hitler ordered and what the German High Command put into effect. That the German military authorities believed, both before and after the landings in Sicily, that there would be an invasion of the Greek mainland is beyond doubt.

In choosing their associates among the different Greek factions Myers and Woodhouse had to act largely on their own initiative, for during the first few months of their stay they had, for various reasons, little radio contact with the outside world. Woodhouse had, it is true, received instructions before leaving Cairo to try to make his way to Athens to contact a group of six colonels. This he did. He found the colonels ready to draw up staff plans for what should be done when the Allies invaded, but with no evident intention to take to the hills.

In Athens he contacted an agent who had been working for the British and who was known by the code-name Prometheus. Soon afterwards Prometheus was picked up by the Italians with his radio set, his codes and his signal plan. As Promethus knew his whereabouts Woodhouse clearly had to take swift evasive action. A meeting had been arranged for him that evening with a clandestine group who, he discovered, were leading figures in the Greek Communist party. Woodhouse explained his predicament, and the two principal members of the group disappeared into another room to discuss whether they should or should not accept responsibility for him. The decision went in his favour, but the rumour that he was dead spread around Greece, and on his way from Athens to Zervas's headquarters he had the unusual experience of entering a church and hearing his own funeral oration pronounced.

By the spring of 1943 the communist-controlled ELAS bands had established a position of such strength that it would have been impossible for Myers to carry out his military directive without their co-operation. He therefore entered on a prolonged series of negotiations, a number of them with a man who had arrived at a position of authority in ELAS in a curious manner. This was Stephanos Saraphis, who had been Greek Military Attaché in Paris and who enjoyed something of a reputation as a soldier, although he had suffered in his military career because of his republican sympathies. Saraphis was made prisoner by ELAS, put into chains and marched through the mountains as an object of ridicule. In spite of this he threw in his lot with ELAS, whose fighting forces he considered the most effective in Greece, and was promptly appointed their military commander. In this role he enjoyed much less authority than the political leaders, but he was allowed to negotiate with Myers, probably on the assumption that soldier could speak to soldier.

Myers pitched his requirements fairly high. He told both Saraphis and Zervas that he wanted all fighting units, which became known as 'bands', to be non-political and unreservedly under the orders of General Wilson as Commander-in-Chief, Middle East. He and Woodhouse then drew up a ten-point programme, calling for co-operation between all bands, while accepting that different bands would have different operational areas. All Greeks were to be free to join whichever band they chose, and supplies from the Middle East would be sent only to those bands which, in the opinion of the British liaison officers, fully honoured the proposed agreement.

Saraphis considered all this would give Myers too much direct authority over Greeks. The proposals were therefore modified to make it clear that while the Greek bands came under General Wilson's command the function of the British in Greece was purely that of liaison officers. When an agreement on this basis was signed GHQ, Middle East, announced publicly that all Greek bands had been 'welded into a united and co-ordinated instrument for the furtherance of the Allied struggle'. It was a statement more of hope than of reality, but the achievement which permitted it to be made at all was a considerable one.

Myers received his first political directive some five months after he arrived in Greece. This made it clear that the King would be regarded as head of the Greek State until the Greek people had had an opportunity to express their will freely in conditions of tranquillity. Myers replied that he would instruct his officers loyally to obey this directive, but pointed out that if the King were to announce that he would not set foot on Greek soil until a plebiscite on the question of the monarchy had been held, it would knock the bottom out of the propaganda of the political controllers of ELAS. More was to be heard of this proposal later.

Some of the radio messages which Myers, with the guidance of Woodhouse, sent to SOE in Cairo in 1943 showed considerable perception and prescience. One stated that only if the British government gave proof of its determination to suppress any attempt at a *coup d'état* by the leaders of ELAS at any time and at any cost could civil war be avoided. The warning was ignored, but within two years British troops had to go into action for the very purpose which Myers had defined. Another message, sent at a time when the British government was considering whether to switch support from Mihailović to Tito, stated that the mission in Greece had 'detected' a determination on the part of communist parties in Balkan countries to set up independent regimes after the war which would be 'unfettered by any major power'.

Leeper continued to mistrust Myers's judgment and prevailed upon the Foreign Office to send what he called 'a proper political adviser' to Greece to serve as Anthony Eden's personal representative. This was Major David Wallace of the 100th Rifles, who was later to be killed in action in Greece. He stayed for a month with Myers and

Woodhouse, established cordial relations with both of them, and showed them in advance the texts of his radio messages, with which they were in general agreement.

SOE also parachuted in its own special observer. This was John Stevens, head of its Greek section in Cairo, who was later to serve with distinction behind the enemy lines in northern Italy. Stevens was a man of unusual ability who after the war became the United Kingdom Executive Director of the World Bank. Unfortunately his return from Greece to Cairo, which began by caique, was seriously delayed, and he finally reached Cairo ten days after Myers himself did. Whether he would have been able, had he arrived earlier, to prevent any of the damage which was to occur during those ten days must be a matter for conjecture.

After exchanges of radio messages it was agreed in the summer of 1943 that representatives of Greek resistance forces should be brought to Cairo for discussions. Myers was ordered to try to construct an air-strip to enable them to be flown out. The man he chose for this task was Denys Hamson.

Hamson, who had volunteered for a single, clearly defined operational mission, was a somewhat reluctant liaison officer with Greek irregulars. It emerges from his book, *We Fell Among Greeks*, that he did not greatly care for many of the Greeks he had to deal with. Nor, it seems, did Tom Barnes. When the two of them were sharing a cave a Greek came to them and said that one day a grateful Greece would erect a marble tablet over the mouth of the cave, on which would be inscribed in letters of gold the names of the visitors who had dropped from the sky. After dragging in Byron he went on to apostrophize 'England, refuge of the oppressed, champion of the weak, dear lover of Greece'. Towards the end of this, and much more, Barnes turned to Hamson and said: 'What's the bastard talking about?'

The construction in Thessaly of the first landing-ground for the use of a large Allied aircraft in enemy-occupied territory in the Second World War was, by contrast, a challenge which Hamson accepted with enthusiasm. He took on 300 men as paid labourers and had 500 troops guarding the surrounding foothills. News that some kind of con-structional work was going on was bound to reach the Germans, and one German prisoner who saw too much was shot. For the rest Hamson relied on his assumption that the descriptions of what was happening would be so embellished that by the time they reached the Germans they would be disregarded. Hamson's camouflage work, which involved cutting down about 1,000 fir trees and staking them into the ground again, was skilful enough to deceive the RAF until full details of the landing-ground were transmitted. It also deceived the Luftwaffe, and landing and take-off of the aircraft were wholly successful.

Inevitably there were disagreements between the various Greek political factions about the choice of those who were to be flown out, but in the end a reasonably representative delegation was chosen. It was accompanied by Wallace and also by Myers. On this point Myers and Woodhouse had almost their only serious difference of opinion. Woodhouse felt certain that Myers, if he ever left Greece, would not be allowed to return. Myers considered it his inescapable duty to accompany the delegates.

The reception of the delegates was deplorable. Myers was blamed, possibly with some slight justification, for not announcing in advance that the political controllers of ELAS would demand three seats in the Greek government, though why such a proposal should occasion surprise might seem barely comprehensible to anyone unacquainted with Anglo-Greek politics in Cairo. From the time of their arrival until they were about to leave Leeper ensured that the delegates were ignored, and even a suggestion by Myers that, as a face-saving exercise, they should be given a conducted tour of the battlefields in the Western Desert was vetoed. The delegates had actually reached Cairo airport to begin their return journey to Greece when a message reached them from Tsouderos, the Prime Minister of the government in exile, that he would like to see them. This was the only positive achievement in an exercise which Sir Orme Sargent, who shortly after the war became the Foreign Office's Permanent Secretary, gently and laconically described as 'an error of judgment'.

Myers himself saw, in fairly rapid succession, the King of the Hellenes, the King of England, Anthony Eden and Winston Churchill. He also gave a lecture to an invited audience in the Curzon cinema in London. The King of the Hellenes greeted him affably, and Myers put to him two suggestions. One was that he should pay a short visit to the mountains in Greece. The King decided he was too old. The other was that he should undertake not to return to Greece until a plebiscite had been held on the subject of the monarchy. On this point the King sought the advice of Churchill and of Roosevelt and was recommended by both to stand firm on his existing position.

King George VI granted Myers a fairly lengthy interview and showed much interest in the prospects of his cousin's return to Greece as King. He also said that his own Foreign Secretary ought to see Myers himself and not receive his information on Greece through subordinates. When Myers did see Eden he was given little chance to say anything, as Eden did nearly all the talking. (Woodhouse, by contrast, found Eden much more receptive to expressions of opinion on wartime Greece than a number of his officials.) Churchill invited Myers to Chequers and said to him significantly: 'Your organization has been meddling in the work of my Foreign Office, and if it had not been for me they would have gone under.'

The lecture which Myers gave in the Curzon cinema was both gripping and disastrous. He began with a lucid and colourful account of life among the Greek guerrilla forces, but then he launched into politics and, as he afterwards wrote, gave the Foreign Office representatives present the impression that he 'knew how to do their job better than they did'.

I was in the audience at the time, and I remember clearly the embarrassment I felt when Gubbins rose at the end to make a peace-keeping speech with such utterances as 'Well, we have this treaty with the King. . . .'

With his lecture in the Curzon cinema Myers finally ensured the Foreign Office's political victory and the fulfilment of Woodhouse's prophecy. He was not allowed to return to Greece, and Woodhouse was appointed head of the British military mission. Thirty-five years later Woodhouse was of the opinion that if Myers and he had been allowed to continue to operate together they would have had a chance, even though a slim one, of maintaining some kind of cohesion between the Greek guerrilla forces. Operating alone, he felt sure, neither of them was capable of doing so.

Addressing the conference which Bill Deakin assembled at St Antony's College, Oxford, in 1962, Woodhouse said that when he looked back to the Second World War he sometimes compared himself with Stendhal's character Fabrice in *La Chartreuse de Parme* who went to considerable lengths to discover whether he had or had not been present at the battle of Waterloo. No doubt he had in mind Greece in the latter part of 1943 and in 1944, when, although fighting continued, a decreasing proportion of it was against Germans.

The reception of the Greek delegation in Cairo and the decision not to allow Myers to return convinced the central committee which controlled ELAS, and which was known by the initials EAM, that the British had no intention of co-operating fully with ELAS in the future. Saraphis was to write that in Cairo Myers had 'shown himself sincere and objective and was regarded as pro-EAM, though this he was not'. He went on to draw a contrast between Myers, the professional soldier, and Woodhouse, whom he described as being 'of the Intelligence Service'.

With the signing of the armistice in Italy large quantities of arms became available in Greece, and ELAS, as the most widespread of the guerrilla forces, secured most of them. These they used, when the opportunity arose, to try to eliminate other groupings. In the process they made themselves so widely disliked that when the Germans formed some new Greek units, known as Security Battalions, they were cheered by the populace as they marched through the streets of Athens.

As their military duties became less demanding the political duties of the British liaison officers became more complex. The responsibility they carried was well described by Woodhouse in his book, *Apple of Discord*. (It is significant that in the title of his book on his experiences in Greece Myers used the word 'entanglement' and that Woodhouse in the most personal, or least impersonal, of his books on Greece included in the title the word 'discord'.) In Greece, Woodhouse wrote, 'the lightest word that falls from the unguarded lips of the youngest second lieutenant in the British Army is assumed to be an inspired declaration of policy'. He added that if three British officers said three different things it did not mean that one of them was wrong or that British policy was confused. It meant that policy was much more intricate than had been supposed.

The British officers who carried out their political duties most skilfully tended to be those who kept at a certain distance from the politicians. Jack Gage, a South African, who had played rugby football for both South Africa and Ireland, was much impressed by the way in which N. G. L. (Nick) Hammond, Cambridge don and future headmaster, under whom he served, handled political problems. When he asked Hammond why he did not live in the same village as the leaders of the forces to which he was attached, Hammond replied that it was 'well worth three hours' march not to be continually on the doorstep of political intrigues'.

Other officers were less discriminating. Donald Stott, the young New Zealander whom Myers had recommended for the VC, went so far as to make contact with a German through the Mayor of Athens in the innocent belief that he could thereby shorten the war. Rufus Sheppard became so enthusiastic about the cause and practices of ELAS that he was regarded almost as their spokesman by SOE in Cairo. Sadly he was killed by a mine laid by the forces he so much admired.

In so far as there was an Allied policy towards Greece in 1943 and

1944 it was almost exclusively a British policy. In the Second World War there was a fundamental difference between the British and American governments in their attitude towards the Balkan countries as a theatre of war. British service chiefs and politicians could see advantages in landings on the Adriatic coast as a prelude to an advance towards central Europe. This was wholly contrary to the strategic planning of General George Marshall and the political thinking of President Roosevelt.

With this important reservation the United States government was for the most part content to let Britain handle Balkan affairs as best she could and gave her loyal support in the process. In the mountains of Greece Saraphis did, it is true, have some success in his attempts to drive a wedge between the British and the Americans by playing on the imagination of a somewhat unsophisticated American cavalry officer, but the success was temporary. The cavalry officer was recalled, and Gerald K. Wines of OSS, a veteran of the First World War, who was appointed head of the American component of the Allied military mission, earned the lasting gratitude of Woodhouse and others for his sympathetic understanding of British problems and his determination to maintain unanimity in Anglo-American policy.

The Soviet presence in Greece was a muted one. Late in July 1944 a Soviet aircraft took off from an Allied base in Italy on what was described as a training flight. It landed near Tito's headquarters, picked up ten members of the Soviet mission in Yugoslavia, dropped two of them into Macedonia, and landed the other eight in Thessaly. The first intimation the British and Americans in Greece had of this venture was when the eight men, whose leader was named Colonel Popov, arrived at ELAS headquarters.

Popov was no more ready to supply ELAS with arms than his counterpart was to supply Tito's Partisans. His mission and the ELAS leaders quickly became disillusioned with each other, and it did not escape the attention of the Greeks that Popov was dependent on the British even for his supplies of vodka. The principal reason for Popov's presence was not known to the Allied military mission at the time. It was to inform the leaders of ELAS, in effect, that Stalin intended to adhere to the bargain he had made concerning spheres of influence in Europe by refraining from overt intervention in Greece. As the bargain was, from Stalin's point of view, an extremely good one, this was a reasonable decision.

In 1944 it was known that Germany had decided to withdraw her forces from Greece in order to concentrate them elsewhere. The two chief immediate aims of British policy were therefore to bring about maximum harassment of German troops as they withdrew and the installation of a representative government in Athens.

In the first aim only limited success was achieved. The people of Greece had suffered greatly during the war. Food shortages had been, and continued to be, as severe as anywhere in Europe. Countless villages had been burnt as reprisals. The peasants and others in the mountains everywhere had treated the Allied missions with unflinching loyalty, never once betraying them to the Germans. Now, when they learnt that the Germans were leaving, it was not surprising that the great majority of the Greek people wanted them to go as quickly as possible and had little desire to delay their departure by further military engagements.

The political outlook for a time seemed hopeful. A new Greek government had been formed in exile under Georgis Papandreou, a liberal of the traditionalist school. The King had finally accepted the need to delay his return until a plebiscite had been held on the subject of the monarchy. So belatedly had the British Foreign Office. In October 1944 Papandreou entered Athens. He was accompanied by a token British force.

SOE officers in Greece knew that ELAS forces were planning a major military operation. Indeed they would have been seriously failing in their duty if they had not known. Yet their warnings seem for a time to have been largely ignored. Then, early in December, ELAS struck. As a counter-measure substantial British forces were despatched to the Greek mainland under the command of Major-General Ronald Scobie. The enemy the British were now fighting was ELAS.

With its decision to resist by force ELAS's attempt to take over control of Greece the British government incurred considerable obloquy. Numerous political commentators, by no means confined to communist countries or their sympathisers, promptly described the far-sighted and unpalatable action taken as a brazen expression of British imperialism.

The episode was also an example of how in certain circumstances resistance could become counter-productive to the main war effort. If General Scobie's troops had not been needed in Greece they could almost certainly have been employed to advantage on the Italian front.

After the war Monty Woodhouse held a number of important posts. He was Member of Parliament for Oxford for several years, Under-Secretary of State at the Home Office and Director of Education and Training for the Confederation of British Industry. Yet he remained a scholar at heart, as his appointments as Director of the Royal Institute of International Affairs and President of the Classical Association indicated. He had had better opportunities than any other British subject of evaluating the Greek wartime scene at first hand, and after the war he made a deep study of the relevant records, Greek and German as well as British. His assessment of the part played by SOE on the Greek mainland must therefore command respect.

One conclusion he reached was that the military significance of Greek resistance had been greatly exaggerated and its political significance underrated. Another was that if there had been no Allied military mission in Greece from 1942 onwards the communists would have been in total control of Greece when the Germans left. If this last judgment is correct the debt which the western world owes to the Allied military mission is an appreciable one.

Time however distorts memories. When he visited Greece in 1971 Woodhouse received an apology from Greek friends for the fact that a local newspaper had described him as having been 'with the resistance'.

In Crete from fairly unpromising beginnings SOE gradually built up an extensive network. A. M. (Sandy) Rendel, a future diplomatic correspondent of *The Times*, who was one of SOE's officers in Crete, later described how in 1944 a number of German deserters were passed from point to point in the course of a four-day journey. Each day they met a new British officer accompanied by a least one NCO with a radio set, all of them dressed in various kinds of Cretan costume. When Rendel himself met the German deserters they seemed to be under the impression, as he put it, that 'every second Cretan was a British officer in disguise'.

Such a state of affairs was made possible by the virtual absence of collaborators with the Germans over large areas of Crete, by the performance of the SOE representatives themselves and, not least, by the judgment with which they were selected. The selections were not of course flawless, but in the main they were very good.

Tom Dunbabin, the Australian who took over from Monty Woodhouse as SOE's chief representative in Crete, was at Corpus Christi College, Oxford, in the early 1930s after attending the Sydney Church of England Grammar School. He studied under Sir Arthur Evans at Knossos and also worked with German archaeologists. One of them he saw in wartime Crete, but as he was himself dressed as a shepherd the German did not recognize him.

Rendel met Dunbabin in Cairo and, believing he held a staff

appointment, was surprised to see him wearing the ribbon of the DSO. Dunbabin was somewhat curt with him, and Rendel later came to understand why. Dunbabin had just returned to Cairo after nine months in Crete and, as Rendel expressed it in his book, *Appointment in Crete*, must have had 'something like the feeling of unreality a man gets when he comes out of prison'.

Dunbabin drove himself mercilessly in Crete and would continue striding across the hills even when all the skin had been removed from the soles of his feet. He mastered Cretan dialects, and his diplomacy and his judgment of the groups to which arms should be distributed seem to have been nearly impeccable.

Dunbabin spent some two years in Crete with only brief interludes between his tours of duty. His exploits were not confined to the work which he undertook solely for SOE. When the Germans constructed an airfield near Tymbaki he made detailed observations from a tree overlooking the runway. The report he subsequently sent enabled the RAF to bomb the airfield with some success.

He thought deeply and made his own individual judgments on a wide range of human activity. The perfect literary humorist for instance was, in his opinion, Chekhov. He may have lacked the flamboyance, and indeed touch of frivolity, which some of the younger SOE officers brought to their work in Crete, but he was deeply respected. Moving around Crete in a long black shepherd's cloak and cowl, he came to be accepted almost as a symbol of resistance.

SOE in Cairo had a special section concerned with Crete which was independent of the main Greek section. It was headed by Jack Smith-Hughes, a barrister by profession, who even in his youth had a portly, comfortable-looking appearance. He had a formidable memory, an incisive mind and a talent for repartee whose speed and wit were sometimes almost Gilbertian in quality.

Smith-Hughes knew Crete well. He was taken prisoner there and escaped and later returned to the island repeatedly. His methods of selecting SOE officers and the questions he put when interviewing them were original. Xan Fielding was a little startled by being asked at a preliminary interview: 'Have you any personal objection to committing murder?' But the quality of most of the people chosen and the care with which plans were made were illustrated by the fact that those who served SOE in Crete or in Cretan waters earned four DSOs between them, yet not a single officer was lost. The total casualties were two NCOs, one of whom was killed in a cave, probably for the money he had with him.

Xan Fielding, who was later to be captured in France and saved by
Christine Granville, was among those who won the DSO in Crete. Yet
the beginnings of his war did not suggest any pronounced desire for
martial glory.

Fielding had been brought up largely on the French Riviera, his
formal education being cut short because of family financial difficulties. When war broke out in 1939 he found himself in Cyprus, where
his jobs had included editing a newspaper and serving as a barman.
He then spent some time on a small Greek island trying, as he later
stated, to decide what attitude to adopt towards the war.

The prospect which he particularly dreaded was, he explained in
Hide and Seek, one of the books he was later to write about Crete, not
a battlefield but an officers' mess. He was in fact commissioned in the
newly formed Cyprus Regiment, serving for a time in a unit which he
described as being 'understandably free from any sense of regimental
pride'. Then he came to Cairo, where he learnt that there were Cretan
civilians fighting against the invaders. 'This concerted rising', he
later wrote, 'of the technically non-combatant seemed to me the most
reasonable and intelligible in the war.'

Fielding had received little military training, but he had other
important qualifications for operating in Crete. He spoke excellent
Greek, and he was short, dark and athletic in build. In these respects
he had the advantage over another officer who accompanied him on
the early stages of his mission and who was one of the more
surprising choices for undercover work. This was a gallant and much-
decorated veteran of the First World War who brought with him a
solar topee, spoke no Greek, and was evidently under the impression
that he was speaking French when he complained to a Cretan guerrilla
leader: 'Mais, mon colonel, vous ne m'avez pas mis dans le tableau.'

Fielding made a decision of some importance soon after his arrival
in Crete. To function properly, he realized, a guerrilla organization
needed a good intelligence network and speedy communications. In
the prevailing circumstances these could be created only with what he
described as 'a certain sacrifice of personal safety'. He therefore
established his headquarters near the northern coastal road. There he
would, he knew, be more accessible to the Germans, but the Germans
would also be more accessible to him.

The decision was vindicated by results and, particularly, by the
growth in the power of the organization with which he was associated. From experiencing what he described as a childish excitement in
'brushing shoulders with members of the Wehrmacht', he advanced
before long to the point of being able to meet the Mayor of Canea in

the town hall, incidentally passing three German officers on his way to the Mayor's office.

.After some time Fielding was joined by a very kindred spirit who was to become a close personal friend. This was Patrick (Paddy) Leigh-Fermor. Both Fielding and Leigh-Fermor were already writers in embryo. Both had travelled widely and alone when very young. Both had been drawn to the Greek classics. Both had acquired a taste for living on the shores of that inland sea variously called Mediterranean, Adriatic and Aegean. Both had had a chequered formal education.

Among the schools which Leigh-Fermor attended was a co-educational one kept by a major who regularly led staff and pupils in country dances which all performed stark naked. Another was King's School, Canterbury, from which he was expelled for a minor peccadillo which today would probably be regarded as indicating nothing worse than a healthy interest in girls. A report from this school described him as a dangerous mixture of sophistication and recklessness, causing the writer of the report to feel 'anxious about his influence on other boys'.

He had thought for a time of becoming a regular soldier and could readily picture himself being seconded for special duties like Strickland Sahib, but given the prospect of having to live on his pay he decided that he was as ill-equipped for thrift in the face of temptation as he was for discipline. In fact, soon after leaving school he set out on a prolonged walk through Europe, which, described some forty years later in his own jewelled and cascading prose, was to become a magical journey. There are some who consider *A Time of Gifts*, the book in which Leigh-Fermor recalled his boyhood travels, over-written. That they do so suggests they suffer from the misfortune of not being able to enjoy the baroque. To others – and I am among them – the book reveals a gift for evoking scenes viewed with youthful eyes which only a few rare spirits, Laurie Lee among them, possess.

In Crete Leigh-Fermor enlivened the scene by singing folk-songs in a number of languages, discoursing on Villon, whom he had translated, reciting the Schlegel-Tieck version of Shakespeare and wearing a royal-blue waistcoat lined with scarlet shot-silk and embroidered with black arabesques. Among Cretans generally he commanded both liking and respect, some even asking him to be godfather to their children. One of these children was given as her names the Greek equivalents of England and Rebellion.

In spite of all his diversions Leigh-Fermor took his operational duties with extreme seriousness, and on being given an opportunity to return to Egypt for a short spell of leave he refused. When he did decide to go back for the first time it was in the company of an Italian general whom he had persuaded to come with him. To achieve this he had to dress in enemy uniform, a venture which no doubt gave him the idea for his next major exploit.

Among the exiles in Cairo during the war was a girl named Zofia Tarnowska, who belonged to one of the best known Polish land-owning families. She met a tall good-looking young Guards officer with a slightly languid air named W. Stanley (Billy) Moss, who was half-English and half-Russian. They were married and set up a temporary home, which was frequented by some of the more colour-ful and spirited young officers who happened to be in Cairo, most of them on leave from the Western Desert or returned from occupied Europe. One of these was Leigh-Fermor.

One evening at an open-air night club under the stars Leigh-Fermor and Moss evolved a plan for kidnapping the much-hated commander of the German garrison in Crete, General Müller. For this purpose they would both dress in German uniform. Moss spoke virtually no German, and when he did eventually appear in the uniform prescribed Leigh-Fermor·described him as looking just like an Englishman pretending to be a German leaning against the bar at the Berkeley. To compensate for these possible shortcomings Leigh-Fermor judged Moss to have the coolness of nerve needed for the enterprise he was planning.

It was agreed that Leigh-Fermor would return to Crete first and that Moss would join him shortly afterwards. In fact no fewer than twelve unsuccessful flights were made with the object of dropping Moss by parachute, and in the end it was decided to send him in by boat. This enabled him to bring some of the books which he and Leigh-Fermor had planned to have with them if possible. They included works by Cellini, Donne, Sir Thomas Browne, Marco Polo and Baudelaire. Billy Maclean, another frequenter of the Moss household, gave them for luck, a Shakespeare and an Oxford Book of English Verse, both of which he had had with him in Albania.

There were objections from a number of quarters to the proposed kidnapping. Widespread reprisals were feared, and in the hope of preventing these Leigh-Fermor undertook to place a letter in the general's car stating that the kidnapping was entirely the work of a British raiding party, who had received no help from Cretans. A certain amount of British equipment would be scattered about as supporting evidence.

The Cretan Communist party was still not satisfied, and Leigh-Fermor received a letter from one of its leaders stating that if he persisted in his plan he would be betrayed to the Germans. It was decided to ignore this threat. Nor was the fact that the original target for kidnapping, General Müller, was no longer in Crete considered of sufficient consequence for the operation to be cancelled. His replacement, General Kreipe, was to be kidnapped instead.

The kidnapping was planned for 24 April 1943, but that day General Kreipe did not conform to his usual routine, on which the planning of the operation was based. The next day he did not leave his villa at all. On the third evening Leigh-Fermor decided to put his plan into action.

The general's car was stopped at a prearranged spot by a length of wire. The wire was connected to a buzzer which served as a signal to Cretan helpers, whose task was to prevent any other traffic from approaching. Leigh-Fermor and Moss, in German uniform, then approached the car. Moss coshed the driver and took over the driving-seat. Leigh Fermor sat in the back and placed the general's hat on his head. Some Cretans held the general down, uttering suitable threats to prevent him from giving any sign of his presence.

Leigh-Fermor then explained to the general that he had been captured by British officers, who intended to treat him as a prisoner of war. The general was clearly relieved and gave his parole not to try to escape. Twenty-two German control posts were then passed, with Leigh-Fermor masquerading as the commander of the German garrison and Moss as his driver.

There followed a long journey over the mountains, which has been well described in Moss's best-selling account of the exploit, *Ill Met by Moonlight*. About a thousand Germans were deployed in an attempt to catch the escaping party. During the journey General Kreipe was clearly impressed by the continual evidence of the popularity of the British and the unpopularity of the Germans in Crete. He was also shocked on learning that the two men who had captured him were not even regular soldiers.

Kreipe was a civilized man. On seeing the sun rising over Mount Ida he began to recite:

> 'Vides ut alta stet nive candidum
> Soracte. . . .'

Leigh-Fermor finished the stanza for him and then added the next five. When he had finished the general said simply: 'Ach so, Herr Major.'

Arrangements had been made for General Kreipe and his escorts to be taken to Egypt by submarine. The signal to be flashed to the submarine to indicate that the party was ready to leave was 'SB'.

The whole kidnapping operation had been planned with care and executed with precision. A dangerous and arduous journey had followed along a well organized escape route. Now, as they stood on the beach ready to be brought to safety, Leigh-Fermor and Moss engaged in a brief dialogue:

'Do you know morse?'

'No. Do you?'

'No.'

They both thought they knew how to signal SOS but felt this would be inappropriate. While they were still trying to decide what to do another SOE officer, Dennis Ciclitira, appeared on the scene. He did know morse.

During the journey across the mountains Leigh-Fermor had been in considerable pain. He learnt later that he was suffering from rheumatic fever, though for some time after his return to Egypt it was diagnosed as poliomyelitis. I remember clearly the shock that was felt in SOE in Cairo when the news was passed in fairly rapid succession that the operation for capturing the German commander in Crete had been wholly successful and that its leader was thought to have contracted polio.

The Germans abandoned nearly the whole of Crete of their own accord, and an invasion by Allied armies was not needed. Many of the preparations for a general rising were never therefore translated into practice. It is questionable too whether the kidnapping of General Kreipe seriously reduced the efficacy of the German garrison.

Nevertheless, when the news was broadcast to the world that the man in command of all the German forces in Crete had been captured by British officers and removed from the island, it was a source of exhilaration and hope to millions. It may also be thought that when General Kreipe, facing Mount Ida at dawn, uttered the words 'Ach so, Herr Major', it was an acknowledgment that the Byron tradition had been richly sustained.

Chapter 7

The Liberation of France

In France, as in the Balkan countries, SOE was confronted with a dichotomy which was partly of its own making. In Yugoslavia, in Albania and in Greece, after help had been given by SOE in different ways and at different times to both sides in their internal conflicts, the British government had eventually to choose whether to support communist-controlled or non-communist forces. In France the issues were more complex, but they also gave rise to conflicts of loyalty.

In an attempt to soften these, and to prevent them from intruding on the prosecution of the war, SOE hit upon the expedient of having two French sections. One was known as F, the other as RF. F Section employed its own agents. RF was a liaison section servicing those who had rallied under the leadership of Charles de Gaulle and who were known for a time as the Free French.

French resistance was an indigenous growth, fostered at first by a few individuals who, appalled by what they had witnessed in the summer of 1940, would not admit that the war had ended at that point. One such was Henri Frenay, a regular officer who came from a family with a strong military tradition. In June 1940 he had seen French soldiers throw down their arms and organize folk-dances in forest clearings, which were watched by passing Germans with looks of astonishment and contempt. He himself had been taken prisoner and had been unable to find a single officer willing to join him in trying to escape. From such unpromising beginnings he built up the resistance organization known as Combat, whose headquarters was in Lyons. Its propaganda staff included Albert Camus.

Emmanuel d'Astier de la Vigerie, a poet who later became French Ambassador in Washington, also began organizing in the unoccupied zone ruled by the Vichy government. At the end of three months, apart from two members of his own family, he had found, as he put it, only five 'disinterested people who were prepared to act without counting the cost'. In Toulouse a group organized by Jean-Pierre Lévy took the name Franc-Tireur, thereby recalling an earlier embryonic resistance

120

movement, that of the men who actively opposed the temporary Prussian occupation after the war of 1870.

It was some time before these and other small, loosely co-ordinated groups looked to Britain for effective support. To many French people the process of evacuation, which became known in Britain as 'the miracle of Dunkirk', seemed no more than an ignominious flight and an act of desertion. As Commander-in-Chief General Weygand had expressed a fairly orthodox view when he told de Gaulle that within a week of the fall of France Britain would begin negotiations with the Germans.

Gradually it became apparent that Britain was continuing the struggle. In France, as elsewhere, the Germans could find no effective means of preventing the BBC from fanning sparks of resistance wherever they happened to be found, while reporting the war news with enough truthfulness to command widespread respect. As a result the problems of Britain's survival and France's future began to be more closely associated in the minds of the thoughtful. Jean Bruller, or, to use his pseudonym, 'Vercors', whose book, *Le Silence de la mer*, was dropped into France by the RAF in large numbers, recorded a conversation in 1940 in which he and a friend agreed that 'if Britain yielded French thought might have to keep alive amid the outer darkness for hundreds of years'.

One man who believed that to promote resistance in France effectively he must first make his way to Britain was Jean Moulin. A skilful cartoonist and a connoisseur of paintings, Moulin was the youngest French prefect at the time of the French capitulation. He refused to append his signature to a statement prepared by the Germans which accused French troops of committing atrocities in the neighbourhood of Chartres, the seat of his prefecture. For this he was so badly beaten that he decided to prevent a repetition of the treatment by committing suicide. He did in fact cut his throat and thereafter had a hoarse voice and a scar, which he usually concealed by wearing a muffler.

The United States still being neutral and maintaining diplomatic relations with the Vichy government, Moulin, in order to further his aims, made contact with the American Consul-General in Marseilles, Hugh S. Fullerton. Through Fullerton he was put in touch with Henri Frenay. At their first meeting Moulin told Frenay that, although he knew a number of opponents of the Vichy administration, he had not yet met anyone who was actually in the resistance.

Fullerton also arranged for Moulin to be given a visa to enter the United States. In fact Moulin went as far as Lisbon, where he had to wait for some time. Then through Gubbins's intervention he was given a seat on an aircraft flying to London. In London he saw representatives of SOE's F and RF sections, and a meeting with de Gaulle was arranged. After close consideration of the various possibilities Moulin came to the conclusion that it was under de Gaulle that he now wished to serve.

Soon after establishing himself in London General de Gaulle formed his own intelligence service. As head of it he appointed André Dewavrin, who had been an assistant professor at the St Cyr military academy. Dewavrin had had no training in intelligence work, but de Gaulle considered this an advantage. Fair-haired, pale-eyed, prematurely bald, Dewavrin had a rather soft appearance. Yet he was a man of strength and resource, surviving the intrigues which seem almost inseparable from administrations in exile and remaining in charge of his department until the end of the war. He also carried out a hazardous operational mission in occupied France. Dewavrin and the senior members of his staff all adopted pseudonyms chosen from the names of the stations on the Paris *Métro*. Dewavrin's choice was Passy, the name by which he is commonly referred to in memoirs and other books on the French resistance.

Dewavrin's department was at first concerned solely with secret intelligence and counter-espionage, to which de Gaulle in the early days of the occupation attached much more importance than he did to the possibilities of subversive action. Even when Moulin reached England in the autumn de Gaulle was still sceptical about the prospects of creating a secret army or other forms of para-military activity.

Moulin made a strong impression on de Gaulle, so much so that when he returned to France he took with him a microphotograph in the false bottom of a matchbox containing a personal message from de Gaulle to resistance leaders. He was also given the title of delegate-general of the Free French Committee and entrusted with the task of co-ordinating all the underground activities of de Gaulle's supporters.

Moulin returned to France on New Year's Day 1942. In the months which followed, in the words of Professor M. R. D. Foot, 'it was he more than any other man – even than de Gaulle – who welded the antagonistic fragments of resistance in France into one more or less coherent and disciplined body'. Had he survived he would no doubt have played a major role in post-war France, probably second only to that of de Gaulle, to whom he was unswervingly loyal.

In fact he was a victim of the political nature of his mission. More than once, in order to achieve agreement, he found it necessary while in France to assemble political leaders in far greater numbers than adherence to rules for security would have allowed. One such meeting, held at a doctor's house in a suburb of Lyons, was attended by more than a dozen people. All, including Moulin, were arrested, only one man escaping. Moulin was subjected to such appalling tortures that he died within a fortnight, having revealed no secrets to his interrogators. The Reichssicherheitsdienst official responsible was severely reprimanded, not for the methods he had used, but for bungling the job so badly that Moulin could not be questioned further.

As resistance in France grew, the responsibilities of Dewavrin's department were extended to include liaison with and, in time, control of resistance organizations. In recognition of its new role it was given a new name, Bureau Central de Renseignements et d'Action. In the last two years before the liberation of France the BCRA was linked with the greater part of the effective resistance forces. It remained dependent on the British and, later, the Americans for arms and other supplies and for most methods of transport in and out of France. Yet, though closely linked with SOE, it was not a part of it, and for this reason details of the exploits of those whom BCRA served or controlled must fall outside the scope of this book.

Within the liaison section known as RF there were a few officers who had operational roles. One of these was J. R. H. (Jim Hutchison, who was put in command of the section in August 1942.

Hutchison, who had served in France and Gallipoli in the First World War, came, like Sandy Glen, from a family of Glasgow shipowners. In the early months of the Second World War he was engaged in fairly undemanding liaison duties in Nantes. He came out through Bordeaux, and later in the summer of 1940 he called on General de Gaulle. It was to be their only meeting, for although Hutchison was for nearly two years in charge of the section of SOE whose sole *raison d'être* was to support the Gaullist forces he never had an opportunity to speak to the general again.

RF Section's day-to-day tasks consisted of providing various facilities, including training, for the BCRA and its agents. It also regularly fought the internal battles which were needed to obtain a reasonable proportion of the exiguous supply of aircraft made available for the support of resistance movements. From time to time it was involved in conflicts of policy.

Moulin's arrest had been preceded by that of the man appointed to command the secret army in France, General Delestraint. De Gaulle decided that a new commander should be appointed, but the British objected on the grounds that, while such a centralization of command might be thought desirable politically, it must give rise to a lack of security which would be unacceptable.

On this occasion the British arguments prevailed. It was agreed that France would be divided into a number of military regions and that fourteen regional commanders would be brought to Britain for discussions and for training. Two of the fourteen, Jacques Chaban-Delmas and Maurice Bourgès-Maunoury, later became Prime Ministers of France.

Hutchison himself began after a time to chafe at having to send other men into France while remaining at a desk himself. Analysing his feelings later in a book of reminiscences which he entitled *That Drug Danger*, he wrote: 'I had no wish to escape but only to join those élite and perhaps also to show that age is a most unreliable method of measuring capabilities.'

His opportunity came when it was decided to form operational units which were to be known as Jedburghs. Jedburghs were to be joint Anglo-French-American groups of not more than half-a-dozen men who were to be dropped to resistance forces shortly before, or in conjunction with, the landing of Allied armies. Their main function would be to provide certain paramilitary skills, but their presence was also to serve as a flag-showing exercise.

Jedburghs were to be dropped in uniform, again partly for propaganda purposes, but primarily because it was believed that if they were captured by German combatant troops, as opposed to secret policemen, they would be protected by the terms of the Geneva Convention. Hutchison was fairly sure that he himself would enjoy no such protection, for he was aware that his name was on the list of those senior SOE officers to whom the German authorities had decided that they would show no mercy. In order to qualify for inclusion in a Jedburgh mission he therefore came to the conclusion that at the age of forty-five he must undergo major facial surgery.

In the London Clinic Hutchison had some bone taken from his pelvis and transplanted on to his chin. To allow the operation on the pelvis to be made and yet provide no evidence of special bodily surgery an old appendix scar was opened up. Marks left on the chin could be satisfactorily explained as a consequence of a car accident and impact with a windscreen. Hutchison's gait too was altered by persistent pain in the area of the pelvis, which caused him to limp. Another change in personality was made by a calligraphic expert, who taught him a new style of handwriting, for Hutchison was aware that specimens of his writing had come into German possession.

Hutchison's confidence in his disguise was much enhanced when he returned to his flat in London and heard his seven-year-old son call out: 'Mummy, there's a man at the door to see you.' His bank manager later queried his signature on a cheque which he had tried, without much success, to write in his old style.

Hutchison was not the only SOE officer to undergo facial surgery before returning to France. George Langelaan, a journalist, who had worked for the *New York Times*, decided he was too well known to be able to move freely in France unless effectively disguised. Photographs of his face before and after treatment, two of which are included in his book of reminiscences, *Knights of the Floating Silk*, certainly suggest, at a first glance, a marked dissimilarity. Langelaan's disguise was in fact penetrated only once. This was when he telephoned an old friend in Lyons who recognized his voice immediately.

The Jedburgh mission on which Hutchison was sent was completed successfully. After the war he entered politics as Conservative Member of Parliament for Glasgow Central. In 1951 Winston Churchill appointed him Parliamentary Under-Secretary of State at the War Office. Yet his name became less well known to the general public in Britain than that of one of his subordinate officers in SOE's small RF Section. This was F. F. E. (Tommy) Yeo-Thomas.

Yeo-Thomas was thirty-eight when the Second World War broke out. Like Hutchison he saw service in the First World War. He then fought for Poland against the invading Bolshevik armies, was captured at Zitomir and sentenced to be shot, but escaped the night before the sentence was due to be carried out.

Yeo-Thomas's family had been settled in France for nearly a century. He himself spoke perfect French and was a director of the couture house of Molyneux in Paris. He was not particularly striking in appearance and might have passed unnoticed in a crowded room, but he gave an impression of quiet forcefulness.

Immediately after the French collapse Yeo-Thomas, as he moved southward from Paris wondered whether he should remain in France and prepare for a future British invasion. As he was in the uniform of the RAF he came to the conclusion that, if he did so, he would probably be posted as a deserter. He therefore returned to England, where he was classified as too old for flying duties. He was, however, commissioned in the RAF and after carrying out some liaison tasks with both French and Polish forces he gravitated rather naturally towards the RF Section of SOE.

Early in 1943 Dewavrin had come to the conclusion that he must himself visit France, partly in order to effect certain necessary reorganizations within resistance groups, and partly to form his own political and other assessments. SIS, with which Dewavrin had a much

closer relationship than he ever had with SOE, questioned the desirability of his return on the grounds that he knew too many secrets, but
its objections were overruled. Dewavrin himself, having been furnished with the lethal dose of potassium of cyanide known as the
L-tablet, felt, as he put it, perfect security in the knowledge that he
could kill himself within five or six seconds.

To accompany him Dewavrin chose a forceful, intelligent journalist,
broadcaster and propagandist for the French Socialist Party named
Pierre Brossolette. He also stated that he would be happy to have with
him as a British observer Yeo-Thomas, on whose knowledge of France
and personal integrity he felt he could rely for a fair and objective
judgment. It was an assessment which was to be vindicated by results.
Dewavrin later described Yeo-Thomas as 'one of the most magnificent
heroes of the war, a valued comrade, a dear friend, with intelligence
and quiet and determined courage'.

When the three men were dropped into France it must have been a
particularly unnerving experience for Dewavrin. He had visited the
training centre at Ringway near Manchester, where SOE agents took
their parachute courses, and had come away with the understanding,
possibly caused by language difficulties, that half the parachutes used
did not open. He had had to console himself with the knowledge that
half did.

Dewavrin and his companions were duly met in France by a reception committee, who relieved them – or so it was thought – of all
compromising material and large sums of money. They then set out on
foot for the next reception point, and after a time Yeo-Thomas asked
Dewavrin why he was carrying two suitcases instead of one, as had been
agreed. It was then discovered that the second suitcase, which ought to
have been removed by the reception committee, contained hand
grenades, revolvers and a radio set.

Before long the three men adapted themselves to life in occupied
France, and Dewavrin had a number of valuable discussions with
resistance leaders. He persuaded them to postpone plans for any sort of
general insurrection and called attention to the advantages of the
British system of rigidly separating secret intelligence from sabotage
and action.

He also learnt at first hand of the lack of understanding sometimes
shown towards operators in the field. During the first three weeks of
March 1943 he, Brossolette and Yeo-Thomas sent some eighty radio
messages to London. In return they received three or four of little
importance from the BCRA. They also met a courier who brought a
long *exposé* of inter-allied differences in Madagascar. This experience

convinced Dewavrin of the need to staff his bureau in London, so far as possible, with officers who had returned from the field.

Yeo-Thomas's role on this first mission was largely that of an observer. During his travels he began to assess the likely effect on resistance of the Vichy government's decree making young Frenchmen liable to be conscripted for forced labour in Germany. This could and did disrupt individual resistance groups. It also drove numbers of young people to adopt, as their only means of escape, a kind of vagabond life in woods and mountains. It was from this more or less forced migration that many of the groups which came to be known as *maquis* developed. Another discovery which Yeo-Thomas made from his first-hand observations was that de Gaulle, who had arrived in England less than three years earlier as a rather obscure military figure, now commanded a large following in France.

After being brought back to England by Lysander aircraft Yeo-Thomas, unlike his chief, Hutchison, was received by de Gaulle, who told him that he had the impression that there was in France 'quelque chose qui s'appelle le gaullisme'. De Gaulle also sent him the Croix de Guerre with palms, but the Air Ministry forbade him to wear this on the grounds that de Gaulle was not a recognized head of state.

After the arrests of General Delestraint and Jean Moulin it was decided to send Brossolette, who had also been brought back to England, on another visit to France. Once again he was accompanied by Yeo-Thomas. This time their tasks were even more demanding, for they discovered that copies of incoming and outgoing radio messages which, contrary to instructions, had not been destroyed had been captured by the Germans together with a list of the names of prominent resistance figures.

During an eight-week stay Brossolette and Yeo-Thomas did much to achieve the decentralization of command within the resistance forces which was so clearly necessary. They also learnt how disastrously ill-armed most of the *maquis* groups were and how difficult it was to convince French resistance leaders that their efforts were given serious attention in London when so few supply drops were made.

Once again Yeo-Thomas was brought back by Lysander, his journey to the landing-field being made on this occasion by hearse. He was by now obsessed by the lack of aircraft for supporting French resistance, and as orthodox methods of asking for more were having little effect he decided to try the unorthodox. His godfather, Major-General E. D. Swinton, had been closely associated with Winston Churchill in the early development of tanks in the First World War and still had enough influence to arrange for Yeo-Thomas to have a personal interview with the Prime Minister. Churchill began by saying he could give Yeo-Thomas five minutes. In fact he gave him fifty-five, during which time Yeo-Thomas explained just what was needed to make the *maquis* an effective fighting force.

Churchill's next visitor happened to be Emmanuel d'Astier de la Vigerie, to whom he was able to state that he had decided to increase substantially the number of aircraft for dropping supplies to France. He did indeed give an order to that effect, and although various reasons were found for delaying the implementation of the order, the business of giving effective support to resistance forces in France was transformed for the first time from the theoretical to the practical.

When he heard that Brossolette had been arrested Yeo-Thomas, who had formed a close friendship with him, decided he must return and rescue him. In France Yeo-Thomas had adopted a number of names and identities. To some people in the resistance he was known as Shelley. In messages he sometimes used the name which Bruce Marshall chose for his biography of Yeo-Thomas, *The White Rabbit*. Now he evolved an additional cover-story which he hoped to be able to sustain if captured. For this purpose he adopted the identity of a certain Squadron-Leader Dodkin, who was on the operational list of the RAF but had reverted to ground duties. In Yeo-Thomas's cover-story Dodkin had been shot down over France.

Yeo-Thomas's plan was to rescue Brossolette with the help of some perfect German-speakers who would wear German uniform. The plan never materialized and Brossolette was never rescued. Instead he committed suicide by jumping through a window. The reason for the failure was that Yeo-Thomas was betrayed and arrested at a prearranged rendezvous.

The tortures to which he was submitted in the weeks which followed have been memorably described by Bruce Marshall. He gave away nothing. He had hoped to have access to his L-tablet, but this was in his signet-ring, which had been removed. At times he found that praying and singing helped him. Eventually he lost count of the number of occasions on which he was subjected to particular tortures, yet emerging through all the accounts are not only the dignity but the ingenuity he showed in resisting. His German interrogators made a practice, whenever he was evidently about to faint with pain, of plunging him into cold water in order to revive him. He therefore carefully observed his own symptoms as he was about to faint and then simulated them in order to reduce the period of torture.

After a time he was moved to Fresnes prison, where at least he had the consolation of being able to communicate with other prisoners by tapping messages in morse on walls. (There were agents who played whole games of chess by this method.) From Fresnes he was moved to Buchenwald concentration camp. This he survived by being one of a small group who, with the connivance of a German guard, exchanged identities with prisoners who had died of typhus. After that he still had the strength and spirit to escape and make his way to the American armies advancing through Germany.

Yeo-Thomas's principal contribution to the prosecution of the war was probably made, not in the field, but in 10 Downing Street, when he persuaded Churchill to provide more aircraft to help the French resistance. His contribution to the history of human dignity is difficult to measure, but it is, and must always remain, heartening evidence that the spirit of man, at its best, is not to be broken by physical torture.

The first agents whom SOE's F Section sent to France were Frenchmen. The first to be parachuted in, Georges Bégué, was dropped early in May 1941. Bégué had attended an engineering college and had acquired an early interest in radio. During the inter-war years he had been unable to find work which provided an outlet for his engineering skills and he was employed in the sales department of the Simca Company. As a reserve officer he was recalled to the colours in 1939, but he found service in the Maginot Line a dispiriting experience. He was glad therefore when his knowledge of English brought him an appointment as liaison officer with British forces. In this capacity he came to England through Belgium and then Dunkirk.

In England he spent some time in hospital and afterwards had convalescent leave with his English wife and their small child, who were living near Hull. This interlude gave him time to consider closely his future course of action. Most of the Frenchmen in England with whom Bégué was in touch at that time wanted to return home to their families, the prospect of service with de Gaulle appealing only to a minority.

Bégué himself visited de Gaulle's headquarters, was not very favourably impressed by what he saw, and declined to take an oath of personal allegiance to the general. Together with a group of some twenty other Frenchmen he enlisted in the British forces, an oath of allegiance to the symbol of the crown seeming a more acceptable commitment than the personal one demanded by de Gaulle.

Bégué was at first enrolled as a private soldier in the Royal Corps of Signals, but his expert knowledge of radio was placed on record, and before long he was called for an interview at one of the War Office rooms used by SOE as cover. Here he was confronted by Thomas

Cadett, one of the pioneer figures in SOE's F Section, who was known to the British public as the BBC's Paris correspondent. Bégué agreed with little hesitation to Cadett's suggestion that he should be dropped into France to provide a radio link. The only proviso he made was that his mission should serve some useful purpose.

The training Bégué received was inevitably much sketchier than that given to agents who went in later. His radio set was cumbersome and not very convincingly disguised in a suitcase. The ration cards he took with him were, he was to discover, not valid. By way of contacts he was given simply the name and address of Max Hymans, a former Socialist member of the Chamber of Deputies, who was known to officials of F Section, and some personal messages which he had to memorize carefully.

Bégué was dropped some ten miles from the landing point chosen. He came down in a ploughed field, where he spent most of the rest of the night, yet as he looked up at the moon and the silvery clouds he decided he had just made the best journey of his life. Lugging the heavy suitcase containing his radio, he made his way to a hotel, which was just inside the unoccupied zone and where a maid gave him some valid bread coupons. After making a number of enquiries he reached the house whose address he had been given in London, only to find that Hymans was away from home.

He had therefore to return later. When he did so he repeated the messages he had memorized, satisfied Hymans of his *bona fides*, and was put in touch first with a chemist and then with a garage-owner. Through these contacts he found a room where he could establish his radio set and the long aerial it needed, and so was able to transmit the first radio message sent to SOE from France.

The radio contact which Bégué established allowed prepared parachute drops to be made, but the maintenance of communications was, for him, continually hazardous. The Germans were quick to exploit the use of detector vans for locating sets which were transmitting. As the resistance organizations grew, radio operators were able to transmit from a number of different sets placed in different houses, and the smaller the sets became the easier they were to conceal when a raid did take place. Bégué had none of these advantages, and he had the added problem of continually having to repair his set without access to suitable spare parts.

To reduce radio traffic Bégué suggested that the BBC should broadcast *en clair* certain prearranged phrases which would indicate to him that a parachute drop would or would not take place or other information of importance. He thereby became one of the originators of a system which would later have widespread application. In time it was even used to inform SOE agents who had left pregnant wives behind of the sex of the children born while they were on operational duty in enemy-occupied territory.

Bégué continued to operate for nearly six months from May to October 1941. When the almost inevitable arrest did take place in Marseilles it was made by the Vichy authorities, not the Germans. Bégué was imprisoned, but through the intercession of the admirable American Consul-General, Hugh Fullerton, was transferred to the Mauzac prison camp. Within the camp he succeeded in rigging up a radio transmitter, which was instrumental in bringing about the escape which was organized for him. He crossed the Pyrenees and reached London.

Here the knowledge he had acquired of the conditions in which radio operators had to function in France was considered of such importance that he was appointed, under the name of George Noble, F Section's signals officer. He was thereby precluded from further operational duties.

An agent who was parachuted in shortly after Bégué had established his initial radio contact was a Frenchman whose background was somewhat different from Bégué's own. This was Pierre de Vomécourt, a member of an aristocratic Lorraine family with a strong anglophile tradition and a long history, recalled with pride, of fighting against Germans.

Pierre de Vomécourt came to England from Brittany in 1940 together with Dewavrin. He met de Gaulle, to whom he put proposals for resistance activity in France. He received no encouragement and was told that what he was suggesting would only lead to reprisals. He therefore approached the British War Office and through the future Field-Marshal and Chief of the Imperial General Staff, Gerald Templer, who was himself to serve in SOE for a time, was put in touch with Gubbins.

Pierre de Vomécourt chose his own first contact in France. This was his brother Philippe, who lived in a castle near Limoges. Philippe de Vomécourt was thirty-seven when war broke out and the father of seven children. Like his two brothers he had been educated in England. The eldest of the three, Jean, had joined the Royal Flying Corps in 1917 by lying about his age.

With a sublime self-confidence and in a manner reminiscent of Julius Caesar the three brothers divided France into three parts for purposes of resistance. Jean was to be responsible for eastern France,

Pierre for the north and west, and Philippe for the territory controlled by the Vichy government.

The groups which Jean de Vomécourt formed carried out some effective sabotage of German E-boats as they passed along canals, but in August 1942 he was arrested. He revealed nothing under interrogation and was about to be released when he was denounced by a traitor. His end came by incineration in a German concentration camp.

Pierre de Vomécourt was able to make a return visit to London in spite of the fact that his radio communications were controlled by the Abwehr. An intermediary he used for sending messages was a French-woman named Mathilde Carré, sometimes known as La Chatte, who was having an affair with an Abwehr sergeant. De Vomécourt dis-covered before long who La Chatte was working for, yet not only did he persuade her to accompany him to London, but her Abwehr controller agreed that she should go in order to continue working for the Germans.

From such exercises in penetration and counter-penetration some-times one side gains the advantage, sometimes another. On this occasion the Allies were clear winners. Mathilde Carré spent the rest of the war in detention in Britain. De Vomécourt was able to give a clear and detailed analysis of conditions in France to SOE officials, to Anthony Eden and to Lord Selbourne, whom Churchill had appointed to succeed Dalton as Minister of Economic Warfare.

Pierre de Vomécourt returned to France, but after a time he too was captured. At his trial he persuaded the German authorities that he and a number of men associated with him should be treated as prisoners of war, and he was eventually liberated by American forces from Colditz. The third brother, Philippe, had a longer stretch at liberty.

The area around Philippe de Vomécourt's castle near Limoges pro-vided the site for SOE's first successful drop of arms and explosives to France. The fact could not be wholly concealed from the local farmers, for whom this was an unprecedented event. As no agents had been dropped de Vomécourt considered it would be a wise precaution for him personally to notify the police of reports that parachutists had landed and to take them on a wholly nugatory tour of possible landing places.

At first de Vomécourt decided to operate under his own identity, and he obtained a post as an inspector of railways. This provided valuable cover for collecting intelligence, organizing sabotage and also for another activity in which he engaged with some success, the repatria-tion of Allied airmen who had been shot down over France.

In the colourful account of his wartime experiences contained in his book, *Who Lived to See the Day*, Philippe de Vomécourt wrote: 'We learned the rules and made the rules as we went along. Some had no time to learn them; their first mistake was their last. At the start, it must be confessed, we thought of the whole business as a game. A serious, deadly one, but a game nevertheless.'

The concept of resistance as a game was dispelled as the arrests multiplied and as new forms of action against the occupying power were devised. According to his own statement, de Vomécourt himself arranged for French prostitutes to supply German pilots with heroin in order to damage their eyesight.

Like his two brothers, Philippe was eventually arrested. The French police who took him in charge informed him that they were doing him a favour by forestalling the only possible alternative, which was arrest by the Germans. He was sentenced to tens years' labour, but in January 1944 he took part in a mass escape involving fifty-four men from a prison in Lot-et-Garonne.

The escaping party was divided into three groups, de Vomécourt being in charge of the only group which had no compass. In his youth he had worked in Zululand helping a Scotsman to run a farm, and he believed his experience of trekking and big-game hunting in Africa would enable him to keep on course. Eventually he led a party of sixteen over the Pyrenees in the worst of winter conditions, he himself suffering from temporary snow-blindness.

Philippe de Vomécourt's debriefing by SOE in London was a spirited affair. He admitted, as he put it, to 'a degree of egocentricity' about his work in France, claiming that this was almost a necessary qualification for success. After making his report he volunteered to return, although he estimated the odds against his survival were about ten to one. He was accompanied by a twenty-three-old English Jewish radio operator named Muriel Byck, who contracted meningitis while in France and died in hospital.

While operating with the French *maquis* de Vomécourt learnt with a mixture of pride and some anxiety that the Germans had put a price of two million francs on his head. Nevertheless he survived, his last important action in a theatre of war occurring when he learnt that an American divisional commander had allowed Germans to make conditions before surrendering.

One of the conditions was that 18,000 German troops who were to give themselves up would be allowed to march through *maquis* territory with their sidearms. De Vomécourt was so incensed that he made his way to General George Patton's headquarters. Although he held only the rank of major in the British Army he soon reached the general's presence and persuaded him to telephone the Supreme Commander, General Eisenhower. Eisenhower agreed that de Vomécourt had his full authority to rescind the order allowing the Germans to retain their arms.

When de Vomécourt reached the divisional headquarters with Eisenhower's order the American general tried to present him to the surrendering German commander. De Vomécourt found this unacceptable. 'It is the German general,' he insisted, 'the commander of the defeated army, who should be presented to *me*, the victor.' The American general did as he was asked, and honour was satisfied.

On one of his missions to France Pierre de Vomécourt met Henri Frenay, the organizer of the resistance group Combat. Frenay later recorded that de Vomécourt said to him: 'The British services are very efficient, much more so than the French – as you've probably noticed. And then, as we all know, the two of them share no mutual trust whatsoever. Anyway, if it's efficiency you're after, the English are the ones who can help you.'

Frenay replied that if the French resistance were to put itself at the disposal of Britain its members would become agents of a foreign power. He added that if de Gaulle were not in London he would probably act in the same way as de Vomécourt.

Such a dilemma was experienced in its most acute form only by the early French resistance leaders. Once de Gaulle accepted the need to promote action inside France, and the BCRA was given this as one of its principal tasks, SOE agreed to renounce all future claims on the services of French citizens. What it was not prepared to accept was any suggestion that it should cease to operate directly in France or, alternatively, to submit such action to the control of the BCRA.

SOE had established with difficulty, and at grave risk to those involved, an embryo organization in France, and it did not intend to withdraw it or to hand over SOE agents, some of whom were British, to the control of a foreign power. This decision, understandable and indeed justifiable operationally, did of course give rise to suspicions, not only in the mind of General de Gaulle, of British political and other motives.

SOE's F Section had from the outset a formidable task in the selection of the right agents. Whereas in the Balkan countries members of SOE were able to operate effectively in uniform, some of them with virtually no knowledge of the local language, agents sent to France had normally to be accepted as French in speech, in habit and in appearance. Once it was precluded from employing French citizens F

Section's recruiting problems were immediately magnified. It now had to look to British men and women who had lived for a long time in France, to people of mixed parentage who held British passports, and to inhabitants or former inhabitants of certain overseas territories. One valuable source of manpower was found to be the predominantly French-speaking British colony of Mauritius, from which came two of SOE's outstanding agents, Claude de Baissac and his sister Lise.

Clandestine operations in France were further complicated by the fact that from the time of the armistice in 1940 until November 1942 most of France was divided into two parts, one occupied by the Germans, one ostensibly ruled by the government headed by Marshal Pétain. There was also a comparatively small area in the south-east of France controlled by the Italians. These divisions resulted in different regulations, different controls, different kinds of officials and, at least as long as the Vichy government retained some authority, different attitudes towards the desirability of resistance.

As a sphere of activity for SOE operations France was also unique among European countries in that it was there that the Allied invasion was to be launched in 1944. Resources had therefore to be husbanded and long-term plans made to cause the maximum disruption shortly before and in conjunction with the Allied landings. Yet it was also necessary, for two years or more before the invasion, to organize sabotage and the continual harassment of the occupying forces. The two requirements, the long-term and the short-, were often mutually contradictory.

These were some of the principal problems confronting the man who, for most of its existence, commanded F Section, and whose name was to become almost symbolic with British involvement in French resistance, Maurice Buckmaster.

Maurice Buckmaster had learnt early in life to cope with the consequences of both success and failure. As his father's business prospered or declined his family made the progression up or down between large and small houses. He was doing well at Eton when his father was declared bankrupt. He was allowed to stay on for a final year through a scholarship and by tutoring younger boys and from then on was entirely dependent on his own resources.

After doing some teaching he made his way to France, where he improved his schoolboy knowledge of French rapidly enough to be taken on as a reporter for *Le Matin*. He was in banking for six years and was then appointed to help establish branches of the Ford Motor Company in a number of European countries. It was while serving as manager of the Ford company in Paris that he brought himself to the point of being virtually bi-lingual. It was while visiting numerous Ford agents that he acquired his exceptional knowledge of the towns and countryside of France.

Buckmaster, who was thirty-seven when war broke out, served with the British Expeditionary Force in France. He came out through Dunkirk and was then involved in the disastrous Anglo-French expedition to Dakar. His introduction to SOE, like that of other distinguished members of the organization, followed a talk with Gerald Templer at the War Office.

A tall man, with a gentle, slightly self-deprecatory manner and eyes which, later in his life, suggested he had seen nearly everything, Buckmaster was thought by some to lack the ruthlessness which a perfectionist might have demanded. No serious person ever doubted his dedication or his awareness of what was owing to his agents in the field.

He worked on average some eighteen hours a day. He sometimes had an evening break, when he would cycle home to Chelsea for an early dinner, returning to Baker Street about 8 p.m. and usually remaining there until about 4 a.m. When considering, after the war, a complaint that the records kept by F Section were somewhat incomplete, he commented that those who finished work at any time between three and five in the morning felt 'little desire to tabulate the events of the day in order to earn the gratitude of some hypothetical historian of the future'.

Buckmaster was deeply aware of the importance of mutual trust between himself and agents who were being sent on missions in which they would feel lonely, would be thrown on their own resources, and would almost certainly begin to doubt whether those in offices at home understood or even greatly cared about their problems. He made a point of presenting agents, as they were about to depart for the field, with a personal gift – gold cuff-links or a gold cigarette-case – which had of course no British markings and which would serve as a reminder that the agent was not forgotten. He would usually add, to avoid embarrassment: 'You can always hock it if you run out of money.' George Millar, a former correspondent of the *Daily Express*, who was among those sent to France by Buckmaster, recalling what the parting gift meant to him, wrote: 'This was a particularly sympathetic and admirable colonel. His talents and industry and kindliness had coloured the whole organization.'

Buckmaster assumed command of F Section in September 1941, succeeding H. A. R. Marriott, a director of Courtaulds' French company. One of his first contributions was to produce a copy of the publication known as Bottin, which was a comprehensive guide to French industry and commerce. He felt that if sabotage was to be organized successfully it would be a useful start to know where the principal targets were likely to be located. From such tentative beginnings F Section advanced under Buckmaster's direction to the point at which it became responsible for the employment of 480 agents.

One of F Section's most important requirements after Buckmaster took over was a training programme which could transform the enthusiastic volunteer into an effective agent within two or three months. Another was the assembling of enough information about documents, regulations and living conditions generally to give agents a reasonable chance of surviving their first few days in France.

While undergoing training F Section's agents were accommodated for the most part in distinguished country houses set in beautiful surroundings and staffed by FANY girls of the kind written about with such affection by one of the agents of the Polish Sixth Bureau. John Goldsmith described his period of training before being sent into France as 'a cross between going back to school and staying at a series of first-class hotels where the shooting, hunting and even fishing were free'.

Potential agents of F Section began their instruction at Wanborough Manor near Guildford. Here they were given some paramilitary training, were accompanied by conducting officers, and observed. At times they were encouraged to relax and have a few drinks. Their conduct then was particularly closely watched, as were their relations with others taking the course. Aptitude tests were given, including the one described by Kipling, in which Kim had to memorize an assortment of articles laid out on a tray.

Wanborough Manor was used partly to weed out the unsuitable. Those who passed through successfully went on to the western Highlands of Scotland. Here they learnt how to live off the land, to poach and to stalk. They underwent assault courses, handled explosives, and were initiated into various methods of killing. The principal instructors in the forms of homicide favoured by SOE were two ex-officers of the Shanghai police, one of whom, known as Bill Sykes, had white hair and the appearance of an exceptionally benevolent bishop. Included in his repertoire was a Chinese method of stifling someone to death which left no visible traces other than death itself. In 1942 the Germans paid him the compliment of producing a pamphlet describing some of the methods he taught.

Those who absorbed all that the course in the western Highlands had to offer emerged capable of destroying a railway bridge, an aircraft or a telephone exchange, of dropping off a train moving at forty miles an hour without serious risk, and of living in the country for days, or even weeks, without needing to buy food. As George Langelaan, the former *New York Times* correspondent, expressed it, his training also enabled him 'to face the possibility of a fight without the slightest tremor of apprehension, a state of mind which very few professional boxers ever enjoy'.

The most intellectually demanding part of an agent's training took place near Beaulieu in the New Forest. Here instruction was given in subjects ranging from ciphers and secret inks to the uniforms of German police and other services and their methods of interrogation. Potential agents were liable to be woken in the early hours of the morning and subjected to a simulated interrogation in which they had to maintain their cover-stories. They might also be required at some stage in their training to enter a prohibited area such as a dockyard or an aircraft factory. If the real reason for their presence had to be revealed to the police it was evidence of failure.

F Section shared most of its training facilities with other country sections of SOE. The quality of the instruction given improved as more and more information was received about living conditions under German occupation. In the assembling of this F Section's agents played a leading part, not least because it was easier to bring people out of France than out of other occupied countries of northern and western Europe.

One of the consequences of the speed with which the Germans completed their French campaign in 1940 was that SIS was virtually bereft of agents inside France. For a time therefore SOE had to depend on its own resources for most of the information it needed.

A valuable first-hand report was received by SOE in London in June 1941. This was brought by a Chilean actress named Giliana Balmaceda. Her link with SOE was through her husband, Victor Gerson, an English Jewish businessman, who had lived for many years in France and who was personally acquainted with Leslie Humphreys, the first head of SOE's F Section. Later in co-operation with Humphreys Gerson was to be the principal organizer of escape routes used by SOE agents who had to leave France. In the early months of the German occupation his wife travelled widely through France, and when she reached London she brought with her such valuable documentation as time-tables and ration cards.

Outstanding among SOE's first agents in France was an American newspaperwoman from Baltimore, whose cover as the accredited correspondent of the *New York Post* was a valuable one. Her name was Virginia Hall. She was a tall woman with bright red hair, an artificial foot, which she named Cuthbert, and a remarkable ability to improvize. Time and again SOE agents, finding themselves in the Lyons area, called on her for help, which she always seemed able to give. One of them, Denis Rake, was later to write: 'Virginia Hall in my opinion – and there are many others who share it – was one of the greatest women agents of the war.' The first service which she rendered Rake was to find him lodgings with a prostitute. Being an undeviating homosexual, Rake had to explain his predicament to the girl, but it was accepted in good part and, so far as security was concerned, the arrangement was an excellent one.

Gradually, from agents returned from the field and from other sources, SOE built up a body of information which enabled those whom F Section sent to France to be better trained, better briefed and better equipped. Dewavrin, himself no lover of the activities of Buckmaster's section, though his personal relations with Buckmaster were fairly cordial, described the technical services of SOE as both more comprehensive and more competent than those of SIS. A point was eventually reached at which SOE was able to put forgeries of a new kind of French ration card into circulation on the same day as the Vichy authorities issued the genuine ones.

The training schools provided detailed reports on potential agents. The opinions of psychiatrists on agents' suitability were also taken into account. But the ultimate responsibility for deciding whether a man or a woman should or should not be sent into France lay with Buckmaster.

Mistakes were made. A professional gambler, who was sent in to obtain information on ration cards, permits and other controls and was given a fairly large sum of money for the purpose, made his way to the French Riviera and was not heard of by SOE again. Another agent became almost paralyzed by fear and hid for days and nights under a bed in the house to which he had been directed. He had eventually to be brought out of France at considerable risk to others. There were too those who failed under interrogation, as many of the rest of us might have failed.

Against these must be set the record of those who succeeded. Some of these were men and women about whom the training schools had expressed reservations, but in whom Buckmaster, for reasons of his own, had confidence. One, as has been seen, was Francis Cammaerts. Of another, Richard Heslop, a training-school report stated: 'This man is disappointing and has not borne out the high promise which one was led to expect.' He was to become in effect joint commander of an army of more than 5,000 Frenchmen operating over an area the size of a rather large English county.

Richard Heslop spent much of his early life in France and later worked in the teak industry in Siam. He was squarely built and of medium height. His features were not very striking, but he was able to convey a quality of leadership under all the different guises which he was to adopt in the field. He was in his early thirties when he began operations in France but looked, certainly by the time he had completed his missions, considerably older.

George Millar, in the course of a long and adventurous journey following an escape from a prisoner-of-war camp, came into contact with Heslop in Upper Savoy. He later wrote of the feelings of pride and patriotism he experienced in watching him at work. Henri Romans-Petit, the Frenchman with whom Heslop was most closely associated operationally, commented on his admirable *sang-froid*. François Musard, a French historian of resistance activity in Upper Savoy, described Heslop as being about forty-five, 'un homme mûr, aux temples gris, aux propos mesurés . . . ancien joueur de rugby aux muscles puissants'.

Heslop began his war service in the ranks of the Field Security Police and was at an officer cadet training unit when he was picked up by F Section's increasingly effective talent-spotting organization. He damaged an ankle on a parachute course, and it was therefore decided to send him into France by sea. He later recorded his sensations before going on his first mission. He was, he decided, no hero; the prospect of pain frightened him; and he would have no friends where he was going.

Heslop went in by one of the regular forms of transport used by SOE to land agents in the unoccupied zone of France. This was a small, slow type of Mediterranean coaster known as a *felucca*. For crewing such vessels General Sikorski had offered Gubbins the services of some Polish seamen whom he described as too rough even for the Polish Navy. Gubbins later recorded that they never gave him any trouble. Two of them were to be awarded the DSO.

After spending short periods in Cannes, where he met Peter Churchill, SOE's principal organizer in the area, and in Lyons, Heslop was arrested by French police in the summer of 1942. At that stage, according to his own judgment, all he had achieved was a holiday on the Riviera at the taxpayers' expense and landing himself in prison where, under torture, he might reveal the names of resistance workers in Cannes. He was also convinced that he had been betrayed by one of

Buckmaster's agents in France. In this, as he was later to discover, he was wrong.

Heslop and another SOE agent named Ernest Wilkinson, who was born in Missouri and who was with Heslop at the time of his arrest, spent three months in a French prison. They were then transferred to a prisoner-of-war camp at Chambaran, where, shortly after their arrival, they learnt that German forces had marched into the unoccupied zone. The French commandant of the camp told Heslop and Wilkinson that he had had orders to kill them both but that he had decided to allow them to escape.

They set off together with an Englishman named Dick Cooper, who had been arrested while working for SOE in Algeria, on a series of long marches. Their destination was Le Puy, where Wilkinson had a friend who had been a chef in the Savoy Hotel in London. On their way they met a German patrol, and Heslop realized that this was the first time he had seen an enemy in uniform.

A number of SOE agents, on escaping from prison or prison camp in France, had little option other than to try to return to Britain after first crossing the Pyrenees, for without documents, contacts and, above all, access to a radio there was little they could achieve. Heslop, by contrast, believed that if he could find Peter Churchill again he and Wilkinson could be brought back into the main stream of activity. Contact was made, first with Churchill, and then through him by radio with London, and it was agreed that Wilkinson should operate in the Dijon area and Heslop should make his way to Angers.

Building up a resistance organization in and around Angers was, for Heslop, a slow and difficult process. For the first parachute drop made to him he could find only two helpers to form a reception committee, a Frenchman and a White Russian. In his original cover-story he had been a timber merchant, but now he found a job in a machine-tool factory as a trainee salesman, and he was able to sustain this role convincingly through a three-hour grilling by both French and German interrogators.

His new occupation enabled him to perform an important piece of espionage, as a result of which details were brought to London of a proposed launching site for VI flying bombs. It also caused him to have an encounter which made such a deep impression on him that he was unable to talk about it for years and did not even mention it during his debriefing in London.

Heslop learnt that details of future German troop movements and of movements of food and ammunition trains were all to be found in one slim file. He decided to steal this and one evening, dressed in blue overalls, he entered the office where it was kept. Suddenly lights went on, and he found himself confronted by a pretty girl in her early twenties, who pointed a pistol at him and told him not to move. Heslop acted quickly. They both fired simultaneously, the girl's shot hitting the ceiling. Heslop's penetrated her left breast.

The girl, Heslop discovered, was a recent recruit to the *Milice*, the sinister paramilitary force established by the Vichy government. She had heard of plans to steal the file and had acted on her own initiative. Heslop knew that his duty as an agent was to finish the girl off and disappear immediately with the file. In fact he knelt for a long time on the floor beside her, cradling her head in his lap. For days afterwards he could not stop trembling and could not eat.

When Buckmaster decided that he should return to England Heslop had long lost the sense of adventure which he had had in his early days. His close friend, Wilkinson, who was to be killed in a concentration camp, was already, he knew, in German hands. For his own part he now regarded himself as a professional, who was able to hate, but to hate with a coldness which kept his temper under control. He had also changed physically. The agent who helped to arrange his departure from France, who was one of SOE's Mauritians, asked him whether he had recently looked at himself carefully in a glass and whether he realized how lined and drawn his face had become.

Buckmaster told Heslop, after a period of debriefing and refresher training, that he wanted him to make contact with a number of *maquis* groups. His first task would be to make a reconnaissance of Ain, Isère, Savoy, Upper Savoy and Jura. He was to be accompanied by Jean Rosenthal, who was also in his early thirties.

Rosenthal's natural inclinations, which caused Heslop to describe him as a playboy at heart, had been tempered a year or two earlier by having to take over responsibility for his family's important fur and jewellery business. He also learnt quickly how to adapt himself to the discipline of clandestine warfare. Soon after his arrival in France he emerged from a restaurant in Annecy after a good meal calling 'Taxi! Taxi!' There were then no taxis in Annecy. Before long Rosenthal, under the name of Cantinier, was to play a major role as a liaison officer with resistance forces.

Heslop's first contacts with *maquis* groups led him to the conclusion that their equipment was quite inadequate and, largely for this reason, that their morale was fairly low. Then in September 1943 he met Henri Romans-Petit, who some nine months earlier had begun to form the *maquis de l'Ain*. Romans-Petit was a man in his forties, who had been decorated in the First World War. Between the wars he had organized publicity for French fashion houses. He and Heslop were to make a formidable partnership. They thought alike on most problems of tactics and strategy, Heslop only occasionally prompting Romans-Petit to take a course of action which differed from the one he had originally favoured.

In October Heslop, who was known in his new theatre of operations as Xavier, and Rosenthal were brought out by a Hudson aircraft. They spent two days in London, which were to be a turning-point in the history of resistance in Ain and Upper Savoy. After their return arms began to be dropped on a scale which, according to Romans-Petit, made his *maquis* the envy of others. All the promises of supplies made to him were, he stated, fulfilled.

By November 1943 an armed force of some 3,000 had been built up under Romans-Petit's command. By the end of the year Germans seldom ventured into territory in which his *maquis* operated. Resistance activity spread too to the towns, and at the specific request of SOE a factory near Annecy making ball-bearings was put out of action for ten weeks.

On their return journey after their short visit to London Heslop and Rosenthal were accompanied by two Americans. One of them, Denis Johnson, was engaged as a radio operator and proved to be a skilled performer with an American carbine. The other, who was to serve as a courier, had, for an American, the improbable name of Elizabeth Devereaux-Rochester. She had been educated in England – very expensively – and complained to George Millar that most of the American and British pilots whom, among her other duties, she helped to repatriate seemed so common.

Heslop was now adopting as his cover the guise of a traveller for a firm of jewellers, a role for which he had equipped himself by taking a course of instruction at Hatton Garden in London. He continued to maintain his standards of perfection even in the somewhat more relaxed atmosphere in which he now found himself. George Millar, when he first met Heslop, had already learnt something about clandestine activity. After escaping from an Italian prisoner-of-war camp he had lived with French workmen of the so-called *Arbeitskommando* in Munich and had even visited the *Daily Express* office in Paris in order to raise some money. Yet when he suggested to Heslop that he should stay in France and work with him Heslop refused adamantly.

Millar, he explained, had not been trained in sabotage, spoke French with a foreign accent, even though he spoke it well, and was too conspicuous in appearance to escape attention. After he returned to England Millar was in fact trained by SOE and was parachuted into

France, where he carried out his mission, which consisted largely of railway sabotage, with conspicuous success.

One resistance exploit which Heslop tried hard to discourage was the occupation of the plateau known as Les Glières. This remarkable formation rises some 500 metres above the nearest valley in the heart of the Aravis *massif*. At first sight it appears almost inaccessible, yet the decision to occupy it by a static force of some 500 resistance troops was contrary to all the teachings about the need for mobility in guerrilla warfare which Heslop and other SOE agents had imbibed.

Nevertheless the occupation took place with an outcome which was inevitable. A vastly superior force of Wehrmacht Alpine troops supported by aircraft and French *Milice* captured the plateau and eliminated its occupants. This whole resistance effort was an example of misguided gallantry, smaller in scale, but comparable in kind with that of the Vercors.

For all his caution Heslop joined Romans-Petit in planning a public display of resistance strength which boosted morale hugely. Word was spread that some kind of parade was to take place in a variety of towns and villages in order to divert the attention of the Germans. Then in the small town of Oyonnax, which had about 14,000 inhabitants, some 200 *maquisards* marched through the streets with standard bearers carrying tricolors, with a band of bugles and drums, and with Romans-Petit dressed in the uniform of a captain in the French Air Force. Later Heslop arranged for a public showing of films which he had had sent to him, including *Desert Victory*, the film of the battle of Alamein.

In time resistance strength became such that every railway line in Ain was cut, and then cut again almost as soon as repairs had been made. One resistance leader apologized personally to Heslop for destroying only fifty-one out of a target of fifty-two locomotives. The volume of supplies by air increased steadily. A British surgeon named Geoffrey Parker was parachuted in and set up a field hospital. On another brief visit to London Heslop convinced SOE that the time had now come to send in mortars and heavy machine-guns.

When the Germans finally withdrew Romans-Petit assumed the post of Prefect of Ain and was closely supported by Heslop, whom he described as 'mon cher anglais' and Johnson ('mon cher américain'). Their authority did not last long. Romans-Petit and Heslop were visited by three representatives of the new French administration who stated that they had orders from Lyons to put Romans-Petit under arrest.

Romans-Petit decided not to resist, 'lthough he commanded the loyalty of thousands of *maquisards*, and did in fact spend some time in prison in Lyons. So many visitors brought him so much food and wine that he described his stay as the best holiday he had ever had. Heslop was told he must leave France within thirty-six hours.

The new administration and the *naphthalinés*, the name given to those who had kept their uniforms in mothballs until the fighting was virtually over, did what they could to erase the memory of what Heslop and those associated with him had contributed, but they did not altogether succeed.

Heslop died while still comparatively young. His request that his ashes should be buried in Ain was duly met. Some three to four decades after the fighting finished anyone who chooses, as I chose, to visit some of the areas in which Heslop operated in 1943 and 1944 will readily find people, none of them young any more, who feel proud and privileged to have enjoyed the friendship or even the acquaintance of the man whom they knew as Xavier.

The SOE agent whom Heslop and Wilkinson had suspected of betraying them in France was Denis Rake, an actor by profession, who began his working career at the age of three as a member of the Sarazini Circus. Rake's father was the *Times* correspondent in Brussels and in the First World War assisted Edith Cavell in helping escaped British prisoners of war. His speciality was forging the signature of the United States consul on papers which enabled the escapers to cross into Holland ostensibly as American citizens. Denis Rake's mother was an opera singer who seems to have been glad to hand over her small son to the care of a circus manager.

As a child tumbler Rake travelled widely over Europe. As a young man he was kept for some time in luxury by a prince in Athens, who finally broke off the liaison because he feared a political scandal. Rake then turned to the musical comedy stage, from which he earned his living for fifteen years under the name of Denis Greer, understudying Bobby Howes and playing the lead in a musical called *Mercenary Mary*.

Rake began his military career in the Royal Army Service Corps. In 1940 he was on board the troopship *Lancastria*, which after leaving St Nazaire for England was successfully bombed by German aircraft. Rake was among those who were rescued from the sea.

While serving as an interpreter with the Free French forces in Britain Rake found himself in a pub in Portsmouth where some airmen were talking indiscreetly about dropping agents into France. The thought of this kind of activity intrigued him, and he succeeded, through an approach to the War Office, in obtaining an interview with

Major Lewis Gielgud, who was a member of Buckmaster's staff and the brother of the great actor.

Rake was accepted for training as a radio operator but was soon described by his conducting officer as 'hopeless'. A crisis in his training came at Arisaig in the western Highlands, where he announced that he was scared of bangs, refused to handle firearms or explosives, yet continued assiduously with his morse practice.

Rake, who all his life had a strong sense of independence, which he attributed largely to his early experiences in a travelling circus, took the view that he was doing SOE a favour by volunteering for service. He wanted to go to France, but he made it clear that he would do so only on his own terms. He was, he told Buckmaster, 'tired of these constant scenes' in which he always seemed to appear as a criminal.

Buckmaster had the breadth of vision to accept that for the demanding job of radio operator Rake was probably of the calibre needed, and he decided that he should continue with his training. This included a parachute course, but in the end the decision was taken that Rake, like Heslop, should go in by the sea route.

His journey from Gibraltar to the French Riviera began in a trawler, whose skipper he recognized as a former chorus-boy in *Mercenary Mary*. He was transferred, first to a submarine, then to one of the *feluccas* crewed by Poles, and finally to a dinghy, which he had to row ashore himself.

In the dinghy he felt fear such as he had never experienced before, but, as he later expressed it, as suddenly as his fear had come his 'common sense' returned. 'Pull yourself together, duckie,' he muttered. 'You'd never live with yourself again if you gave up now.'

Rake, whose cover was that of a music-hall artist, was to serve as a relief or emergency radio operator. This was an exceptionally dangerous task. In countries in which SOE representatives operated in a paramilitary role in uniform radio operators commonly had the rank of army sergeant. In wholly clandestine conditions they tended also to have subordinate roles because they had not been chosen as leaders. Yet there were few agents who were more exposed to risk. An organizer could, and sometimes wisely would, lie low for a period. A radio operator served a useful purpose only when he or she was receiving or transmitting, ciphering or deciphering. Because of the detection system every transmission was hazardous.

For a time Rake served as a relief operator for Ted Zeff, a man in his fifties who had owned a haberdashery shop in Paris. Zeff sometimes consoled himself with the observation that the Germans could kill him for being a radio operator, or they could kill him for being a Jew, but they could not kill him twice. On one occasion during this period of service Rake was stopped by a French policeman while carrying his radio set in a suitcase. With the help of a bribe of 20,000 francs he succeeded in persuading the policeman to accept his story that he was a thief and that his suitcase contained antiques.

When he learnt that one of the SOE circuits needed a radio operator in Paris Rake volunteered to go there, and Virginia Hall made the necessary arrangements. While trying to cross from the unoccupied to the occupied zone he was arrested once again. This time he was imprisoned in Dijon, was badly knocked about, and lost a number of his teeth. With the help of a priest he escaped from the prison concealed in a swill-bin. He returned to Lyons, again sought the help of Virginia Hall, and again tried to make for Paris. This time he succeeded.

One of Rake's first actions after arriving in Paris was to visit *Le Boeuf sur le toit*, where he had been a member before the war. The barman recognized him at once and introduced him to a German, who, he said, came from an ancient family and was violently anti-Nazi. Rake soon discovered that he and the German had much in common in addition to their sexual inclinations. They were both lonely, and they both hated war. Before long Rake found himself more emotionally involved than at any time since the end of what he described as his 'Greek experience'.

It was from the time that he learnt that he was living with a German that Wilkinson's serious antipathy to him, as opposed to mild disdain, dated. Nevertheless the two men travelled together from Paris to Lyons, where Virginia Hall was now able to present Rake with a new and much smaller radio. Rake had found it painful to leave his German friend Max and later said that had it not been for the war they would have remained together for many years, 'if not for ever'.

Rake was arrested for the third time in Limoges. Heslop and Wilkinson had a rendezvous with him there, and when he did not turn up they made the mistake, which their instructors had warned them against, of waiting instead of leaving at once. They too were arrested, and when they learnt that Rake had already been picked up, and their French interrogators told them they were known to be British agents, they understandably assumed that Rake had told them all he knew.

In fact, in spite of having a number of bones in his right foot broken while being interrogated, Rake had revealed nothing about the others. There was, however, more incriminating evidence than there ought to have been. Rake and Wilkinson had divided between them a number of new banknotes, which, it is thought, came to them from Lisbon and which were numbered consecutively. It was also discovered that their identity cards, with which they had been provided locally and which had ostensibly been issued in different towns, were made out in the same handwriting.

Rake was transferred from the same prison to the same prisoner-of-war camp as Heslop and Wilkinson. His foot hurt him greatly. So too did the cold-shouldering he received from his fellow-agents, and when the chance of escape was presented Wilkinson refused to have Rake with him.

Rake therefore made his way across the Pyrenees, spent some time in an internment camp in Spain, and was eventually brought into the presence of the British Ambassador, Sir Samuel Hoare, who made the memorable comment: 'Really, I think you SOE people are more trouble than you're worth.'

After returning to England Rake spent some time in hospital in a state of nervous and mental exhaustion. When he had recovered, and SOE was satisfied there was no truth in the suggestions that he might have betrayed either Heslop or Wilkinson, Buckmaster offered him a job as a conducting officer accompanying potential agents on courses. It was in this role that he met an Australian named Nancy Wake, with whom he was to form a remarkable operational partnership.

Nancy Wake was a strongly built girl with an exuberance and a zest for living which led some people to wonder whether she could really be equipped for the role of secret agent. She was later to tell her biographer, Russell Braddon: 'My war was full of laughter and people I loved.' She had worked as a journalist in Sydney and as a nurse in a mental hospital. At the age of twenty-two she married, shortly after war broke out, a rich Marseilles businessman named Henri Fiocca.

In 1940 she served for a time as an ambulance driver. Later she became involved in helping the escape of British prisoners of war. She travelled regularly between Marseilles and Cannes to organize escape routes; the Fiocca flat in Marseilles was a refuge and a rendezvous for escapers; and she came under the control of the Belgian, Albert Guérisse, who also used the name of Patrick O'Leary and who was, arguably, the greatest of all the organizers in the Second World War of escape routes for prisoners of war in Europe.

Nancy Wake was arrested by French police and handled their interrogation skilfully. (The fact that she could do so without training was to influence the judgment of those who had to decide whether she should or should not be employed by SOE.) But she was considered too heavily compromised to remain in France. She succeeded in crossing the Spanish frontier at the fifth attempt.

After a period of training, during which her sheer vitality was at times found almost overpowering by her instructors, Nancy Wake was parachuted into the Auvergne at the end of February 1944. It was clear to her and to the regular British Army officer, J. H. Farmer, who was in charge of their mission, that the people among whom they found themselves could develop into a powerful *maquis* organization. They were, however, presented with problems of deciding which groups most merited support. Soon after her arrival Nancy Wake overheard one conspirator suggest to another that he should seduce her and then murder her and take her money. The incident understandably influenced her judgment of where and to whom arms should be delivered.

While serving as conducting officer to Nancy Wake and others Denis Rake asked Buckmaster whether he could return to the field. Buckmaster agreed, and it was decided to send him to join Nancy Wake, with whom he had established something of a *rapport*. She habitually referred to him as 'Den-Den'.

With the arrival of Denis Rake and the establishment of direct, regular radio contact the status of both Farmer and Nancy Wake was considerably enhanced. Nancy Wake supervised parachute drops on six successive nights and had a major part in deciding how and where the arms and ammunition were to be distributed.

For Rake the role he had to play was a new one. A man whom he had met in his Spanish internment camp, and whom he now encountered again, told him that he must regard himself not as a secret agent but as a brigand. He did not accept this new role unquestioningly. When he learnt that in one *maquis* the genitals of captured members of the *Milice* were being burnt with red-hot irons he decided to have nothing further to do with it. But he responded to the bangs, of which he had said he was so frightened, with apparently growing indifference, and he continued to operate his radio set calmly and efficiently. When the Allied invasions began there were some twelve thousand *maquisards* in the Auvergne. Denis Rake was to write: 'It is no exaggeration to say that Nancy Wake armed and supplied the vast majority of them.'

After the war Nancy Wake contested a parliamentary seat which had been held by the Australian Prime Minister, Dr Herbert Evatt, with a majority of some 23,000. She reduced it to 127. Denis Rake was more modest in his aims. After being a ship's steward for a time he became butler to Douglas Fairbanks Junior, a post which he seems to have filled to perfection. One day a letter arrived at the Fairbanks' English home addressed to Major Denis Rake MC. Rake looked at it and said: 'I hoped you wouldn't know about all that nonsense.'

The agents employed by Buckmaster's section were probably more varied in age and in character, in background and in occupation, than those employed by the other sections of SOE. Their motives for serving also differed considerably. One who analysed his motives more carefully than most was Harry Ree, the schoolmaster who had originally introduced Francis Cammaerts to SOE.

Ree, like Cammaerts, had been strongly inclined towards pacifism, but after volunteering to serve in minesweepers he had been enrolled after the fall of France in the ranks of the Field Security Police. When asked by a colonel in that force whether he had any interest in security work, he replied that he had no interest at all and that his sympathies were likely to be with those he had to watch. Among his duties was accompanying certain SOE agents in training, and this led him to volunteer to serve in France himself. He had taught French and German at school, but he spoke neither language perfectly.

During a symposium held at the University of Salford in 1973 Ree spoke of the agents who had trained with him. A number of them, he said, had been sent, although in uniform, to safe places in Britain while their wives endured bombing in the cities, and they wanted 'to jump the gun to get into action'. If they were to be exposed to dangers they preferred, as he did, to go where they would be their own masters and not have to advance into a screen of machine-gun bullets in fulfilment of orders with which they disagreed. 'We were all', he said, 'individualists.'

When Ree was parachuted into France one of the containers dropped with him was caught on a pylon and was later rescued by a farmer who happened to be in the resistance. The first safe address he was given was that of a hotel which, two weeks earlier, had been taken over by the Gestapo. The agent whom he had been sent to meet in Clermont-Ferrand, on hearing his French, recommended him to leave town as soon as possible.

Ree added to his own difficulties by declining to have a radio operator, considering the job a dangerous and dull one, which somebody else would have to perform. When he learnt how well the business of crossing the Swiss frontier was organized, even in peacetime, he preferred to communicate with London through Switzerland.

In spite of all these difficulties and handicaps Ree remained in France for some nine months in 1943. He trained and operated with *maquisards* in the Franche Conté. He was responsible with others for exposing a traitor whose activities had led to the arrest of some seventy people. He devised a brilliantly successful form of sabotage of an entirely new kind. He finally had to escape in a manner which defied all probability.

The traitor was a self-styled resistance leader of whom Ree had immediately felt suspicious on hearing him say that he only worked for the resistance so that men would talk about him. Ree accepted the decision that the man must be liquidated, though after he had done so he wondered how the *Manchester Guardian* and the Lord Chief Justice would have viewed what was done.

The unique form of sabotage took place in the Peugeot works at Sochaux near Montbéliard. A motor-car factory in peacetime, it was engaged in production for both the German Army and the German Air Force. The RAF chose it as a target for an attack on 14 July 1943. No bomb landed within a kilometre of the factory, but a number of French civilians were killed.

Ree, who was sitting under a peach-tree some miles away when the bombing took place, decided he must find a better way of putting the Peugeot factory out of action. He succeeded in contacting Robert Peugeot, whose pro-Allied sympathies were fairly well known, and suggested to him a pact whereby effective internal sabotage would be carried out against an assurance that the factory would not be attacked again from the air.

Peugeot naturally asked for evidence of Ree's good faith and of his power to guarantee immunity from bombing. Ree therefore asked him to choose his own code-phrase which the BBC would then transmit at a prearranged hour. When the BBC did so Peugeot decided to trust Ree and give him plans of the factory and the necessary inside contacts.

A team of saboteurs was assembled, for whom Ree arranged an escape route to Switzerland. While waiting outside the factory gate for someone to produce a key the saboteurs played a game of football against some uniformed German guards. When a home-made bakelite bomb fell out of a saboteur's pocket a German guard politely handed it back to him.

Extensive and carefully selected damage to the factory was caused. The RAF, which had initially accepted Ree's plan with reluctance, duly maintained the embargo on bombing, although SOE's suggestion that the Sochaux experiment might be repeated elsewhere did not meet with approval. Ree's contribution was evidence of what a highly intelligent man – he was later to be appointed Professor of Education at York University – who had strong pacifist feelings, courage and resource, could achieve as an act of war.

When a German came to arrest Ree he realized he had a chance to fight and took it. The fight was held in a kitchen, with crockery falling about the contestants. The only weapon available to Ree was a bottle of armagnac. He tried to remember some of the tricks he had been taught while training, but failed and had to rely on memories of *King Lear* as he tried, unsuccessfully, to gouge his opponent's eyes out. He succeeded in escaping but was shot several times.

One bullet penetrated a lung. Another grazed his heart. Four others inflicted minor wounds in an arm, a shoulder and a side. Yet he swam across a swiftly flowing river and crawled for four miles through woods and fields. A doctor who treated him shortly afterwards considered the achievement barely possible, and it was in spontaneous and heartfelt admiration that he exclaimed: 'Ah, les anglais!'

Another analyst of his own motives, who differed widely from Ree in his views on politics and society, was Hugh Dormer, whose wartime diaries were published posthumously. 'This war', Dormer wrote at one point, 'is far more of a Crusade than the Crusades were.' The Germans, as he pictured them, were striking at religion and national culture because cathedrals and schools were the centres of the spirit which they were trying to destroy for ever. His own inspiration to join SOE came from seeing the French coast from the deck of a destroyer.

Dormer, who was educated at Ampleforth and Oxford, served as an officer in the Irish Guards before joining SOE. He recorded in his diary that he believed it was important to show that his own social class did not lack courage and endurance. 'I feel', he added, 'that more than ever before our class today is on trial before the world.' While waiting to be sent on his first mission to France he read Shakespeare's *Henry V*. He continued reading it in the aircraft before being dropped.

Dormer's assignment was to lead a party of six to attack a synthetic petrol plant near Autun in August 1943. Although dressed in civilian clothes the assault party resembled a small Commando unit in its task and composition rather more than it did the normal kind of mission sent by SOE to France. Dormer himself spoke painstaking French and other members of his group were even less fluent.

The plant was found to be so heavily guarded by Germans, probably because news of the proposed attack had reached them, that Dormer prudently accepted the need to abandon the whole project. He and his party then became dependent on Victor Gerson's escape organization, which was able to bring some, though not all, out over the Pyrenees.

Dormer was one of those who returned home. He was persuasive enough to convince SOE that a second attempt should be made on the same target. This time some damage was inflicted, but of the operational party only Dormer himself and a sergeant, who accompanied him on his return and who – deplorably, it may be thought – spoke no French, avoided capture and came home via the Pyrenees route.

Dormer clearly did not find his spiritual home in SOE. As the time for the Allied invasion of France approached he was torn between returning to his regiment and becoming part of one of the Jedburgh teams which SOE was assembling. In the end he chose his regiment.

'Guerrilla fighting', he recorded in his diary, 'often breeds a race of professional mercenaries who love war.' Until this point in his military career he had undertaken clearly defined tasks with whose purpose he was in full agreement. The prospect of leading 'armed bands of hungry, desperate men eager for revenge' had been, he wrote, a nightmare which had often haunted him. Having made his decision, he took part in the Normandy landings with the Guards Armoured Division. He was killed in action in July 1944.

In contrast with the tone and contents of Hugh Dormer's diaries, John Goldsmith, who was perhaps better suited to the prevailing atmosphere in SOE, gave his own book of reminiscences the title *Accidental Agent*.

Goldsmith was born and brought up in France, his family background being largely dominated by horses. Among the posts he had held before the war had been that of manager of the polo club in Lille. He described his father as a horse-dealer and expressed the opinion that, if more SOE agents had had some knowledge of horse-dealing, there would have been more who were capable of outwitting their captors by telling them convincing stories.

Goldsmith was brought into SOE after his sister-in-law spoke of his knowledge of France to a solicitor who happened to be one of SOE's recruiting agents. He entered France on his first mission by the *felucca* route. The smell aboard the *felucca* struck him as being worse than that of any stable he had known, and he admired the fortitude with which another agent, Sidney Jones, who was no longer young and who had worked for Elizabeth Arden before the war, endured it.

Buckmaster had accepted Goldsmith's suggestion that he should begin with a period of acclimatization in the unoccupied zone. This included taking advantage of the Riviera sun to acquire a suitable tan. His cover at this stage was that of a black-market operator, and he reflected that he could easily retire from clandestine activity and set up in business in the manner suggested by his cover-story. In fact evening after evening he gave instruction in Rivera flats in the handling of Sten guns and the use of plastic explosive.

Among those whom Goldsmith met on the Riviera was an artist named André Giraud, with whom Peter Churchill had been in contact for some time. The lack of security within Giraud's organization, which in theory was a very large one, became known before long to

French, British and German authorities alike, but to his personal charm there have been numerous testimonies. Goldsmith described him as 'bursting with ideas', but added: 'The trouble was that they followed so closely on the heels of each other that nothing ever came of them.'

One of Giraud's ideas was that Goldsmith should establish a branch of the Giraud organization in Corsica. Once he was convinced that this idea too would never be translated into reality Goldsmith accepted an assignment to escort a French general and two members of his staff into Spain. All four were arrested by a French policeman, to whom Goldsmith made it clear that he did not deal with underlings. He was thereupon taken to the local mayor, who signed all the permits the party needed.

This technique for dealing with officials was one which Goldsmith was to adopt, with variants, later. On his second mission in France he regularly travelled in first-class railway compartments, choosing, wherever possible, one in which there were German officers. He even had the effrontery to address a Gestapo official, who had arrested him, as one officer to another and as one gentleman to another, and the technique worked.

Apparently accepting the inevitability of being imprisoned, he suggested to the official that he should be allowed to spend one night in a hotel under complete guard. To indicate that he realized the Germans had won and his cover-story could no longer be sustained he registered in the hotel under his correct name and military rank. Shortly afterwards he escaped by jumping through a window.

For a month after his escape he remained in hiding in the flat of a Roumanian actress in Paris. The only book in the flat appeared to be a French translation of *Gone with the Wind*. He read it five times.

Goldsmith paid three visits to France, arriving once by *felucca* and dinghy, once by Lysander, and once by parachute. On his third arrival, in 1944, he was much impressed by the way in which the resistance had developed since what he called 'the melodramatic days of 1942, when everyone was learning the business', and since 1943, when the tension was highest and the German counter-measures most efficient.

When he had been on the Riviera in 1942, for a long time only one family knew Goldsmith's real identity. In 1944 the more people who knew he was a British officer the safer he felt himself to be. A battle fought by the *maquis* in the Vaucluse region, in which he was involved, seemed to him the culmination of everything he had worked for since joining SOE

Goldsmith's reminiscences contained none of the expressions of high ideals to be found in Hugh Dormer's diaries. Yet he was faced with the kind of moral dilemma which Dormer was spared by his decision to rejoin his regiment.

Two Frenchwomen, a mother and a daughter, were known beyond doubt to have been guilty of betraying members of the *maquis* to the Germans. After seeing the horribly mutilated corpse of a seventeen-year-old *maquisard*, who had been tortured by the Germans, a *maquis* leader whom Goldsmith greatly liked and respected took it upon himself to shoot the daughter, who was pregnant. To Goldsmith was assigned the task of shooting the mother.

He carried it out and then vomited into nearby bushes. 'Had I refused', he afterwards wrote, 'on the grounds that executions were not part of my job and were beneath the dignity of a British officer, I have no doubt that I would have been put on a plane for Algiers the following night.'

Philippe de Vomécourt, French land-owner; Richard Heslop, teak-forest overseer; Denis Rake, musical-comedy actor; John Goldsmith, racehorse trainer: all carried out their missions, avoided capture or escaped from captivity, and were present to take part in the final acts of liberation in France. There were others too who similarly succeeded and survived.

George Starr, a man in his early forties who had worked in the mining industry in Belgium, arrived by *felucca* and dinghy in France in October 1942. Less than two years later he was marching at the head of 1,000 *maquisards* on Toulouse. During his career as a secret agent he had the unusual distinction of being asked to become deputy mayor of a village near Avignon. His radio operator, Yvonne Cormeau, transmitted and received over a period of thirteen months with impunity, largely because of an unswerving adherence to all the rules she had been taught.

Roger Landes, an architect who used his knowledge of buildings to plan their destruction meticulously, became the effective commander of a private army of some 5,000 men. He also played a significant part in preventing German plans to destroy the Bordeaux docks from being implemented. When de Gaulle arrived in Bordeaux he told Landes that as an Englishman his place was not there. In a two-minute interview the newly appointed French Minister of War gave him two hours in which to leave France.

Robert Boiteux, who before the war had simultaneously owned a women's hairdressing establishment in Mombasa and held the fly-weight boxing championship of Kenya, armed, organized and fought with *maquis* groups in the Marseilles area. One of the principal training grounds he used was the Marseilles zoo. Anthony Brooks, who had spent his childhood in Switzerland and who was too young to have had any profession before the war, found himself at the age of twenty-three an experienced saboteur and *maquis* fighter and the holder of the DSO, the MC and the rank of major.

Ben Cowburn, an oil technician from Lancashire, one of the earliest and most resourceful of Buckmaster's agents, arrived in France clandestinely no fewer than four times. Pearl Witherington, who had worked in the British Embassy in Paris, was parachuted in as a courier, effectively took command of 2,000 *maquisards*, and survived in spite of the fact that the Germans put a price of a million francs on her head.

The statistical chance of such successes and survivals were not high. Buckmaster calculated that the losses incurred within his section were 'equivalent to those sustained by a regiment of the line in constant action'. Some agents were killed fighting, other in concentration camps. Their losses could be attributed to misfortune, carelessness, treachery, the skill with which the Abwehr penetrated SOE circuits, or a combination of two or more of these factors. Some agents were victims, in part at least, of political pressures.

Michael Trotobas, one of SOE's principal organizers in the Lille area, performed an outstandingly successful act of sabotage in a loco-motive works in a Lille suburb. Entering the factory at night with a Gestapo pass, he persuaded the watchmen that he and his companions were checking security arrangements. While apparently making a detailed examination of the premises they placed a large number of explosive charges. One of these went off prematurely, and Trotobas quickly turned the incident to advantage. He told the watchmen they must take no action until he returned with firemen and investigators. He and his companions then left and did not come back.

Trotobas was known to his closest associates as Capitaine Michel. One of them betrayed him under duress, and Trotobas was killed when German police raided the house where he was staying. Buckmaster visited Lille in October 1944 and found a large banner suspended over the Avenue de la Liberté with the initials O.F.A.C.M. These, he learnt, stood for 'Organisation française des amis du Capitaine Michel'.

Another casualty was a girl whom Buckmaster described as 'really beautiful with a porcelain clarity of face'. This was Violette Bushell, who spent much of her childhood in Paris, where her English father drove a taxi. The family later settled in Brixton, where Violette attended a London County Council school which she left at the age of fourteen. She spent the first winter of the war, when she was eighteen, working in the scent department of the Brixton Bon Marché store.

Violette Bushell married an officer in the Free French forces named Etienne Szabo, who was killed at Alamein shortly after their daughter was born. Apart from her excellent French her most evident qualification for service in SOE was an exceptional talent for shooting, which caused her to be banned from some of London's West End galleries because she won too many prizes. Nevertheless Selwyn Jepson, to whom she had been recommended, thought she might be a suitable recruit. His principal doubt arose from the readiness with which she volunteered for service. He wondered for a time whether she might belong to a category which he had learnt, with reason, to distrust, that of agents with a suicidal urge.

On her first mission Violette Szabo was directed by Philippe Liewer, a former correspondent of the Havas news agency, to make a study of resistance possibilities in the Rouen area. She completed her task in spite of twice having to explain her movements to French police, who had arrested her, and was brought back to England.

Her second parachute drop into France took place almost immediately after the Normandy landings. Her role was now a paramilitary one. While giving covering fire to a French *maquis* leader, who had an important mission to fulfil, she engaged in a gun battle with Germans until her ammunition ran out. From a French prison she was sent to Ravensbrück concentration camp, where she was killed.

On board the train which eventually brought her to Ravensbrück there were a number of SOE agents. Yeo-Thomas, who was one of them, later recorded how Violette Szabo, while chained to another girl, crawled along the train corridors to bring water to her fellow prisoners. A survivor of Ravensbrück described her as outstanding even among the thousands of women in the camp.

A loss which those responsible for planning SOE operations in France felt particularly severely was that of Francis Suttill, whom Buckmaster described as 'calm, conscientious and of a logical mind'. Suttill was a barrister and was born in Lille. His mother was French, but his own French accent was not perfect, although he could pass as a Belgian. This limitation imposed additional demands on his principal courier, Andrée Borrel, who was the first woman agent of SOE to be parachuted into France and who, like Nancy Wake, had already had experience of helping escaped prisoners.

Suttill established a number of SOE circuits in the Paris region. He also made contact with some communist groups and arranged to supply them with arms. His network spread steadily to different parts of

France, but so in time did penetration by the Abwehr. Numerous arrests followed, including that of Suttill himself, who was horribly tortured. He was eventually hanged in Sachsenhausen concentration camp. Andrée Borrel was also arrested, taken to a concentration camp and killed.

The communist groups which Suttill helped to supply continued to operate successfully, but among the others the damage was grave. Buckmaster admitted that SOE never succeeded in restoring its organization in the Paris region to the standard of efficiency which it reached at one stage under Suttill's leadership. That Suttill expanded his organization faster than strict compliance with considerations of security would have allowed was attributable, in part at least, to political pressures to produce more concrete evidence of effective action in France. Suttill himself was fully aware of the likely consequences of trying to produce the evidence.

Of the SOE agents who were captured in France and sent to concentration camps few survived. Perhaps the most famous of those who did was a French girl, Odette Brailly, who had married an Englishman named Sansom by whom she had three children. She was parachuted in to serve as courier to Peter Churchill, a Cambridge ice-hockey blue, who had been operating over an extensive area of southern France.

Both were arrested. Odette Sansom succeeded in convincing her interrogators that it was she and not Churchill who made the decisions and, as the citation for the George Cross which she was awarded stated, that it was she and not Churchill who should be shot. In fact they both survived, not least because of the skill with which Odette Sansom caused her interrogators to believe that Peter Churchill was related to Winston Churchill and that she was Peter Churchill's wife. They were indeed to be married later.

The arrest of Peter Churchill and his courier was one of the triumphs of an Abwehr official named Hugo Bleicher, who was sometimes known as Colonel Henri but who never rose higher than the rank of sergeant. He was also responsible for the penetration of many of Suttill's circuits. Bleicher was skilful in his choice and exploitation of French traitors, and he could pose skilfully as an opponent of Nazism.

His achievements in combating the work of SOE in France were far less than those of his opposite numbers in the Netherlands and in no way comparable with those of counter-intelligence in Britain, where after a time all German agents, would-be spies or would-be saboteurs, were operating under British control. But he was a formidable antagonist.

He would have been even more dangerous but for the continuous struggle between the two which impaired the efficiency of both the professional Abwehr and the purely Nazi Reichssicherheitsdienst. One consequence of this was a journey made with impunity by Nicholas Bodington, a member of Buckmaster's staff and a former Paris correspondent of the *Daily Express*. Bodington was a very courageous man who more than once visited France to make his own assessment of resistance problems. On one occasion his presence in Paris was known to the German authorities, yet he was not arrested. Evidence from German sources indicates that the omission was less part of a calculated waiting game than a consequence of the German security services' mutual antagonism. He returned to England safely.

An agent who also survived a concentration camp was Christopher Burney, who spent much of his prolonged stay in Buchenwald in building up, together with a Viennese journalist and a Dutch Olympic athlete, a potential resistance movement within the camp, to which arms were in fact smuggled. Another survivor was a man whose record of misfortune and courage it would be difficult to surpass.

This was Harry Peulevé, who before the war was a BBC television cameraman. On his first mission to France he broke his leg while parachuting in. When he reached hospital he insisted on being treated without an anaesthetic as he feared that while unconscious he might talk indiscreetly. He came out over the Pyrenees. Others who made this journey in wartime, including fit and trained soldiers such as Hugh Dormer, found that, because of the distances which had to be covered in any one night, it taxed their physical and moral resources to the utmost. Peulevé made the journey on crutches.

After spending six months in internment camps in Spain he returned to England, apologized to Buckmaster for having failed in his mission, and asked when he could be sent to France again. On his second mission a man who thought he was a Jew denounced him as such to the Germans. He was shot through the thigh – he later removed the bullet himself with a soup spoon – captured, and sent to Buchenwald. He survived, as did Yeo-Thomas, by being allowed to exchange identity with a prisoner who had died of typhus.

Peulévé died young of a heart attack in 1963. He must be classified as a delayed casualty of the war, as were Yeo-Thomas, Heslop and others. Indeed one of the penalties of service in SOE was learning repeatedly, in the 1950s and 1960s, of the sudden and early deaths of friends and colleagues who had endured extremes of hardship as agents on the run, in prisons or in concentration camps.

It has been estimated that the combined activities of French resistance kept eight German divisions permanently away from the battlefields following the Allied landings in northern and southern France. General Eisenhower stated that these activities served to shorten the war in Europe by nine months. General Maitland Wilson estimated that resistance in south-eastern France reduced the strength of the German forces which the regular armies had to overcome to half what it would otherwise have been. In a combined report to the Chiefs of Staff the American General Bedell Smith and the British General F. E. Morgan wrote: 'Without the organization, communications, material, training and leadership which SOE provided, "resistance" would have been of no military value.'

It is by such military criteria that SOE's efforts in France should mainly be judged, for the political part it played was at all times muted. Had there been any strong possibility of a communist take-over in France, or had the British Foreign Office supported a regime which was clearly unpopular among French people generally, SOE's task might have been politically more complex. But such difficulties did not occur, and SOE's agents in France were instructed to steer clear of politics wherever possible. In obeying these instructions many of them were following their natural inclinations.

The French Communist party was slow to go into action against the Germans. In July 1940 its principal newspaper, *Humanité*, was calling for a Franco-Soviet pact to supplement the German-Soviet one and recommending French workers to fraternize with German soldiers in bistros and on the streets. After the German invasion of the Soviet Union the communist element within the French resistance grew steadily in strength, but some of the political ground which had been lost earlier was never made up, and with Stalin's acceptance of France as falling outside the Soviet sphere of influence the likelihood of communist domination was never grave.

In 1941 SOE made it clear to the British Cabinet that in its judgment a major resistance movement could be brought into being in France only by working with and through de Gaulle and the Free French. This policy, which was adhered to, may seem in retrospect to have been the only logical one. Yet the American State Department, which for a long time had much better opportunities of assessing French opinion than were available to any British agencies, was unwilling to endorse it.

The maintenance of diplomatic relations with the Vichy government after the French defeat in 1940 meant that the United States had accredited representatives with access to large parts of metropolitan France. In Algeria new opportunities were created. The State Department representative there, Robert Murphy, reached an agreement with the French authorities that the United States should supply certain French colonial territories with badly needed imports. To prevent these supplies from falling into German hands it was also agreed that their distribution should be controlled by State Department officials. The officials were given vice-consular rank and intelligence assignments.

This penetration of French North Africa by the American State Department, and later by OSS, played an important part in facilitating the Allied landings in November 1942. But the opportunities for judging where and how to give support to particular French political groupings were strangely squandered. American backing was given not only to General Giraud, a gallant soldier though a mediocre politician, but to even less suitable claimants to the power which de Gaulle increasingly enjoyed.

R. Harris Smith, a historian of OSS, stated that in wartime Washington de Gaulle was regarded as 'a British creation with dictatorial ambitions and little support among the French people'. Whether this really was the prevailing opinion or not, it is a fact that as late as the middle of 1943 the State Department official in charge of French affairs expressed surprise to de Gaulle's representative in Washington that de Gaulle was unable to understand that all that remained for him was to take command of an armoured division.

A number of British agencies contributed to de Gaulle's political success, SOE being one of them. Indeed no institution in the world gave him better opportunities for rallying his supporters than did the BBC. But that he acquired and maintained the authority he had was of course due primarily to his own extraordinary personal qualities. Emmanuel d'Astier de la Vigerie, often a severe critic, gave one of the most vivid portraits of de Gaulle in wartime London when he wrote of him as a man motivated by one historical idea, the greatness of France, whose voice seemed to replace all others, 'the voice of God, man, progress and all ideologies'. He went on to state how much he regretted not having known de Gaulle during the few days at the end of June and the beginning of July 1940, when he had 'incarnated France'.

That a man of such stature and such grandeur should have behaved so meanly towards Richard Heslop, Roger Landes and other SOE agents, who had clearly played both honourable and effective parts in helping to bring about the liberation of France, may seem strange. Yet it is also readily explicable.

De Gaulle's many great qualities did not include any serious understanding of British traditions, British institutions or British habits of mind, and there is little evidence that he made much effort to remedy this shortcoming. He seems to have accepted from the outset a stereotype picture of a nation, and the accuracy of his picture was no doubt confirmed for him in the aircraft which brought him to Britain after the French defeat in 1940. On that occasion he was given a cup of coffee, took one sip, and announced that he did not drink tea. Several years after the war was over, when writing his memoirs, he was still capable of making the statement that to the British 'intelligence is a passion as much as a service'.

In a letter to General Koenig, the Commander of the French Forces of the Interior, in June 1944 de Gaulle wrote of Frenchmen who had 'committed the error of executing orders given them without right by foreign services'. Any Frenchman incorporated in the French forces by virtue of an ordinance of 9 June 1944 would, he made clear, be exposed to the full rigour of the law if he 'should continue to consider himself dependent on a foreign power to carry out its orders or instructions'.

From such a doctrine there was no reason in logic to exclude the activities of SOE officers. They themselves may have wanted nothing more than to celebrate victory together with their companions in battle, but this did not preclude them from being regarded as agents of an alien intelligence service, whose malevolent tentacles extended almost everywhere.

That SOE succeeded militarily in France can hardly be denied. Its collective political judgments were also predominantly sound. Nevertheless in the late 1950s SOE's activities in France were exposed to some severe criticisms, mainly by women writers and mainly because of the number of women agents whose lives were lost. These criticisms were based on information which, perhaps inevitably at the time when they were made, was somewhat sketchy. But they were brought to the attention of Dame Irene Ward, Member of Parliament for Tynemouth, a lady of massive goodwill and an engaging readiness to charge into parliamentary battle, albeit at times rather impulsively, on behalf of those who sought her help.

In questioning the competence of SOE Dame Irene referred to it derisively as an 'amateur wartime organization'. Buckmaster later issued a dignified statement, accepting with justifiable pride the epithet 'amateur'. The parliamentary replies were, understandably, restrained, largely because it was not at that time Government policy to make known how overwhelmingly the British defeated the Germans in the Second World War in all forms of clandestine activity. The fact that for years the British had read German high-grade ciphers was still kept secret. Nor had it been publicly revealed that the control of German agents in Britain was such that, in order to maintain the confidence of Hitler and his advisers in these agents, British counter-intelligence arranged for acts of sabotage to be committed in Britain, the results of which could be photographed by newspapers and reported by the controlled agents.

There was one useful outcome of the parliamentary exchange initiated by Dame Irene Ward. This was an undertaking by Harold Macmillan as Prime Minister that an official history of SOE in France would be published. The task of writing it was entrusted to the Oxford historian M. R. D. Foot. The outcome was a work which is indispensable to anyone who wants to understand what SOE was and how it operated. The obvious requirement for official histories of SOE's activities in other theatres of war remains unfulfilled.

One of the charges made in the attacks which came to the attention of Dame Irene Ward was of indifference, once the war was over, to those who had worked with and for SOE in France and elsewhere. There is some measure of truth in this charge. SOE was wound up, understandably and on the insistence of the Foreign Office, with the least possible delay, and there was no official organization to take its place. Of this aspect of British post-war policy Professor Foot was to say that the British did little to retain the affections of thousands of sub-agents 'who had been proud to handle, on the orders of British officers, British weapons brought to them by British air crews'.

There was, it is true, one member of Buckmaster's staff who had an official position in the immediate post-war years which enabled her to maintain some kind of continuity with her earlier work. This was Vera Atkins, a senior staff officer.

After the war Vera Atkins had the gruesome task of moving from concentration camp to concentration camp, discovering what the fate of SOE agents had been. A number of Germans found her to be a formidable interrogator. Hugo Bleicher of the Abwehr, for instance, considered her interrogation of him was the most skilful of any to which he was subjected. Peter Churchill, himself a former concentration camp inmate, wrote that, as a result of Vera Atkins's enquiries, the friends and relations of those who had died in concentration camps because of their associations with SOE could at least be assured that nothing was spared in trying to discover the full truth of what had taken place.

With those who survived contact had to be maintained through private initiative. In ensuring that the association formed in war between SOE's F Section and members of the French resistance was not allowed to wither and die two men made major contributions. One was Buckmaster. The other was a Frenchman named Jean-Bernard Badaire.

Badaire was only twenty-two when the war ended, but he had already experienced life in a concentration camp as a consequence of his resistance activities. While serving in the French Air Force after the war he was appalled to discover that not only was he expected to forget his past, but that his association with SOE was considered tantamount to serving as an agent of a foreign power. He was determined to rectify this injustice, not simply for himself but in so far as it affected thousands of other French people, and he spent much of his life in doing so.

Largely as a result of his efforts the old comrades' association of the Gaullist resistance known as the Amicale Action finally accepted, and even fused with, the Amicale Libre Resistance (sometimes called Amicale Buckmaster). Nearly forty years after SOE was founded Buckmaster himself was still dealing with some twenty-five to thirty letters a week from people in France in some way concerned with resistance. E. H. Cookridge in his thoroughly researched and informative work, *Inside S.O.E.*, stated that twenty years after the war there were still forty-six Amicale Buckmaster clubs.

It was André Malraux who coined the phrase 'resistance owes no debt'. Not everyone in France agreed.

Chapter 8

Other European
Theatres

In the Netherlands the efforts of SOE met with disaster to an extent not experienced anywhere else in the world. The country, having no mountains and with only about 7 per cent of its land surface covered by forests, affords no natural terrain for guerrilla warfare. It was therefore particularly important that in clandestine activities in the Netherlands all possible precautions should be taken to enable agents to operate with some prospect of success.

The requirements imposed by topography were reinforced by political considerations. There was early evidence that the Dutch intended to resist German occupation. It soon became standard practice, whenever a German entered a bar, for all the Dutch people present to leave. Underground newspapers flourished, and in February 1941 there was a short-lived general strike in Amsterdam as a protest against the public beating and subsequent deportation of Jews. Nevertheless the Dutch government in exile did not welcome the prospect of reprisals for overt acts of sabotage, and SOE could hope to win its confidence and support only by advancing with extreme caution.

A number of Dutch agents were trained in Britain, and parachute operations began in the autumn of 1941. Among the agents trained and dropped was a radio operator named Hubertus Lauwers. The Germans located his set in a suburb of The Hague. When the flat in which he was living was raided the owner of the flat dropped the set out of a window, hoping it would land in some rose-bushes. In fact it was caught in a clothes line.

Lauwers was arrested soon afterwards and acted as he had been instructed to do. This was to appear, after a brief show of resistance, to be co-operating with his captors and to give the prearranged warning signal which would make it clear to SOE that he was acting under duress. The warning took the form of a deliberate mistake in every sixteenth word transmitted.

Lauwers had acquired during his training what he afterwards described as 'an almost mystical belief' in the skills of the British Secret Service, which was what he supposed SOE to be. Naturally therefore he expected his warning had been understood. But, being an extremely brave man, he decided, at considerable risk to himself, to make his position even clearer by including the word 'caught' in his transmissions on three separate occasions. Neither this nor his initial warning signal was heeded.

Because of the conditions in which transmissions often took place in occupied territories radio procedures agreed in advance were not always put into practice in the field. SOE staff officers had therefore to use their own judgment from time to time when deciding whether messages were genuine. A number of instances could be cited which showed that assessment of the personality of an agent could be a more reliable guide than strict interpretations of the rules. Nevertheless the failure to recognize Lauwers's warnings is difficult to excuse. Its consequences were calamitous.

The Abwehr chief in the Netherlands, Hermann Giskes, regarded his task as a formidable one. He was, as he afterwards wrote, confronted both by a British enemy 'unexcelled in his skill in the conduct of underground warfare' and by 'an élite of Dutch volunteers willing to risk their lives'. He was also continually conscious of what he described as 'the cursed duplication without which nothing could be done under Nazi rule', although in fact co-operation between the Abwehr and the Reichssicherheitsdienst in the Netherlands was much smoother than it was in most occupied territories. The capture of Lauwers and the fact that SOE appeared to be regarding his signals as genuine provided Giskes therefore with an advantage which he had never expected. For nearly two years he exploited it with skill and success.

By the end of February 1942 the ascendancy of Giskes over SOE was such that the first parachute drop to the Netherlands wholly controlled by the Abwehr took place. In time there were fourteen Abwehr-controlled radio links between the Netherlands and SOE, and 570 SOE containers, with radio equipment, Sten guns and half a million rounds of ammunition fell into German hands. Giskes was even able to indulge in the kind of deception practised by MI5 in Britain when he arranged for a ship to be sabotaged in broad daylight in Rotterdam.

All this stemmed from one initial oversight on the part of SOE, followed by a period of somewhat ingenuous trust. As Giskes himself was to point out, a party dropped unannounced in the Netherlands with instructions to watch the next arranged drop could have destroyed at once the whole of his exercise in deception.

Other services besides SOE suffered from the deception. One of the principal escape routes for prisoners of war was penetrated, and because the Germans knew in advance when and where parachute drops were to take place they could virtually decide how many RAF aircraft to destroy.

Losses of aircraft in the controlled drops were in fact about one in three. This was a proportion compatible with the maintenance of Giskes's deception, but it was not one which was welcome to the British Chiefs of Staff, particularly when the true reasons for it became known. Indeed there are grounds for believing that if SOE had failed in one more country in the way it failed in the Netherlands the whole policy of air support for its operations would have been called into question.

The beginning of the end of Giskes's successful deception came with the escape of some agents from the Netherlands. Two of them, Peter Dourlein and J. B. Ubbink, broke out of prison in Haaren and made their way through Switzerland, France and Spain to London. When he learnt that they had escaped Giskes duly planted the information that they were really working for the Germans, and their immediate reception in Britain was chilly. Once their *bona fides* were accepted the truth of what was happening in the Netherlands began to emerge.

A recovery was later made by SOE and OSS acting in conjunction, and about a hundred agents and some 35,000 weapons were successfully dropped. But all the efforts of two years were unnecessarily wasted. Fortunately for the efficacy of the resistance generally the Dutch communists and other underground groupings were largely unaffected by SOE's failure.

Giskes's responsibilities extended to northern France and Belgium. In recalling his triumphs in the Netherlands he conceded that in the other territories with which he was concerned the underground war was won beyond doubt by the Allies. The secret armies which they had learnt to mobilize behind the German front would, he wrote, 'appear everywhere but could nowhere be pinned down'.

When the Belgian forces laid down their arms towards the end of May 1940 the great majority of the population clearly believed that Germany would win the war. A Belgian government was established in exile with the approval of King Leopold III, but the king himself remained in Belgium as a somewhat ambiguous, virtually neutral figure, for whom a good deal of sympathy was felt in Belgium in the early days of the occupation.

In the First World War a number of underground newspapers had been produced in Belgium, and the experience gained then was soon exploited in the Second World War. An underground paper appeared as early as 15 June 1940, and in the course of the war no fewer than 650 different newspapers were published clandestinely in Belgium, some in French, some in Flemish, and even some in German.

There was, however, no twentieth-century experience of armed resistance to an occupying power, and the few officers who insisted that the surrender of the Belgian Army was only a temporary interlude in the war had at first little except their own hopes to support them.

After the war was over no fewer than fifteen Belgian resistance movements received official recognition. The choice of which embryo resistance groups to support in the early days was therefore one of the most demanding of the tasks facing the head of SOE's Belgian section. This was a regular soldier named Claude Knight. His second-in-command, who was later to succeed him as head of the section, was Hardy Amies, the future Dressmaker to the Queen. Amies was a man of sufficient resource and versatility to be able to continue to do some dress-designing while serving as an officer in SOE.

SOE's choice of resistance groups to support did not always please the Belgian government in exile. When a delegate from the body which later came to be known as the Secret Army, Charles Claser, reached Britain in the spring of 1942 he was warmly greeted by Knight and cold-shouldered, for political reasons, by the Belgian authorities. Nevertheless he was returned by SOE via the sea route to the south of France and then over one of the established land routes to Belgium. The representative of the Belgian government deputed to deal with all British secret organizations temporarily broke off relations with SOE.

Efforts to support a number of organizations in Belgium did serve to dissipate effort, but that SOE's judgment was predominantly sound is indicated both by results and by enlightened individual testimony, in particular that of Henri Bernard, who was later to be appointed professor at Belgium's Royal Military Academy.

Bernard was for fifteen months the joint chief of a Belgian underground intelligence group, which was formed as early as the autumn of 1940. He witnessed the beginnings of the Secret Army, came over to Britain, worked closely with SOE as head of the Belgian government's section dealing specifically with resistance, and then returned to Belgium.

In an analysis of resistance as an episode in Belgian history Bernard wrote of SOE and other British clandestine bodies that they 'speedily and with a breadth of vision surprising in services of this kind gave their confidence to Belgian organizations which initially had little expertise'. Thanks to SOE, he added, Britain became the arsenal, the bank and the headquarters of Belgian resistance.

Belgian resistance played an important part in the deception exercises staged before and in the early days of the Allied invasion of Normandy in 1944. In one night of January that year a Belgian resistance group put out of action so many high-tension cables that the repair work was estimated to have required ten million man hours. That so much planning and so much effort were put into the attack on the cables gave credence to the assumption that the Allied landings would take place in the Pas de Calais rather than Normandy.

The speed of the Allied advance in September 1944 precluded the Belgian Secret Army from coming into action in the manner for which it had prepared. But the seizure of the port of Antwerp by Belgian underground forces prevented the elaborate German plans for the destruction of the port installations from being put into effect and saved an incalculable number of lives. It was an achievement which, in Bernard's judgment, compensated for all the efforts and all the sacrifices made from 1940 onwards.

The first plans for the encouragement and support of resistance in Denmark drawn up in Britain met with firm official obstruction. Their authors were two naval officers who had left Denmark at the time of the German invasion, Frank Stagg and Ralph Hollingworth. Appreciating that the invasion was strongly resented and that there was widespread pro-British feeling in Denmark, they proposed the formation of an Anglo-Danish council in Britain to co-ordinate resistance. This was vetoed by the British Foreign Office.

Danish forces had been ordered to cease resistance on the day of the German invasion; there had been no declaration of war between Denmark and Germany; and in the view of the Foreign Office Denmark was a neutral country, with its own government, on whose soil it would be improper for a British agency concerned with military activities to be seen to be operating. Hollingworth was posted to Iceland, and the Foreign Office intimated that others with expert knowledge of Danish affairs were liable to find themselves in South America.

A former rubber planter in Malaya, Werner Iversen, also had plans for stimulating Danish resistance. Stagg introduced him to Charles Hambro, the future head of SOE, who decided to go to Stockholm to investigate at first hand the possibilities of establishing links with Denmark.

In Stockholm Hambro met Ebbe Munck, the correspondent of the *Berlingske Tidende*. For some time after this meeting Munck was to act as the Stockholm link between Danish clandestine organizations and Britain. He passed, at first legally and later clandestinely, in and out of

Denmark and became one of the outstanding figures in Danish resistance.

One of the earlier attempts by a Dane to establish links by making his way to Britain on his own initiative also had a discouraging reception. A pilot named Thomas Sneum decided to fly a Tiger Moth aircraft, whose engines had not been run for a year and which had to take off within earshot of German guards, to Britain, relying for his navigation on a map which he had torn from an atlas. He landed safely near Berwick-on-Tweed, but the whole episode seemed so improbable that he was regarded with understandable, though quite unjustified, suspicion. SIS had him confined for a time in Brixton prison, and the cine film of German radar installations, which he had brought with him, was largely destroyed in the processing. Stagg later described the treatment of Sneum as 'a disgraceful chapter'.

For some time after the German invasion the efforts of Danish underground organizations were directed mainly towards maintaining a clandestine press and the gathering and passing of secret intelligence. With easy access, including a regular telephone link, to the neutral country of Sweden information of various kinds could be passed on without great difficulty.

Within SOE it became apparent that active resistance in Denmark could be stimulated, and Gubbins persuaded Dalton to use his influence to have certain Danish specialists recalled from their virtual exile in Iceland and elsewhere. Hollingworth was appointed head of SOE's Danish section. Another SOE officer, Ronald Turnbull, was sent to Stockholm with diplomatic cover and instructions to remain in close contact with Ebbe Munck. The Danish Council was established in London, and in 1942 a leading politician, Christmas Møller, was brought out of Denmark to give it added weight.

Contrary to its practice in the Balkan countries and in France, SOE's policy in dealing with the Low Countries and Scandinavia was to rely, for operational purposes, on the nationals of the countries concerned. Of the fifty agents sent to Denmark all were Danes. The role of the British was confined to recruiting and training agents, supplies, communications, transport and strategic direction. The outcome was a form of co-operation between the Danish resistance and SOE which was in a number of respects a model one.

The Danish government remained in power until Germany assumed total control of the country on 29 August 1943, Danish underground organizations being, until then, financed largely by civil servants who had access to government funds. When it considered the time was ripe, the Danish resistance, as Gubbins explained at the post-war conference held at St Antony's College, Oxford, informed SOE that the sabotage campaign could be intensified. This, it was rightly believed, would compel the Germans to take control and treat Denmark as a hostile country.

When a Freedom Council met clandestinely in Denmark within a month of the formal German assumption of control it was considered proper, and indeed natural, that someone sent to Denmark by SOE should be included. This was Flemming Muus, who earlier in the war had come to Britain from Liberia and who had the unnerving experience of seeing the aircraft which dropped him into Denmark shot down in flames. Some years after the war a Danish historian of the resistance, Jørgen Hæstrup, was to say: 'I wonder whether they ever realized in London what magic the words "London thinks" implied. For many London became a sort of mysterious, supreme authority.'

Communications between Britain and Denmark were greatly improved when a Danish radio engineer named Arne Duus-Hansen developed a high-speed radio transmitter which could send some 800 words a minute and which the Germans failed to detect. During the last six months of the war all clandestine communications from Denmark were by this method, and SOE had no need to send in any radio sets or operators.

In spite of the flatness of much of its territory, and the consequent lack of natural cover, the proportion of successful parachute drops was higher in Denmark than in any other European country. At sea it was found possible from time to time to transfer sabotage material to boats returning to Denmark in exchange for components for war production factories which were brought back to Britain.

To the Danish people as a whole the most welcome benefit of good clandestine communications was that bomber aircraft could frequently be directed to the right targets and lives could thereby be saved. One method by which this was achieved was the placing of the homing devices known as Eureka permanently in the steeples of Danish churches. Ultimately the confidence of both the Danish resistance and the RAF in the possibilities of guiding aircraft to their targets was such that it was decided to mount an operation for the destruction of a single building in Copenhagen.

This was the Gestapo headquarters. The central part of the building was totally destroyed. So too were the records of thousands of Danes, and several Danish prisoners escaped. It was highly selective, highly skilful bombing, yet the number of Danes killed was about a hundred. Eighty-three of them were children in a nearby school, which was hit after one of the low-flying aircraft struck an overhead cable.

Perhaps the greatest contribution which the Danish underground made towards winning the war in Europe was the sabotage of railways in Jutland. This seriously hampered the bringing of German reinforcements to the battle of the Ardennes. Its principal contribution towards winning the war as a whole was almost certainly facilitating the escape of a scientist who was to play a major role in the construction of the atom bomb.

The scientist was Professor Niels Bohr, to whom a message from Sir James Chadwick, advising him to escape, was conveyed on three specks of film. These had to be placed on a glass slide and read through a powerful microscope.

Bohr accepted Chadwick's advice and agreed to be taken to Sweden. In his hurry to leave he forgot to bring with him a bottle of heavy water and some important notes. All were safely recovered by the Danish resistance.

The principle, generally adopted by SOE in northern Europe, of encouraging the people of occupied territories to carry out their own acts of resistance and sabotage, rather than sending in British nationals who might have been all too conspicuous, was varied when a young Englishman volunteered to be sent to German-occupied Estonia.

His name was Ronald Seth. He had worked in Estonia before the war, spoke the language well, and had the extreme fairness of hair and complexion sometimes to be found among Estonians. He was in fact almost indistinguishable physically from an Estonian seaman, whose identity he chose to adopt. He even learnt to forge the seaman's handwriting and served as a steward in a merchant ship to acquire the necessary background knowledge.

Seth's largely self-imposed task was to organize resistance in Estonia, primarily with a view to sabotaging the shale-oil mines. In fact he spent twelve days in the country, for most of the time wandering in dense forests, before being captured and horribly tortured. His mission at least caused the Germans to wonder where agents of the enemy were likely to appear next.

In Norway, although ultimately all resistance was in the hands of Norwegians, the British were involved in some of the important early stages of organizing opposition to the Germans. This was a consequence of the short and, from the Allied point of view, disastrous campaign in Norway in 1940.

During the campaign a number of Norwegians attached themselves in one capacity or another to the independent companies which Gubbins commanded. One of these was a well known actor in the Oslo

National Theatre, Martin Linge, who was appointed liaison officer with the British forces at Andalsnes.

Linge, who was then in his forties, was a man of strong personality and power of command, so much so that he had the distinction of having a fighting force named after him. This was the Linge Company, which consisted of Norwegians who came to Britain to continue the struggle. From these volunteers were to emerge some of the outstanding saboteurs of the Second World War. The Linge Company was later renamed Norwegian Independent Company No. 1 and continued to be under SOE's control. Linge himself was killed in action in a raid on the island of Maaloy towards the end of 1942.

A number of the early recruits to MI(R) were sent to Norway. They included Malcolm Munthe, the son of the famous writer and doctor; Andrew Croft, the explorer; and Peter Fleming, who served under Carton de Wiart and was described by him as the perfect staff officer, 'dispensing entirely with paper'.

Munthe served as liaison officer with the Norwegian Army in southern Norway. After the Germans captured Stavanger he was given some civilian clothes by a member of the staff of the British Consulate. He hid his military identity card and other documents in an accordion and set off on his own. After a time he joined some Norwegian forces who were continuing the fight, and was wounded in both legs. He was captured by the Germans but escaped with Norwegian help. A Norwegian then carried him slung over his shoulder into a forest.

For a time Munthe was housed in Bergen next door to the German naval Commander-in-Chief, Admiral Raeder, whom he frequently observed in his garden. Various attempts which Munthe made to reach Britain by sea failed, and Norwegian friends brought him to a clinic in Oslo, where his wounds were treated. From Oslo he followed an escape route, which had recently become established, to Sweden.

In Stockholm Munthe was taken on the staff of the British Embassy as an Assistant Military Attaché. After a time he received a visit from Charles Hambro, who told him something about SOE, appointed him as his representative, and provided him with a private code based on the works of Ruskin. Munthe found Hambro's visit both encouraging and refreshing. 'He was enormously tall', he afterwards wrote, 'and athletic, with broad shoulders, broad eyes and a broad smile; and when he left the room I got the impression that the war was a cricket match'. Hambro had in fact captained Eton at cricket.

Munthe secretly trained Norwegian would-be saboteurs in the use of explosives in woods near Stockholm. To provide himself with some sort of cover he invented a figure known as The Red Horse, who was supposed to be responsible for clandestine activities in which the British were involved. Thereafter he stamped his communications with his red horse symbol.

In time word spread among Norwegians who intended to make their way to Stockholm that they could expect a much more helpful reception in the British than in the Norwegian Embassy. Among those who passed through Munthe's hands was a young Norwegian named Odd Starheim, who had been trained as a ship's radio operator.

In March 1942 Starheim and a number of his friends captured a 620-ton coastal steamer named *Galtesund* off the Norwegian coast and brought her successfully to Aberdeen. He then returned to Norway to contact a resistance group. One of the leaders of this group, Gustav Tomstad, maintained regular contact with Germans by being ostensibly a prominent member of the Nazi-type Norwegian National Front and regularly wearing its uniform. Not the least of the group's achievements was sending the first information that the *Bismarck* was at sea and heading north. As a consequence of this the operation was mounted which led to the sinking of the *Bismarck* in the Atlantic.

When Starheim reached Stockholm after his second departure from Norway Munthe was already regarded with disfavour in certain Swedish circles. His departure was insisted upon when tentative plans for the assassination of Heinrich Himmler during a visit which he was expected to make to Oslo came to light. Munthe therefore returned to work for a time in Britain. So did Starheim.

In charge of SOE's Norwegian section when Munthe returned was Frank Stagg, whose proposals for stimulating resistance in Denmark had had such an icy reception. Stagg knew Norway well and had written extensively about its history. He was assisted by a naval reserve officer named James Chaworth-Musters, who had a large red beard, was an enthusiastic fisherman, and had a country home in Norway, where he was a neighbour of Martin Linge.

The man in command of the Scandinavian sections generally was Jack Wilson, the former Director of the International Boy Scouts Bureau. Odd Starheim, who was later to return to Norway on a mission in which he was killed at sea, had been a dedicated Scout since his boyhood. To him it was a memorable thrill to meet, in Wilson, a man who had actually known Baden-Powell. His two principal boyhood heroes had been Baden-Powell and Nansen.

SOE Norwegian Section's most important establishment was at

Lunna Voe, some twenty-seven miles from Lerwick in the Shetland Islands. From there, and later from Scalloway, a unique form of transport service operated, which came to be known as the Shetland Bus. 'To take the Shetland Bus' was the phrase adopted by Norwegians who for one reason or another had to leave Norway and make their way to Britain.

The Lunna Voe base was established in the autumn of 1941. Six Norwegian fishing boats were requisitioned and a number of Norwegian fishermen and merchant seamen were enrolled as civilians. Their task was to provide a ferry service for men and materials between Shetland and occupied Norway. In charge of the base was a young man in Army uniform named Leslie (Bob) Mitchell. He had thick-lensed spectacles and a slight stoop and proved to be a highly successful commander of a unit for whose organization there were no precedents.

Mitchell's second-in-command was a tall young naval reserve officer named David Howarth, who had a peculiar talent for dealing with marine engines. He also had a considerable talent for words and after the war was to write a number of books. One of these he entitled *The Shetland Bus*. Another, *We Die Alone*, was an account of the extraordinary powers of endurance of a Norwegian named Jan Baalsrud, who was the sole survivor of an unsuccessful sabotage party landed by one of the fishing boats from Shetland.

Baalsrud endured avalanches and frostbite and gangrene. He lay in a sleeping-bag in the snow for twenty-seven days. He cut off his gangrened toes with a penknife, using brandy as an anaesthetic and disinfectant. He was carried 3,000 feet up a mountainside by a Norwegian resistance group in a specially designed sledge. He was brought to the Swedish frontier by some Lapps, who gave him an escort of hundreds of reindeer, and was back on active service before the war ended.

The fishing boats of the Shetland Bus service were 50 to 70 feet long. They sailed alone through the northern winter, and if they were attacked from the air and sunk their crews had little hope of survival. Inevitably in those waters in winter they had to face prolonged periods of gales. In November 1941 these lasted for five days and five nights, with wind speeds at times exceeding 100 miles an hour.

Mitchell and Howarth had no power to impose orders and no sanctions which they could apply. They were dealing with fishermen, and, as Howarth expressed it, 'no fisherman of any nation can be driven; he is brought up to depend on nobody and to call nobody his master.' They quickly realized therefore that it would be pointless to try to apply the standard disciplines of armed services.

This suited them both temperamentally. Of Mitchell Howarth wrote that he had 'too much sense of the ridiculous and of his own fallibility to be a good parade-ground officer'. Howarth himself, for sound practical reasons in the prevailing climate, usually dressed as a fisherman, and on one occasion, when wearing flannel trousers, without a collar and with a large quantity of cement in his hair, he was accosted by a visiting British admiral, who asked him where he could find a naval officer named Howarth.

At one stage it was decided that the Shetland base should be brought under the control of the Norwegian Navy, and a Norwegian naval officer was appointed to take charge of the boats. He was a disciplinarian and insisted on saluting and the scrubbing of decks. The fishermen simply refused to take any notice of him, and the boats reverted to SOE control. In their dealings with the British Navy Mitchell and Howarth received maximum co-operation and minimum evidence of any desire to interfere with administrative arrangements. This Howarth attributed to the Navy's sense of security in its own traditions of discipline, which enabled it to tolerate certain necessary irregularities.

The fishermen at the Shetland base elected their own skippers. They usually chose well, largely because it was so necessary that they should do so. One skipper, Leif Larsen, who had fought in the Spanish Civil War and in Finland and had been skipper of a Bergen ferry, was given the rank of sub-lieutenant so that he could receive some ciphers which were issued to officers only. He refused to attend any officers' training schools and became, in Howarth's words, 'the most unofficer-like and most successful sub-lieutenant one could imagine'.

Larsen received more decorations for gallantry than any other Norwegian or British serviceman. They included the DSO, the DSC, the DSM and bar, the Conspicuous Gallantry Medal and a number of Norwegian decorations. Howarth described him as 'a humble, gentle and peaceful person'.

Through three winters the fishing boats continued to make their crossings, which sometimes took as long as three weeks. They had to operate in the winter because it was necessary to approach the Norwegian coast under cover of darkness. The Germans had imposed a fifty-mile limit within which fishing was permitted, and the boats of the Shetland Bus service, although heavily armed with hidden machine guns, had, in all respects, to appear to be normal Norwegian fishing boats and to be seen to abide by the regulations.

In the third winter of operations, 1942–3, losses were alarmingly heavy. Five fishing boats – that is to say half the number normally kept in commission – were lost. So were forty-two of the men who sailed regularly. German vigilance became steadily greater; because of fuel shortages fewer Norwegian boats were allowed to fish; and the boats of the Shetland Bus service became increasingly conspicuous. No acceptable vessels to take their place seemed to be available from British sources, and as the struggle inside Norway intensified the prospects of maintaining supplies by sea appeared to grow steadily worse.

The difficulties were resolved by the United States Navy. Admiral Chester Nimitz made three submarine chasers available from Miami, which had a cruising speed of 17 knots and a maximum speed of 22. They were found to be nearly ideal as transport vessels for crossing the North Sea. They were even fitted with refrigerators and electric toasters, thereby giving the crews of the Shetland Bus service an experience of comfort at sea which was wholly new to them.

The transport provided by the boats from the Shetland base was supplemented by a limited number of aircraft, and it was by parachute that Norwegians assigned to some of the most important missions of all were infiltrated. One such mission followed a report sent from Norway by a professor of physics named Leif Tromstad. In this he stated that the Germans were increasing the production of heavy water at Rjukan with the obvious intention of manufacturing an atom bomb. The report in itself was of major importance in influencing the United States government in its decision to produce the atom bombs which were later dropped in Japan.

The problem of how to put the heavy water plant out of action was referred by the British War Office to the staff of Combined Operations, and the decision taken was to mount a glider-borne operation. This was a disaster. One towing aircraft crashed into a mountain, and the whole crew were killed. The remaining members of the British operational party were captured and, although they were in uniform, executed.

Four Norwegians who had been sent in by SOE did, however, survive. They spent fourteen months living on the countryside and maintaining their morale and cohesion by such devices as giving each other lectures. One subject chosen was tact and good manners. Another was the art of shooting reindeer.

Once it was known that the glider-borne assault on Rjukan had failed SOE undertook to mount another operation to attack the same target. This called for perfection in both planning and training, for there was no doubt that the Germans would be prepared for a second attempt. Not only was this a natural assumption, but maps had been found with the bodies of the British party killed showing rings round the name 'Rjukan'.

When the Germans invaded Norway in 1940 the Norwegian people had no tradition of underground resistance and no first-hand experience of warfare of any kind. This relative innocence was soon compensated for by a readiness to learn. The Norwegian agents trained by SOE were nearly all exceptionally conscientious. They surprised some of the most experienced instructors in the schools in the western Highlands by their powers of endurance, and Polish parachutists were much impressed by the way in which Norwegians dropped with their skis on in order to make a quick get-away.

No agents took more pains in their training than those chosen to attack the heavy water plant at Rjukan. They were helped by the presence of Professor Jomar Brun, the former chief engineer at the plant, who had been brought out through Sweden and who ensured that they all carried an exact mental picture of its layout and contents.

Six men were chosen to join the four who had already been waiting for months. Their leader was named Joachim Ronneberg. One of the members of the party and its future chronicler, Knut Haukelid, was the twin brother of a well known film actress, Sigrid Gurie. He was a man who delighted in solitude and open spaces. When Gubbins visited him in Norway after the war Haukelid took him to his home, explaining before he did so: 'I take the train for a day, and then I motor for a few hours, and then I walk over the mountains, and then I am in my home, and nothing can spoil it.' The radio operator of the party, Knut Haugland, was later to join the *Kon-Tiki* expedition.

Ronneberg's group duly joined the men who had been sent in advance. They all agreed that if anyone was wounded in the attack he would immediately take his L-tablet. The passwords they chose for distinguishing members of their operational group from everyone else inside or guarding the factory were 'Piccadilly' and 'Leicester Square'.

The attack was a total success. The plant was put out of action for several months; 350 kilograms of heavy water were destroyed, and not a man was lost. After the attack the Germans deployed some 12,000 men in a search for the saboteurs. They failed to capture any of them, largely because, as Haukelid recorded, the saboteurs had learnt to live in much the same manner as reindeer. General Falkenhorst, the German Commander-in-Chief, described the operation as the best coup he had known.

After more than four months the Germans succeeded in getting production of heavy water under way again. Bombing of the plant was therefore ordered, the most successful attack being a daylight raid by 150 American aircraft. They destroyed very little heavy water, but they seriously disrupted production. The raid also led to a German decision to remove all the heavy water so far produced to Germany.

Two SS companies were given the task of guarding the train which transported the heavy water, and detailed inspections were made of all the railway lines along which it had to travel. The Norwegian response to this was to concentrate on the ferry which was to transport the load across water. It was prepared for demolition, and the timing was so perfect that the ferry exploded and sank at the deepest point. All the heavy water was lost.

Ironically it was learnt later that the methods the Germans proposed for producing atom bombs would probably not have succeeded. Had they in fact been advancing along the right lines, the attacks, first on the Rjukan plant and then on the ferry, might have been among the decisive actions of the war.

One Englishman who was established in Norway when the country was invaded by the Germans was later to play major roles in SOE operations in other theatres of war. This was Gerard Holdsworth, an early recruit to Section D.

A man of medium height, strongly built, with decisively cut features and a quiet air of authority, Holdsworth spent seven years in Borneo, at first as a planter and later in the Colonial Service. After returning home he became one of the comparatively few people in Britain who in the 1930s earned their living by making films for advertising agencies. It was through filming for the Philips Company in the Netherlands, an activity which led to fairly frequent visits to Germany, that he received what he and others described as 'the tap on the shoulder' and was placed on the strength, although not on the payroll, of Section D.

Holdsworth was an expert small-boat sailor, and on his first visit to Norway he surveyed a number of the fjords. Shortly before war broke out he was set up in Norway, ostensibly as a buyer of brisling and slid. This gave him the opportunity to contact a number of Norwegians who were willing to co-operate with the British if the Germans invaded their country.

As Holdsworth did not speak Norwegian his instructions were to leave the country before it was overrun by Germans. After the invasion therefore he set off for Sweden and by chance fell in with an escaping party which included the President of the Norwegian Parliament, whose name, like that of the future head of SOE, was Hambro. The party crossed the frontier successfully, and from Sweden Holdsworth was able to go to Finland. There he had another helpful chance encounter.

This was with a Finn whom he had proposed as a member of the Royal Thames Yacht Club and who was ADC to Finland's great national hero, Field-Marshal Mannerheim. The ADC told Holdsworth that the easiest way for him to return to Britain would be through the Soviet Union. This prospect did not appeal to Holdsworth, and when he was taken to see Mannerheim the Field-Marshal fully appreciated his misgivings. He therefore arranged for Holdsworth to be taken to Petsamo, from which a ship was due to sail to Kirkenes and then to England. The ship reached Barrow-in-Furness after a three-week journey, most of it in fog. During the journey Holdsworth learnt of the defeat in France and the evacuation from Dunkirk.

On his return he reported to Lawrence Grand and was instructed to go to Penzance to investigate the possibilities of transporting agents to and from the Brittany coast in small boats. The outcome was the so-called Helford Flotilla.

The Helford river provided good anchorage and, at that time, comparative freedom from casual observation. A suitable house for accommodating agents and crews was found, Holdsworth's beautiful, blonde wife, who had herself worked in Section D, being put in charge. Her porcelain-like complexion and almost fragile appearance did not at first sight suggest an intimate knowledge of explosives. In fact she was so intimately acquainted with them that as a skilled commercial artist she had made detailed drawings on such subjects as 'how to construct a home-made mine' for a handbook for saboteurs.

Holdsworth's crews were assembled by word of mouth and from a variety of sources. They included a black-bearded Channel Islander named John Newton; a Norfolk man named Tom Long, who had served in coastal trading vessels; Pierre Guillet, a Breton fisherman, who was produced for Holdsworth by Thomas Cadett of SOE's French section; and a number of Cornish fishermen suggested by the Royal Navy.

For his second-in-command Holdsworth chose Francis Brooks Richards, a young naval sub-lieutenant, who had been injured in an explosion aboard a mine-sweeper and who was to accompany him on all the flotilla's missions. After the war Brooks Richards, like Peter Wilkinson, was to fill the exacting post of British Ambassador in Saigon.

Holdsworth himself, who held an Army commission, now became a naval officer. The buttons of his uniform were somewhat unusual in that one concealed a compass and another a hacksaw. On operational duty he normally appeared as a Breton fisherman.

Satisfactory crews were more easily found than satisfactory vessels. The first boat which Holdsworth was told could be made available was a Belgian river launch. This he described in an official report as 'of the type frequently seen on the Thames in the Henley reaches'. After a time, through the help of the Royal Navy in Plymouth, he found a 65-foot French tunnyman named *Mutin*, to which he later became deeply attached. *Mutin* and a French drifter, which was also acquired, needed re-engining and other modifications before they could be put into service. The first of the Helford Flotilla's operations was therefore carried out in a seaplane tender which Holdsworth had obtained from the RAF.

Operations were mounted to take agents and stores ashore and to bring out agents and, incidentally, intelligence. On one mission Holdsworth had a rendezvous off the coast of Brittany with a boat which had an old man and a boy aboard. After passwords had been exchanged the boy handed Holdsworth a German gasmask containing some papers. These had been given to the old man by an agent of Polish intelligence and consisted of plans of the German installations at Brest and details of the disposition of troops.

Landings had to be carried out in darkness with no buoys or other navigational aids and usually with no knowledge of whether a beach was mined. At times the presence of the Breton, Pierre Guillet, was of the utmost value, for he had the gift, which some fishermen possess, of knowing exactly where he was on a particular coast by little more than feel and smell. The only signals which could be risked from the shore came from blue, muffled torches. Strict silence had to be observed on landing, the crews wearing canvas shoes and recognizing each other's presence by small, luminous perspex balls, about the size of golf balls.

Inevitably the boats periodically came under enemy attack. On one occasion a German aircraft swept *Mutin*'s deck with machine-gun fire, killing the boat's engineer. Another time the attack came from an E-boat in mid-Channel. Again the fire was intense, and when it was over Holdsworth put his right hand to his side to take some cigarettes from his pocket. The pocket had been shot away, and a moment later he found he had no left-hand pocket either.

After some time it became clear that landings could be made on the Brittany coast with any likelihood of success only in winter, to maintain contact by sea with the French resistance in summer a new system was devised. This involved the co-operation of the French fishing fleet in the Bay of Biscay. Holdsworth was given the use of a small island in the Scillies as a forward base, and *Mutin* was reconverted so that she once again had all the appearance of a tunnyman and could appear inconspicuously amid the French tunny-fishing fleet. In this capacity she delivered sizeable quantities of plastic explosive disguised convincingly as fish.

In the autumn of 1942 Holdsworth was instructed to prepare himself for a new role. This was to be in the Mediterranean and would follow the landings in North Africa. He therefore sailed *Mutin* to Gibraltar, where he met two men who were being held in readiness to go into Spain if German troops entered the country. One was an Anglo-Spaniard named Adrian Gallegos. The other, Charles MacIntosh, had spent much of his life in South America. Neither was of course required in Spain, and both were later to serve with distinction under Holdsworth in a new capacity.

For a time Holdsworth was engaged in small-boat operations in the Mediterranean, one of which brought him to Corsica. These ended when he was appointed to the command of No. 1 Special Force, whose headquarters were for a time in Malta and were located later in Monopoli near Bari. No. 1 Special Force was the cover name for the SOE organization concerned with promoting and supporting resistance in Italy.

The support of resistance in Italy presented certain problems which were not encountered elsewhere. Until Mussolini was removed from office towards the end of July 1943, and an armistice followed, Italy was a hostile power. Later she was given the status of co-belligerent, but the Germans remained in effective control of parts of the country until the end. A number of prisoner-of-war camps were located in Italy, and after the armistice was signed many of the prisoners were virtually let loose on the countryside. Some of them on their own initiative became involved in resistance activities.

Italy was unique too in being the only country in Europe in which SOE and OSS operated on more or less equal terms. Elsewhere the active support of resistance from outside had begun before the United States entered the war, and it was only natural that OSS should follow where SOE had led. An SOE mission did land in Italy by parachute as early as December 1942, but its members were captured before long. Support of resistance on a significant scale did not begin until both American and British armies were established on the Italian mainland. By then OSS in Europe was already an active body. The co-operation between SOE and OSS in Italy was at times harmonious and at times not.

SOE's first British-led operational unit in Italy was under the command of Malcolm Munthe, who, having spent some time on staff duties in the Norwegian section, had volunteered for more active service. The unit came with the first wave of the armies which landed in Sicily in July 1943. Its principal task was to contact anti-fascist elements, and in trying to fulfil this the unit found itself in Salerno rather earlier than had been planned, before in fact the American Army reached the city.

Munthe's unit was a cosmopolitan one. Not only was he himself half-Swedish, but of the three other officers one, Adrian Gallegos, was the Anglo-Spaniard whom Holdsworth had met in Gibraltar; another was a Frenchman named Boutigny; another was an Italian, Massimo Salvadori, who held a commission in the British Army and was known as Max Sylvester.

After the Allied occupation of southern Italy Munthe's unit, which remained in touch with forward troops, operated variously from Ischia, from Naples and from Capri, where Munthe, as the son of the distinguished doctor who had lived there so long, was received with much affection and much respect.

One of the more memorable of the unit's achievements was bringing the great liberal philosopher and courageous anti-fascist, Benedetto Croce, safely into contact with the Allies. Croce was living in Sorrento, which was at that time behind the German lines. Guided by the Mayor of Capri, Gallegos set off from the island in a boat, rescued Croce, and brought him back to Capri. Munthe himself rescued Croce's wife and daughter.

When Allied forces landed at Anzio in January 1944 Munthe's unit was again in action. By this time its strength had been increased, and it included a young British captain named Michael Gubbins, who was Colin Gubbins's son. Soon after the Anzio landings the unit came under heavy shell-fire. Michael Gubbins was killed and Munthe was seriously wounded.

Massimo Salvadori, the Italian officer in Munthe's unit, represented much that was best in the Italian liberal, anti-fascist tradition. He was born in England, but came from an Italian aristocratic, Protestant family. In 1922, as a boy of fourteen, he had his first sight of Mussolini and heard his father describe him as looking like a gorilla. Two years later father and son were both beaten up by Blackshirts after the father had published two articles in an English weekly describing acts of violence in Italy. The son continued his education in Switzerland.

In Geneva Massimo Salvadori found the indifference of his fellow-students to political issues surprising. He himself was already formulating some of the ideas which he was to spend much of his later life in propagating and defending. One of these was that 'liberty is the greatest good, not for the benefits it brings, but because only a free man is fully a man'. Another was that those who believed in liberty had no right to sit back and do nothing while free institutions were threatened. Salvadori was a profound admirer of Croce, and his own broad picture of modern history, which he described in later life, was of a centuries-old march towards liberty being gravely impeded when the two great totalitarian powers, Germany and the Soviet Union, reached an agreement and war followed.

In 1929, now aged twenty-one, Salvadori returned to Italy as the secret representative of the exiled politician, Alberto Tarchiani, one of the leaders of the Justice and Liberty party. For three years he carried on underground activities, first as a student at Rome University and then while doing military service. He formed secret groups and distributed pamphlets and codes, although he already knew that he had a personal dislike of conspiracies and secret societies.

Salvadori was arrested by the OVRA, the fascist secret police, in 1933 and imprisoned. His release followed an intercession by a British cousin, and he then spent some three years farming in Kenya.

When war broke out in 1939 Salvadori was already in touch with British intelligence, and he was given the task of contacting Italians in the United States who were thought to be sympathetic to the Allied cause and who might at some later date be sent in to Italy. While on the American continent he indulged in such incidental activities as sabotaging a radio transmitter, which was being used by the Germans in Central America, and he was in Mexico City when, in January 1943, he learnt that his application to be allowed to enlist in the British Army had been approved. It was therefore as a British captain and a member of SOE that in 1943 he set foot on Italian soil for the first time in ten years.

While serving with Munthe's unit Salvadori contracted jaundice and was withdrawn from the fighting front. Harold Macmillan, who was then British Minister Resident at the Allied Headquarters in Italy, suggested that he should become an Under-Secretary in the new Italian government, but he preferred to remain on active service until the war ended.

Early in 1945 Salvadori was parachuted into northern Italy. The two British officers who accompanied him were both killed, but Salvadori made contact with the Italian resistance groups whose command came to be known as the National Liberation Committee. He entered Milan clandestinely and decided to remain there. The Germans knew that there was a representative of the Allied command in the city, but they were unable to find Salvadori, even though he saw some fifty to sixty people a week.

After the war Salvadori was given the freedom of the city of Milan. This and the award of the DSO were some compensation for a painful encounter he had had earlier. In June 1944 he visited, after a long absence, the home of his parents at San Tomasso and met his father, from whom he had first learnt of the need to sustain the fight against fascism. His father greeted him frostily and addressed him contemptuously as an agent of a foreign power.

Few of those who served in No. 1 Special Force had such compelling political motives as Salvadori. One man, who fought with distinction while serving as a liaison officer with Italian Partisans, had no doubt in his own mind that his principal reason for volunteering to be parachuted into northern Italy was the prospect of being able to climb some interesting mountains. This was the well-known mountaineer and explorer, Harold Tilman, who had led the Everest expedition in 1938.

Tilman was in his late forties when he was dropped into Italy. He had served on the Western Front in the First World War. In the Second World War he fought both in France and in the Western Desert. Then, learning from routine orders, which emanated from Cairo, that volunteers were wanted for special service duties, he put his name forward, was accepted, and was parachuted into Albania.

His chief complaint about life with the Albanian Partisans was that for much of the time it was, as he put it, 'indecently dull and placid'. To relieve the tedium he made long journeys in which, against Albanian advice, he normally dispensed with guides. One reason why he preferred to go alone was that he considered Albanians to be very poor walkers, continually stopping for a chat or a smoke or a drink of water. Nor could he understand why they chose to wear several sweaters and thick, homespun trousers when he was satisfied with a pair of shorts.

Nevertheless, through its very topography, Albania approximated a little to Tilman's ideal of perfect territory. This he had found in the Assam Himalaya. Of it he wrote in his revealing work, *When Men and Mountains Meet*, that it was 'not easy to reach, but neither were Christian's Delectable Mountains, nor is any place that is worth reaching. By this I mean country which is more or less unknown, sparsely or not at all inhabited, inhospitable, difficult to move in, and, of course, mountainous.'

Tilman was accompanied on his drop into Italy by a young Gunner officer, who when war broke out had been reading medicine at Cambridge and who, Tilman supposed, had volunteered for service in Italy from a desire 'to blow something to bits'. This Tilman found under-standable. What puzzled him was that the same officer, 'although young, strong, and in full possession of his senses, was strangely inappreciative of the mountains'.

In *When Men and Mountains Meet* Tilman recorded little of the fighting with the Nanatti Division of the Italian Partisans which led to his being awarded the DSO and the freedom of Belluno. He did, however, mention *en passant* that he spent seventy-two hours without food and with frozen feet. He also made an illuminating comment when he wrote: 'Everything that makes life tolerable for the regular soldier, that sustains his morale in quiet times and in battle gives him a reasonable chance of survival, was absent from the life of the partisans.'

Another member of No. 1 Special Force had served for more than eleven years in the French Foreign Legion. This was Dick Cooper, who was born in Baghdad of an English father and an Italian mother. His nomadic career began when he was kidnapped at the age of six and spent a year with wandering Arabs.

He became fluent in Arabic, Turkish, French, Greek, Italian and Spanish, speaking English with a foreign accent. Schools could not hold him for long, and he was apprenticed to a shipping company but took an early opportunity to jump ship at Gulfport, Mississippi. He worked in the United States for a time as a dishwasher, but then joined another ship and reached Algiers. There in October 1914, at the age of fifteen and under the influence of an early hangover, he joined the French Foreign Legion, giving his nationality as Mexican and his age as twenty-one.

Cooper was wounded in the Dardanelles campaign and decorated for gallantry. He later joined the British Army and was wounded again. After the First World War he returned to the life of a *légionnaire*.

His first stable civilian employment gave him the opportunity of entering SOE by an unusual method. In 1940 he was working in London as a telephone operator dealing with calls to and from Europe when he overheard a conversation between two British officers. One of the officers was in London, the other in Bordeaux, and they were discussing, most indiscreetly, the difficulties of finding people who could be sent to France and pass as French. Cooper noted the number of the London end of the call, discovered the address, and obtained an interview with SOE. His initiative, added to his past military ex-periences and his knowledge of languages, ensured that he was later taken on SOE's strength.

Cooper was sent by SOE to Algeria, where he was soon arrested by the French Second Bureau. He was later transferred to the camp near Grenoble where Richard Heslop and Ernest Wilkinson were held for a time. He was allowed, just as they were, to escape and had a gruelling journey on foot similar to theirs. In Italy he was concerned with the training and infiltration of agents.

Cooper later described his colourful life in two autobiographical works. Towards the end of one of them he made the engaging comment: 'I do not think it sad that I survived into old age.'

When the gates of the prisoner-of-war camps in Italy were thrown open the British Chiefs of Staff had no clear policy for the employment of the men who emerged. Most of them were soldiers, and it was War Office doctrine that a prisoner's duty was to try to escape and make his way to the nearest British base for further employment on active service. No instructions were given on the subject of joining Partisan groups, and in so far as the War Office had any influence on the ex-prisoners at large in Italy it was exercised in favour of bringing them home.

Missions were in fact despatched to Italy for this specific purpose, and they achieved a certain success. Some servicemen escaped through Yugoslavia, some by sea, and some by passing through the German lines. There were others too who preferred to lodge peacefully with Italian families, and a comparatively small number, estimated to have been about fifty in all, became actively involved in resistance.

One of these was Major Gordon Lett, an officer in the East Surrey Regiment, who had been captured at Tobruk. Lett's original intention, on being freed from a prison camp, was to make his way to the coast in the hope of an Allied landing. When he came to the valley of Rossano he had other thoughts. He had a few British troops with him; Italians gave them shelter; and they were joined by three Poles, who had escaped from doing forced labour for the Germans in the Todt Organization. Then Lett received a visit from a representative of the Liberation Committee in Genoa, who discussed with him the possibility of forming what was already described as an international brigade.

Before long every man in the immediate neighbourhood who had a firearm of any kind called to see Lett. The cosmopolitan nature of the force which was developing was maintained by the accession of two Yugoslavs, a Peruvian and a Somali, who had escaped from a ship in La Spezia and whose general attitude was one of mild bewilderment. The Germans offered an award of 5,000 lire, later supplemented by two months' rations of food and tobacco, to anyone who brought about the capture of an Allied serviceman alive or dead. More and more people came to know about Lett's presence, but no one betrayed him.

One of the missions whose task was to bring out ex-prisoners made contact with Lett, and a number of servicemen, including an army colonel, were taken out. The mission also provided Lett with a means of communication with the Allied command, and before long he learnt that an operational group with two radio sets was being sent to him. This came from No. 1 Special Force.

With the establishment of radio communications Lett's military and political standing were immediately heightened. His personal standing was already of the highest. He became a kind of unofficial governor, being called upon to register births and deaths, settle private disputes, and deal with problems of public health. On one occasion a man called on him and said he wanted a divorce from his wife. Lett pointed out that divorce was illegal in Italy, but the man replied that that was so under the fascists, but now in the Rossano valley 'the Signor Maggiore makes the laws'.

As more and more arms became available the Partisan groups which Lett in effect commanded became increasingly active. There were a number of successful ambushes of enemy troops, and after a time Lett learnt that the Germans called off other anti-Partisan operations in order to concentrate on punitive expeditions against his Rossano groups. Of Lett's own part in these actions Roberto Battaglia, historian of the Italian resistance and himself a distinguished Partisan commander, wrote that his gallantry would never be forgotten.

One episode which gave Lett particular pleasure was an act of preservation, not destruction. He was approached by the Bishop of Pontremoli, who asked him if he could persuade the Allied High Command to spare Pontremoli from bombing. Lett replied that his influence was limited, but any intercession he might make was likely to be more effective if he could report exactly where German troops were billeted in the area. This might enable targets to be selected more carefully. The bishop replied that as a priest he could not supply such information. Not long afterwards a Partisan brought Lett a detailed list of all the German billets and garrisons in the region which, he said, he had found under a tree. Pontremoli was largely spared.

Lett was given the freedom of Pontremoli. A few years after the war was over he returned there and witnessed what was described as a march-past of Partisans. To his dismay and sorrow he did not recognize a single face among those taking part. 'We have been forgotten,' he wrote in his exceptionally attractive book of reminiscences, *Rossano. An Adventure of the Italian Resistance*, 'and our place taken by the rank and file of the Communist party, who are making political capital out of our good name. There is not very much we can do about it.'

In a report on the Italian campaign Holdsworth, in describing resistance activities, divided them into three main phases. In the first, which preceded the armistice, achievements amounted to little more than causing nuisance and helping prisoners to escape. In the second, which ended in the late autumn of 1944, specific targets were given to resistance groups to attack and enemy troop movements were seriously impeded. In the final phase much of Italy was liberated.

In the first phase SOE was involved in one action which had important consequences. This followed the parachuting in of a young officer named Dick Mallaby, who was half British and half Italian. Mallaby had a gentle, almost dreamy manner and had been employed by SOE for some time in the Middle East as a sergeant-instructor teaching radio operators. One of his pupils was Christine Granville.

Mallaby was dropped into one of the Italian lakes and was soon captured. Mussolini's government decided that he was to be executed as a spy and that, to serve as a deterrent, the execution should be given maximum publicity. Mallaby was taken under escort to Rome, but while this was happening secret negotiations were being conducted in Portugal to bring the state of war between Italy and the Allies to an end.

On reading one of the telegrams about the negotiations Holdsworth noted that Marshal Badoglio, on whose behalf the Italian negotiators in Portugal were acting, had no direct channel of communication with the Allied High Command. He therefore suggested that Mallaby should provide the link, using the radio set, ciphers and crystals which he had taken in with him.

This was what happened. Mallaby stayed with King Victor Emmanuel and Badoglio while the armistice negotiations were being conducted, finally emerging with them to meet Allied representatives, including Holdsworth, in Brindisi.

The support given by the British to the King and Badoglio was one cause of OSS distrust of what SOE in Italy was doing. Within OSS the opinion was widely held that the British were more concerned with preventing the communists from gaining control in Italy than with taking advantage of the considerable contribution which the communists could make towards winning the war. This policy seemed to a number of Americans fully in line with the established British practice in the Second World War of supporting monarchies, no matter how discredited they might be. Members of SOE for their part contended that the principal beneficiary of OSS activities in Italy was likely to be the Mafia. There was some substance in the complaints on both sides.

At the beginning of the winter of 1944–5 Field-Marshal Alexander, the Supreme Allied Commander, made a broadcast to the Italian Partisans in which he told them they should, in effect, hibernate until the spring, giving as his principal reason the difficulty of sending them supplies in winter. The broadcast gave widespread offence to Italians and was commonly interpreted, not without reason and not only by communists, as intended to limit the growth of communist power.

Some of the recruiting methods of OSS in the early months of its existence seemed almost designed to benefit the Mafia. According to the OSS historian Harris Smith, Americans of Italian descent were recruited by OSS from such organizations as Murder Inc. and the Philadelphia Purple Gang. He added that 'their one desire was to get over to the old country and start throwing knives'. An OSS lieutenant and his sergeant, a former New York factory worker of Italian descent, were later tried by an Italian court *in absentia* for the murder of an OSS major and convicted.

Real though the differences were both politically and in the methods of supporting resistance, Anglo-American co-operation in the Italian theatre of war generally was predominantly good. Co-operation with Italian resistance was both closer and more productive than had commonly been expected. SOE alone sent in no fewer than forty-eight missions. Of them an Italian historian said at the conference at St Antony's College, Oxford, organized by Bill Deakin: 'To have a British mission was a matter of pride for the Partisans and was something more important even than weapons.'

During the second phase referred to in Holdsworth's report the Partisans were not fighting against a retreating and demoralized army but against one which maintained its cohesion and discipline admirably. Some of the fighting was in consequence extremely fierce. John Stevens, the former head of SOE's Greek section, was dropped into northern Italy in the middle of a battle. When the battle ended only 14 Partisans remained out of a force estimated to have numbered 4,000.

In the final phase no fewer than 100 towns were liberated by resistance forces before the Allies arrived. In Bologna, in particular, the street fighting was intense. In a country which until the middle of 1943 had been at war with the Allies these were formidable achievements. They also indicated where the sympathies of the great majority of the Italian people lay.

In the final stages of the war the Italian resistance forces had an important counter-sabotage role, particularly in preventing the destruction of the hydro-electric works in the north. Resistance forces were also, like the regular forces, faced from time to time with agonizing problems arising from the need to liberate great cities while minimizing damage to their architectural and other treasures. Nowhere was this problem more acutely felt than in Florence.

At the beginning of August 1944 an operational party of six from No. 1 Special force set off for Florence in an American scout car. It was led by a man whose recruitment into what eventually became SOE took place in Venezuela. This was Charles MacIntosh, who was born in Uruguay of New Zealand parents and was educated at the Dollar Academy in Scotland and Cambridge. He was working for Shell in Venezuela when war broke out and was interviewed in Maracaibo by a man who was ostensibly acting for the British War Office. In retrospect MacIntosh believed he was working for MI(R), for on reaching England he himself was immediately put through the standard officers' training course, followed by instruction in various SOE schools. As a member of any operational group which SOE might have to send into Spain MacIntosh was an obvious choice. His selection for No. 1 Special Force was largely a result of his chance meeting with Holdsworth in Gibraltar.

Florence formed an important part of the German defensive system known as the Arno line. When advancing Allied troops entered the southern suburbs of Florence on 3 August 1944 there seemed every likelihood that the Germans would defend the city street by street. They had already destroyed four bridges across the Arno and had prepared a fifth, the tenth-century Ponte Vecchio, for demolition. In the north of the city they had substantial forces, including elements of a parachute division, SS troops, artillery and tanks.

The immediate tasks of MacIntosh's unit were to enter the city, make contact with resistance groups, reconnoitre and report. Direct contact between the resistance in the area and No. 1 Special Force had been broken off since June, when a radio operating from the southern part of the city had been located by detector vans. The members of the group operating it had been killed, some before, some after capture.

On 4 August an Italian Partisan officer named Fisher, who was later to tell MacIntosh that he was of English descent, made his way into the forward headquarters of the German SS commander, which were the thirteenth-century Palazzo Vecchio. He did so with the help of an Italian policeman, who was himself a Partisan in disguise.

The Medicis had built their own secret passage from the Palazzo

Vecchio to the Palazzo Pitti on the other side of the river. It is approximately two miles long. Fisher knew of its existence and decided to make his way along it. Towards its end the passage joins, and indeed becomes, the upper floor of the Ponte Vecchio. At the southern end of the bridge Fisher found that nothing of the passage-way remained. He had had the foresight to bring a rope with him, and he used this to let himself down to ground level. He then crossed a minefield and returned to the Allied lines. There he met MacIntosh.

MacIntosh's immediate problem was whether to believe Fisher's colourful story. He decided to take a chance and accompanied him to the Ponte Vecchio. The end of the rope by which Fisher had lowered himself was still in position. Fisher climbed it; MacIntosh tied the end of the rope to the handle of a suitcase containing a telephone and three hundred yards of wire, and then joined Fisher.

For six days the telephone and wire brought by MacIntosh and the secret passage-way built by the Medicis provided the link between the Partisans who had been infiltrated into the German SS headquarters in the Palazzo Vecchio and MacIntosh's party. The radio of MacIntosh's unit was placed in a kind of no-man's land in another part of the city, where reception was better than in the southern half. Communication with the radio operator was maintained by the American scout car.

Telephone and radio traffic were almost continuous. Information was passed about enemy troop locations and movements and about roads and bridges mined or prepared for demolition. The German password of the day was regularly given to the Partisans, and a message was conveyed from the Bishop of Florence to the Supreme Allied Commander asking for food, water and medicines for the civil population. MacIntosh had a disturbing moment when he found Fisher's name spelt 'Fischer', but a detailed inspection showed that the telephone wire was in order, and he continued, rightly as it happened, to trust the man who had first brought him to the Medicis' secret passage.

On 11 August MacIntosh learnt that the Germans were withdrawing from some of their positions near the River Arno. Fearing this might lead to a premature Partisan rising, he made his way along the secret passage as far as the Palazzo Vecchio. He was not stopped on the way and was able to confer with the Partisans who had been operating the Palazzo Vecchio end of the telephone line. They took him to yet another palace, where he met members of the National Liberation Committee. By this time the Allied High Command was sufficiently impressed by the possibilities of Partisan action for MacIntosh to be instructed to report directly to the Allied corps commander. It was also apparent that one of the immediate reasons for the German withdrawal had been to avoid having to deal with partisan forces in the narrow streets of the oldest part of the city.

MacIntosh informed the National Liberation Committee that an Allied crossing of the River Arno in strength could not be expected immediately, even though three companies of the Indian Brigade did establish themselves on the northern side on 13 August. In the drawing-up of plans to carry out the directives of the Allied High Command MacIntosh found himself in almost complete agreement with the Partisan commanders, but the orders to limit objectives were not always carried out.

Street fighting continued for some two to three weeks. Casualties were fairly heavy, but most of the oldest part of Florence was spared. It was not until 1 September that tanks of the 6th Armoured Division passed through Florence unopposed and the city was finally liberated. Before that happened MacIntosh, whose relations with the Army commanders were of the best, had been ordered to assume responsibility for civil administration over the heads of the officers of the Allied Military Government who had been sent in for that purpose.

That Partisan forces played a major part in the street fighting which preceded the final liberation of Florence is beyond dispute. That they made a major contribution towards sparing much of Florence from destruction is at least arguable. If they did, posterity's debt to them is evident.

When the Italian campaign was over Holdsworth returned to England and was given a new assignment by Gubbins. This was to form some kind of post-war association of men and women who had served in SOE. Gubbins's immediate concern was to establish some method whereby people with particular qualifications could be swiftly contacted in the event of a new war or other emergency. He also hoped members of SOE could have opportunities to continue to meet socially.

Several decades passed during which there was, happily, no need to revive SOE in any operational capacity. A social club did, however, come into being. It was located in London near Harrods and was known as the Special Forces Club. Apart from a few plaques it is hitherto the only physical memorial erected in Britain to SOE.

Chapter 9

The Far East

In 1941, a few months before the Japanese launched their attack on Pearl Harbor, SOE established an instructional centre at Tanjong Balai some ten miles west of Singapore. It was known as No. 101 Special Training School. The commandant, J. M. L. (Jim) Gavin, was a regular officer in the Royal Engineers and one of the pioneers in the training of irregular troops. The second-in-command had already established something of a reputation as an explorer and mountaineer. This was Freddie Spencer Chapman, a man of unusually complex character.

Spencer Chapman's mother died shortly after he was born. His father, a solicitor, was declared bankrupt and emigrated to Canada. He himself was brought up, together with his brother, by an elderly, childless couple, a clergyman and his wife, in the Lake District. Much of Freddie Spencer Chapman's subsequent life consisted of a search for an ultimate security, which had to be reached by continually courting danger.

As a child he seems to have been fascinated by danger and much concerned with his own reactions to both danger and pain. His biographer, Ralph Barker, later described how his contemporaries at school were encouraged by Spencer Chapman to hit him on the head with a cricket bat to discover how much he could endure. The school was Sedbergh, which had an exceptionally rugged regime. Spencer Chapman added to the rigours by frequent and, where possible, dangerous excursions over the moors.

Spencer Chapman was tall, handsome and impressive in a manner which transcended mere good looks. Sir Olaf Caroe, the distinguished colonial governor, who was a profound admirer of Spencer Chapman's personality and achievements, described him as having the 'far-away gaze of the visionary always looking to a dream beyond the horizon'. He added that he was one of the few men of whom 'it is right and just to say that he was beautiful to behold'.

At Cambridge, where his academic record was undistinguished, Spencer Chapman became interested in exploration, and on coming down from the university he joined the British Arctic Air Route Expedition of 1930–1, which was led by Gino Watkins. It was during this expedition that Augustine Courtauld showed what could be achieved by self-discipline and good planning when spending four and a half months alone through an Arctic winter, forty-five days of which he was under snow. Spencer Chapman was in charge of the first exploratory journey across the Greenland ice-cap.

From Arctic exploration Spencer Chapman moved to Himalayan climbing. In 1937 he startled climbing circles by an individual and successful assault on Mount Chomolhari in a manner which some experts dismissed as foolhardy. It was a disappointment to him that he was not included in the Everest expedition of 1938 led by Harold Tilman.

He taught for a time at Gordonstoun School, where the future Duke of Edinburgh was among his pupils, and was commissioned as a territorial officer in the Seaforth Highlanders. In 1940 he took a course at the training school in Scotland where Jim Gavin was an instructor, and this led to his being chosen for a mission which was sent to Australia. Its purpose was to train Australian and New Zealand independent companies of the kind which Gubbins had commanded in Norway.

A training camp was established on Wilson's Promontory, the southern tip of Victoria. Here Spencer Chapman devised a programme which comprised, as he later described it, 'a new conception of fitness, knowledge of the night sky, what to wear, what to take and how to carry it, what to eat and how to cook it, how to live off the country, tracking, memorizing routes, and how to escape if caught by the enemy'. From Australia he was transferred in 1941 to the training school near Singapore.

SOE's prospects of being able to achieve anything of use on the Malayan peninsula in the event of a war between Britain and Japan were at first discouraging. The Army command evinced no interest in guerrilla warfare. A plan was put to it in August 1941 for establishing some kind of stay-behind organization. This would consist of European planters and policemen as well as Malays, Chinese and Indians. Its tasks would include sabotage, propaganda and attacks on Japanese lines of communication. The plan was considered at the highest level and turned down.

The principal objection raised was that the very existence of such a force would be taken to infer that a successful Japanese invasion was likely. Concern was felt at the prospect of giving arms to Chinese communists. It was also considered that a stay-behind organization would drain away too much European manpower and that Europeans would be too conspicuous to be able to operate successfully.

SOE could therefore do little at first other than train a few people whose services might be needed if war did break out in the Far East. Some of these were planters, among them a Frenchman named Pierre Boulle, who was later to spend nearly two and a half years in prison for undertaking a hazardous and clandestine mission in Vichy-controlled French Indochina, and who was later still to achieve fame as the author of *The Bridge over the River Kwai*. Students who attended subsequent courses included Chinese communists, some of whom showed an exceptional aptitude for the methods in which they were being trained.

When the invasion did take place and large areas of Malaya were quickly brought under Japanese control a few British officers were instructed to organize and lead reconnaissance and operational parties behind the enemy lines. One of these was Spencer Chapman, who soon came to the conclusion that small parties, provided they included at least one man who knew the territory well, could inflict appreciable damage on the enemy lines of communication.

This was a shrewd deduction. Nearly three-quarters of Malaya is covered by the high, continuous forest known as rain forest or, more popularly, jungle. There was no European tradition of conducting guerrilla warfare in this territory, and Spencer Chapman was himself fairly new to it. He had, however, given thought to the whole problem of survival in the jungle, and at No. 101 Special Training School a list had been drawn up of suitable supplies for units operating behind the enemy lines. It included food for three months, seeds and gardening and forestry tools. There can surely have been no previous military manual which listed seeds and gardening tools among the stores prescribed for lightly armed combat troops.

Spencer Chapman also made his own assessment of the Japanese soldiers. The belief was soon to grow up, fostered by the extraordinary speed of the Japanese advances, that in jungle warfare Japanese troops were somehow almost invincible. Spencer Chapman came to the conclusion that the enemy he would have to deal with consisted for the most part of good second-class troops, who were well trained but poorly equipped.

When it was agreed that he should himself lead an operational party Spencer Chapman decided that its discipline and organization were to be those of a polar or climbing expedition. To accompany him he chose two planters named Harvey and Vanrenan and a Chinese radio operator named Ah Sing. He had a prejudice, which was not altogether reasonable, against the use of regular soldiers for irregular warfare, but he did include one of them in his party. This was John Sartin, a Sapper, who had, he considered, acquired sufficient irregular qualities through being an instructor for five months at No. 101 Special Training School.

Spencer Chapman's party was successfully infiltrated and began a series of attacks on enemy communications. For explosives they used gelignite obtained from tin mines. To make themselves less conspicuous the British members of the party dressed as Tamils and darkened their faces with a mixture of lamp black, iodine, potassium permanganate and coffee. So far as they were aware they were never recognized as Europeans.

Spencer Chapman recorded the destruction or near-destruction of 7 trains, 15 bridges and 40 motor vehicles and the killing of some hundreds of Japanese during a short period of action, of which he afterwards wrote: 'We all agreed that the last fortnight had been the most marvellous time of our lives – far more exciting and satisfactory than hunting or big-game shooting.' As a contribution towards the slowing-down of the enemy advance the effect of all this was minimal, but at least it had been proved that small bodies of irregular troops could operate successfully in the jungle.

His role as a leader of an operational party in action was not one which Spencer Chapman was able to play for long. Japanese reprisals against the local population were thought to be too severe to justify continued sabotage of railway lines, and when the other members of his party were taken prisoner Spencer Chapman was on his own. What followed until he re-established contact with SOE towards the end of 1943 was only marginally related to the conduct of the war. But it was to provide, like the survival of Jan Baalsrud in Norway, new evidence of what the human body can be prevailed upon by the human spirit to endure.

Following an attack of pneumonia in the jungle Spencer Chapman was unconscious for seventeen days. Later he contracted blackwater fever and two men had to hold him down to counteract the violence of the rigors which he could not control. The malaria from which he suffered was virtually chronic, and he was also afflicted by tick-typhus. At one stage he marched for six days without food. Jungle conditions in some places were such that it took him twelve days' hard marching to cover ten miles. In the course of his service in Malaya he was twice wounded, was captured, and escaped.

Yet he survived. So too did most of the notes and diaries which he kept. His keeping of diaries was of course a breach of security regulations, mitigated only slightly by his practice of writing some of his notes in Eskimo in order to baffle the Japanese if he should be captured. Fortunately he disregarded the regulations and the record remains.

Much of the thought which Spencer Chapman gave to the problems of survival in Malaya was epitomized in the inspired phrase which he used for the title of his book, *The Jungle is Neutral*. Most soldiers, he learnt, who were cut off from their units and left in the jungle, expected to be dead within a few weeks and were. Yet survival was possible. The jungle did not, as was sometimes supposed, offer luscious fruits for the taking, but it did provide plenty of fresh water and unlimited cover. The cover was available to both friend and foe, and it was in this that the jungle's neutrality consisted.

Spencer Chapman survived through his own willpower and also because of the presence of Chinese communist guerrillas. Shortly after the Japanese invasion the Malayan Communist party had offered in discussions with the colonial government to raise a military force to fight the Japanese. The offer was at first refused, but was later partially adopted. Those who enrolled were nearly all Chinese, who constituted nearly 40 per cent of the population of the Federated Malay States.

The guerrilla forces which continued to fight after the Japanese had occupied Malaya were also nearly all Chinese, and most of them were controlled by the Communist party. They were armed at first largely with weapons which the retreating British forces abandoned.

In July 1942 in the course of his wanderings Spencer Chapman reached one of the communist guerrilla camps and stayed there for some months. He was understandably regarded with suspicion and was assumed to be a spy left behind by the colonial government to report on the doings of the Malayan Communist party. His efforts to learn Mandarin Chinese were frustrated by an ingenious system whereby he was taught a different Chinese dialect every day. The guerrillas also accepted personal responsibility for his safety, thereby effectively impeding his movements. Nevertheless they kept him and fed him, although he could bring them no promises of support from outside and had no money with which to pay.

In Johore Spencer Chapman came across another type of Chinese encampment. The occupants of this were unashamedly bandits. He found them cheerful and likeable and free from the austerity and earnestness which characterized the communist guerilla camps, but he also discovered that nearly half of them were heavy opium smokers and all of them were undisciplined.

The communist guerrillas spent much of their time in political speech-making and singing. The political leader in any group outranked the military commander, and the second most important figure was likely to be the chief teacher-propagandist. Nevertheless these guerrillas were disciplined forces, and only in them was to be found any prospect of effective resistance to the Japanese.

It was primarily in order to make contact with these forces that SOE sent in its first missions when it was once again able to operate in Malaya. The names of the leaders of the first two missions were John Davis and Richard Broome. Though supplying and supporting the Chinese guerrillas was to be their principal task, they were also instructed to try to find two Englishmen who were thought to be still alive in Malaya. One was an ethnologist named Pat Noone, who had made a prolonged study of the Senoi, a somewhat primitive tribe of Australoid type living in Malaya and sometimes referred to as the Sakai. The other was Spencer Chapman.

John Davis, a shortish man of athletic build with lively eyes and a quick mind, joined the police service in the Federated Malay States shortly after leaving Tonbridge School. He had been ten years in the police, including two spent in China in order to learn Chinese, when Japan entered the war in December 1941. He had a good knowledge of various parts of Malaya, which he had acquired not only from his official duties, for he tended to shun the conventional club life of the expatriate British and to spend his leaves exploring the interior of the country.

Richard Broome came to Malaya in the Colonial Service soon after coming down from Cambridge. He too was a capable Chinese speaker. He had a lean body, a caustic wit and an original and inventive mind. He was later to relieve the tedium of a Chinese communist guerrilla camp by composing a Gilbert-and-Sullivan-type operetta about camp life, making up crosswords and carving a set of chess men out of bamboo.

Late in 1941 Broome was approached in Singapore by Basil Goodfellow, a former employee of Imperial Chemical Industries, who also held the post of honorary secretary of the Alpine Club, and asked whether he would like to take service with SOE. Shortly before this Broome had been asked to join SIS, but he chose SOE in preference because he thought the prospect of the work it offered more exciting. Broome and Davis were close friends, Davis having been best man at Broome's wedding, and Broome suggested to Goodfellow that Davis should be enrolled in SOE too. This was done.

From early January to early February 1942 Davis and Broome were engaged in placing parties of Chinese, some of whom had recently been released from internment by the British, in different parts of Malaya. As the primary task of SOE was still considered to be sabotage, the Chinese parties were given plenty of explosives and a limited number of small arms. Later experience was to show that arms would have been much more useful than explosives.

Between them Davis and Broome had successfully infiltrated between 300 and 400 Chinese by the time Singapore was invested and the mainland cut off. They made their way to Sumatra with the intention of continuing to supply their Chinese parties by junk from the Sumatran coast, but in the meantime Singapore surrendered.

The man in charge of irregular operations in the area at the time was a colonel in the Royal Marines named Alan Warren. He went to Sumatra with Davis and Broome and when Sumatra also fell to the Japanese he ordered some twenty officers and others, including Broome, who was put in charge, and Davis, to try to make their way to India in a Sumatran *prow*. Warren himself took charge of the remnant of British troops and was later captured by the Japanese.

The *prow* was a ten-ton vessel some forty feet in length. Broome and his party brought her successfully under sail to Ceylon between the south-west and north-east monsoons. Among those who made the journey was Broome's former houseboy, Loo Ngiap Soon. He was later to be trained as a radio operator and parachuted back into Malaya.

When they reached India Davis and Broome re-established contact with Basil Goodfellow and almost immediately began planning their return to Malaya. Their principal requirements were now suitable Chinese recruits to accompany them on their missions and adequate transport.

The problem of finding recruits was largely solved by the arrival in India of Lim Bo Seng, a Straits Chinese who had been educated at Hong Kong University and who came from an influential family of manufacturers. Lim Bo Seng was strongly anti-Japanese – he was later to be captured by the Japanese in Malaya and died in captivity – and had excellent contacts with the government of General Chiang Kai Shek. These he used to recruit Straits Chinese for SOE's purposes. Davis and Broome both had an immediate *rapport* with Lim Bo Seng and the three became in effect joint chief planners under Goodfellow's general guidance. (It was characteristic of the easy relationship between Davis and Broome that, whereas Broome had been in charge of the party which escaped from Sumatra to Ceylon, it was accepted by both of them that Davis would be in operational command when they returned to Malaya.)

No Liberator aircraft were available to SOE in the Far East before 1944. Until then the only acceptable method of bringing an operational party from Ceylon to Malaya was by submarine. The only submarines which could be spared were provided by the Royal Netherlands Navy.

It was therefore by submarine that in May 1943 Davis and five Chinese reached the Malacca Straits. As SOE had no radio link with Malaya there was no reception party to meet them where they landed. Davis had been out of the country for well over a year and could only guess at how he would be received. Japanese surveillance of the coastal areas was strict. Later, when a representative of the Malayan Communist party came out for a meeting aboard a junk with an SOE officer named Claude Fenner, he deemed it necessary to conceal information which he had brought with him in a tube of toothpaste. He returned with messages hidden in the brain cavity of a dried fish.

Nevertheless Davis's party successfully made its way into the interior and established contact with Chinese guerrilla forces. Davis's mission was at first exploratory, and before long he came out to report, having a rendezvous with Broome aboard a submarine, which brought them back to India. In July 1943 Davis returned to Malaya. He was now furnished with a letter accrediting him as the chief representative in the country of Mountbatten as Supreme Allied Commander in South-East Asia.

Broome joined Davis in Malaya in September. Before long they made contact with some of the Chinese whom they had infiltrated eighteen months earlier and who now led them to the central, mountain region, where a camp was established. On Christmas Day 1943 Davis and Broome were suddenly visited in the camp by Freddie Spencer Chapman. He looked fitter than they had expected him to, and they learnt that there was at least one other white-skinned officer who had survived in the jungle. This was Frank Quayle, a New Zealand mining engineer.

Spencer Chapman was older than Davis, and when they had last met Spencer Chapman had been the senior officer. He now accepted with good grace Davis's position as the officer in command. Nor did he envy Davis his task, which was to become increasingly political.

Davis, who was later to describe Spencer Chapman as the greatest adventurer of his generation, quickly realized that he needed some form of activity which would take him away from the monotony of camp life. A solution was found when they agreed that he should set off on a search for the ethnologist, Pat Noone, a mission which might be said to have a humanitarian aim but was unlikely to be of much military value.

It was later learnt that Noone was still alive when Spencer Chapman went to look for him, but before long he was killed by a member of the tribe whose habits he was studying and one of whom he had married. It was during his search for Noone that Spencer Chapman was captured by the Japanese.

The officer commanding the troops who made the arrest, on learning that Spencer Chapman held the rank of major, jumped to attention and saluted. He then asked him if he knew a Colonel Chapman, whom he described as the head of all the communists. Spencer Chapman replied that that was his elder brother. The Japanese guards were too polite even to tie Spencer Chapman's hands, and he had little difficulty in escaping.

The task of Davis and Broome was now to co-ordinate, so far as possible, Chinese guerrilla activity with the aims of the Allied High Command and, in particular, to ensure maximum disruption of Japanese communications when the time came for an Allied invasion.

They had some bad setbacks in March 1944, when a number of Chinese agents with whom they were in communication were arrested. As a result of a Japanese attack, in which they lost much of their equipment, they were out of radio contact with SOE for months. When contact was re-established in December, following the production of a new and somewhat primitive generator, SOE in Ceylon doubted whether Davis and Broome were still at liberty and indicated this through a prearranged signal. Davis's radio operator repeated the identification checks and added a message from Davis, which read: 'If you don't believe us now, you bastards, come and pedal this bloody machine yourselves.' The phraseology of the message was accepted as evidence of its authenticity.

By March 1945 negotiations between Davis and his mission and the Chinese guerrilla leaders had reached a point at which a full-scale conference could be held. At this agreement was reached on methods of military co-operation. The Chinese accepted strategic control for the remainder of the war and the subsequent period of military rule. For their part they asked principally for financial support to supplement the money which they extracted locally for the maintenance of the guerrilla forces.

With the advent of Liberator aircraft the guerrillas began to receive more and more arms. They became an increasingly effective force and by their very presence tied down an appreciable number of Japanese second-line troops. This, however, was to be the extent of their contribution to the defeat of the enemy. The Allied invasion for which they were preparing never took place, for the dropping of the atom bombs brought the war to an end before any regular Allied troops reached Malayan territory.

Some of the arms supplied by SOE were certainly used by communist Chinese in their prolonged fighting against the British after the war, in the course of which the British High Commissioner, Sir Henry

Gurney, was ambushed and killed. Nevertheless Davis, whose first-hand experience included being the chief Allied representative with the guerrillas at the time of the Japanese surrender, was convinced then, and remained convinced later, of the beneficial effects on the immediate post-war settlement of the relationship established between the guerrilla leaders and members of the SOE missions. Spencer Chapman was of the same opinion. So was Broome.

When he returned to Malaya after a short spell at home Broome received a welcome which he described as 'rapturous'. No such welcome awaited most of the Dutch when they returned to take control of their colonies. The contrast between the reception which the British and the Dutch had in South-East Asia at the end of the war cannot be attributed wholly, or even largely, to the presence of a few British missions during and immediately after the fighting. But the two were not unrelated.

After the war Davis and Broome remained in service in Malaya. Spencer Chapman had a more varied and a more nomadic life. With the publication of *The Jungle is Neutral* he became a famous figure, and he wrote much and lectured widely. Yet he continued to vacillate between his search for security and the lure of adventure.

Security beckoned in the form of headmasterships, those who offered him the appointments having to balance his personal distinction and reputation against his third-class honours degree and his innate restlessness. Among the headmasterships which he held for a time were those of a school near Kiel for the children of officials in the military government of Germany and of St Andrew's College in Grahamstown, South Africa. The urge to travel asserted itself when at the age of forty-five he set off with his wife and three children under the age of five to spend six months on the African continent in a caravan.

In December 1963 Spencer Chapman was made the subject of the television programme, *This is Your Life*. The presenter of the programme, Eamonn Andrews, announced that it had not been found possible to condense the story of Spencer Chapman's life into the normal half-hour programme and that it would be spread over two half-hours. He added that this had happened only once before in nine years.

Of the many posts which Spencer Chapman filled after the war the one which perhaps gave him the greatest satisfaction was that of warden of a Pestalozzi Village for war orphans of different nations. Here, as he told his wife, he found it easy to establish a *rapport* with the children largely because of memories of his own deprived childhood.

Spencer Chapman's physical and mental condition deteriorated steadily. Sometimes during the caravanning period in Africa he would wake in the middle of the night screaming. Latterly, in the words of his· wife, the spring went out of his step. He became obsessed by a belief that he faced a complete breakdown in health, and on 7 August 1971, at the age of sixty-four, he put the barrel of a gun to his head and committed suicide.

A medical report stated that 'this ex-officer's very sound mental make-up suffered as a result of his privations and his suffering was a prime cause leading to his death'. This and the strenuous exertions of Colin Gubbins ensured that he was deemed to have been a war casualty and that his widow was treated accordingly.

Unlike Malaya, where preparations were made for an invasion which never happened, Burma was reoccupied by the British some three years after their expulsion. It was also the scene of one of the largest irregular operations in the area of the South-East Asia Command. This operation, in which SOE was involved from the outset, was made possible by the peculiar relationship which existed between the British and one of the hill peoples of Burma, the Karens.

The Karens, who are thought to have migrated from eastern Tibet and southern China, have retained their racial identity and language. They have, or had, relatively little in common with the Burmese, who tended to describe them contemptuously as wild men. They actively helped the British in their Burmese campaigns in 1826 and 1852, and a considerable number of them, perhaps 15 to 20 per cent, embraced the Christian faith. This was largely brought about by American Baptist missionaries but was also influenced by a Karen legend that their golden book would one day be returned to them by a white man. Before the Second World War Karens provided about half the recruits for the Burma Rifles. The British whom they encountered at that time were nearly all foresters or officials, missionaries or soldiers.

The Englishman who became most closely identified with the Karens in the Second World War was an officer in the Burma Rifles named Hugh Seagrim. The son of a Norfolk clergyman, Seagrim came from a family with a strong military tradition. One of his brothers was to win the VC in the Western Desert. He himself had the reputation among his fellow regular officers before the war of being likeable, slightly eccentric and with an unusually enquiring mind. He was an impressive figure physically, being 6 feet 4 inches in height.

Seagrim formulated his own plans for raising guerrilla forces among the hill peoples in Burma, and shortly after war with Japan broke out he came into contact with SOE's Far East Mission. The head of this mission at the time, Val St John Killery, was one of the numerous employees of Imperial Chemical Industries to serve in SOE. Most of the members of the mission had been withdrawn from Singapore to Burma and would later have to continue their retreat to India.

With one of the members of the mission named Ronald Heath, Seagrim drove to Papun in Karen territory. They quickly enrolled some 200 Karen volunteers, to whom they distributed firearms, most of which had been captured from the Italians in North Africa. This guerrilla group and others delayed the Japanese advance slightly, but the scale of their operations was at this stage relatively small. As the Japanese advance continued Seagrim made it clear that he intended to remain with the Karens, although he had no radio contact with the outside world.

For nearly three years Seagrim continued to live in Karen huts. He sent out messages, which he hoped would reach India, stating that whenever he saw an Allied aircraft near Pyagawpu, which was his main base, he would lay out the letters KV to indicate the presence of Karen volunteers. But for months no Allied aircraft came within sight. He drew up a secret register of Karen volunteers and made preliminary plans for their employment when Allied forces returned.

Another European had remained with the Karens. This was a French missionary named Father Calmon. His presence and that of Seagrim caused the Japanese some concern. A report received by the Japanese-controlled Burmese administration stated that the Karens hoped that the British would return before long and were being fortified in this hope by the presence among them of an English captain and a Roman Catholic priest. Seagrim also learnt that some of the Japanese believed there were 2,000 British troops concealed in the hills.

While sharing the life of the Karens Seagrim became more and more deeply imbued with his Christian faith. He was said to have read the Bible through from beginning to end twelve times. Every evening he and his companions held prayer meetings in English and Burmese. These were followed by religious discussions. His intention, when the war ended, was, as he told a number of his associates, to leave the Army and spend the rest of his life as a missionary in Karen territory. He seems also to have been continually of good cheer. His biographer, Ian Morrison, later spoke to a number of Karens who had known Seagrim during the war. The adjective which some of them chose for describing him was 'smiley-faced'.

During most of 1942 nobody in India knew whether Seagrim was dead or alive. People with an understanding of Burma believed, however, that he could rely absolutely on the loyalty of the Karens. This belief was to be amply vindicated.

Early in 1943 SOE in India was able to begin implementing its plans for re-establishing contact with whatever resistance forces there might be in Burma. Two British officers, Jimmy Nimmo and Eric McCrindle, were chosen to be parachuted in. The two men were close friends. Both were Scots, and both, on coming down from Cambridge, had joined the timber firm of Magregor & Co.

SOE had little information about conditions in Burma. It was not known whether there was any effective resistance or whether Europeans had any chance of remaining at liberty for long. It was therefore decided that the first mission should be led by a Karen subaltern named Ba Gyaw, who would be dropped with three other Karens. Their task would be purely reconnaissance, and they would not take with them anything as incriminating as a radio.

If they decided that more men and supplies should be sent in they were to lay out agreed ground signals. The next drop would bring a radio operator and set, and after that missions led respectively by Nimmo and McCrindle would follow. If Seagrim was found to be alive all those sent in were to place themselves under his command.

On the night of 18 February 1943 Ba Gyaw and his three companions were successfully dropped. The flight was a difficult one into a narrow valley, and several attempts to drop other parties failed, usually because mist prevented the ground signals from being seen. Month after month during the full-moon period flights continued. Nimmo went as a passenger on several of them, and he finally persuaded SOE to dispense with one of the preliminary missions and to allow him to drop with five Karens, including a radio operator, at the first opportunity.

On the night of 12 October Nimmo and his party were parachuted in. They soon found both Ba Gyaw and Seagrim, and within three days the first radio link between Burma and SOE in India was established and Seagrim was again able to communicate with the world outside.

He warned SOE of the dangers of precipitating a premature rising and explained in some detail how he wanted the prospective guerrilla forces to be armed: 8,000 weapons should be dropped to British missions established in the hills two months before the British invasion and 12,000 more to arm ex-soldiers when the offensive began.

One of the first consequences of establishing radio contact was that the RAF, acting on information received, was able to bomb Japanese airfields with some accuracy. In December McCrindle was dropped with four more Karens and more radio equipment, and Seagrim felt himself in a position to call a meeting of his closest followers, and of those who had been parachuted in to him, to discuss operational plans. It was an unusual kind of meeting of resistance forces. It began with a religious service in Karen and ended with three Karen parachutists singing *Rock of Ages* in harmony, followed by the Lord's Prayer.

The Japanese became aware before long that there were British parachutists in the hills, and they made determined efforts to locate them. These included the arrest and torture of individual Karens and the burning of villages. One ex-soldier in the Burma Rifles named Maung Wah was tortured for three days and gave nothing away. He was then told that he must go up to the hills and that if at the end of a week he had not returned with full details of Seagrim's whereabouts reprisals would be taken against his family.

Maung Wah came to Seagrim and asked to be supplied with arms. Although he had warned SOE of the dangers of sending in arms prematurely, Seagrim, who had of course no knowledge of when the invasion of Burma would take place, asked by radio whether the time had or had not come for arms to be dropped. On learning that he could expect nothing immediately he advised Maung Wah to return to the Japanese and tell them all he knew. He himself then moved northwards.

McCrindle's whereabouts was discovered by the Japanese. A Japanese force closed in on him and he was killed in action. Not long afterwards Nimmo too was surrounded and killed. Reprisals against Karen villages became even fiercer, and Seagrim decided that there was now only one course for him to take. This was to give himself up to prevent further slaughter.

In March 1944 therefore he called on the local Japanese commander, Captain Inoue, said that he himself was responsible for all that had happened in the hills, and asked him to treat the Karens generously. Inoue, who later described Seagrim as 'a gentleman, a man of high character', sent him to Rangoon, where he was held in prison.

In prison Seagrim made a deep impression on those who met him. He was known to some of the Japanese prison staff as 'Big Master'. A fellow prisoner, Flight-Lieutenant Arthur Sharpe, who had been shot down over Burma, said of him: 'I believe him to be the finest gentleman I have ever met. He had a complete disregard for his own life and the greatest concern for the Karens.' It is not known for certain whether Seagrim was tortured, but others in the prison were. Yet Seagrim was able to lead his fellow-prisoners in praying for their Japanese guards with the words: 'Father, forgive them, for they know not what they do.'

Seagrim was killed by a Japanese firing squad. The Japanese attempts to suppress the Karen resistance movement were for a time successful. Yet within a year of Seagrim's death a Karen guerrilla army was in effective and widespread action.

During and immediately before the British Army's thousand-mile retreat through Burma early in 1942 various efforts were made, most of them hurriedly, to create some kind of guerrilla force or stay-behind organization. For this purpose a body known as V Force was brought into being by the Army command. It included several colonial administrators, and its immediate task was to harass the enemy's lines of communication.

The very speed of the retreat prevented V Force from achieving much in its original role, but it was kept in being for purposes of military intelligence, small units being sent behind the enemy lines to observe and report. One of its officers, Anthony Irwin, who had served with Commandos and glider-borne troops and was himself the son of a general, described the *esprit de corps* of V Force as better than that of any other fighting force he had known.

When the British Fourteenth Army returned to Burma units of V Force, equipped with small portable radios, acted as advance patrols. Responsibility for organizing resistance and guerrilla forces now rested entirely with SOE or, as it was known in the area of the South-East Asia Command, Force 136, to which a number of V Force officers were transferred. One of these, John Gebhard, who later took his mother's name of Bowen, was to be parachuted in to Karen territory and to describe in a book entitled *Undercover in the Jungle* how the seeds sown by Seagrim over nearly three years came to fruit in 1945.

The best known figure of all those engaged in stay-behind missions in Burma was a member of SOE named J. H. Williams. He had been in the Camel Corps in the First World War and later spent twenty-five years living with elephants. He was generally known by the title he gave to his autobiographical work, *Elephant Bill*.

Williams learnt from first-hand experience that the teak industry provided a good training ground for service in SOE. Soon after his appointment as assistant manager for a teak firm in Burma he found himself responsible for an area larger than most English counties. He also learnt that continuing to work while suffering from malaria was an accepted part of his duties. In 1931 he was chosen to explore the forests of the North Andaman Islands to discover whether they were suitable territory for elephants. The favourable report he submitted was the outcome of spending three days and three nights with a female elephant and collecting a specimen of every plant she ate.

Williams was appointed Elephant Adviser to the Fourteenth Army. In this capacity he received permission to remain behind the Japanese lines with a South African named Harold Browne. In the course of their journeyings Williams and Browne brought out to Assam, through jungle country and over heights as great as those traversed by Hannibal when crossing the Alps, a party consisting of 45 elephants, 40 armed Karens, 90 elephant riders and attendants, and 64 refugee women and children.

Not the least of Williams's contributions was preventing elephants from falling into the hands of the Japanese. As elephants were used for laying causeways, preparing airfields and hauling back to pathways vehicles which would otherwise have had to be abandoned, their military as well as their commercial value was considerable.

The task of saving the elephants was for Williams a naturally congenial one, as his book, *Elephant Bill*, an exceptionally attractive contribution to the study of human–elephant relations, indicates. In this he wrote: 'There is no more lovely sight than to see a fourteen-year-old boy riding a newly trained calf elephant of six. The understanding between them is only equalled by that of a child with a puppy, but the Burmese boy is not so cruel to his elephant as most children are with puppies.' He also wrote that living for twenty-five years with 'the most magnificent of all animals' had given him a deep reverence for the jungle and all jungle creatures.

Burma was also the scene of operations which, in the words of the OSS historian, R. Harris Smith, 'provided a model for Allied harmony in clandestine services'. The OSS unit on the Burma front was known as 101 Detachment. Its commander during much of the war, Colonel William R. Peers, wrote of it: 'Such a unit had never been organized within American history. There was nobody trained, qualified or, for that matter, anybody who knew much about carrying on irregular warfare.'

The first commander of the detachment, Carl Eifler, had been Deputy Director of Customs in Honolulu and had lived for a time among Chinese and Japanese. Only two other members of the detachment had been in the Far East before. Yet they learnt with exemplary speed, largely because they were wise enough to accept advice from people with long experience.

While still in their training camp in Maryland they received instruction from Donald Fairbairn, the former chief of police in Shanghai, who with Bill Sykes developed SOE's standard methods of unarmed combat and silent killing. When they reached India Peers was surprised to find that there seemed to be no SOE report or file considered too secret for his eyes. In order to learn about local conditions members of 101 Detachment lived for a time among British tea-planters in Assam. They employed a number of Anglo-Burmese agents, some of whom were infiltrated four or more times. In the end, after starting in almost total innocence, 101 Detachment achieved the considerable distinction of helping to arm, and fighting in association with, some 9,000 guerrilla troops in the hills of Burma.

Those whom OSS armed were mostly Kachins, another of the hill peoples who before the war provided much of the manpower of the Burma Rifles. SOE continued to expend most of its efforts on arming the Karens, and early in 1945 contact, which had been broken off after the loss of the parachutists sent to Seagrim, was re-established.

The first British officer dropped into the Karen hills in 1945, Major R. G. Turrall, was a mining engineer, who had won the MC in the First World War and had spent a number of years in Southern Africa. Some of those who followed had served with SOE in Greece or the French *maquis*; others, like Gebhard, had been transferred from V Force. One of those dropped, Bill Nimmo, was the brother of the man who had already been killed in Karen territory.

Quantities of arms were also dropped, and it was decided to send in two officers with the rank of lieutenant-colonel named Peacock and Tulloch, who were soon in command of substantial forces. The Commander-in-Chief of the Fourteenth Army, General Slim, had set himself the target of capturing Rangoon before the May monsoon. To achieve this he had to make a rapid advance through Burma with the danger always present that the Japanese would sever his lines of communication.

It was to prevent this from happening that the Karens were mainly deployed, and for one important week they successfully held the Japanese back. It was an exploit which Gubbins, in a foreward to a book on Norwegian resistance, picked out as one of the outstanding achievements of SOE. 'The Karen army', he wrote, 'of 16,000 men behind the enemy lines held up a whole Japanese division at a vital moment. . . . In these operations they killed 16,000 Japanese.'

One of the SOE officers who had served with the French *maquis* and was parachuted in to the Karens was named Duncan Guthrie. Before the war he had been an actor, a journalist and a playwright. Guthrie broke his ankle when landing and was immobilized for weeks. He was 200 miles behind the Japanese lines and became wholly dependent on the Karens. So too did two other injured men, an English sergeant and a Karen rifleman, who were hidden with him in a forest.

Japanese patrols soon began searching for the British parachutists. They threatened to burn every village whose inhabitants refused to say where the British were. Nobody betrayed them, and day after day Karens secretly brought food to them in the forest, where they lay on sheets made of parachute silk with orchids overhead.

Guthrie's foot did not heal properly, but he was able after a time to hobble with the help of a long bamboo stick, to ride on an elephant, to receive arms drops, and to train Karens in the use of arms and explosives. By then he had grown a large spade-shaped beard, and John (Gebhard) Bowen, on meeting him in the Karen hills, thought he looked like Robinson Crusoe. Karens commented that Guthrie was beginning to resemble Seagrim and treated him with evident respect.

Guthrie kept a diary which was published after the war. At one point he wrote: 'I do not think there is a single man in all the mountains of Karenni who would not do everything in his power to help the British.' Later, of his own treatment by the Karens, he added: 'I knew that there was charity of this order in the world. But I did not ever expect to meet it myself.'

In a broadcast which he made after the war Guthrie stated that the loyalty of the Karens towards the British could not be surpassed 'even between Englishmen born and bred in England'. He added: 'It takes two to make a loyalty. On the one side it is due to men like Seagrim; on the other to the character of the Karen people.'

A number of Karens told Seagrim that they hoped, when the war was over, to have their own state, of which he would be the first governor. Other SOE officers learnt too of the Karens' wish to have their own country, which would be independent of the Burmese and closely associated with the British. It was a wish which was not, of course, to be fulfilled. The Karens became part of the independent country of Burma; they staged a long and damaging rebellion; and they had to accept no more than a limited degree of autonomy.

The head of Force 136 for most of the war, Colin Mackenzie, had won the Chancellor's Medal for English verse at Cambridge and gained a first-class honours degree in economics. He lost a leg in the First World War and was later employed by J. & P. Coats, for whom he travelled widely. In his capacity as head of SOE in South-East Asia he had the wisdom to remain a civilian and was thereby able to exercise an authority and command a respect which might not have been granted to him in any service rank which he might have held. Mackenzie's second-in-command, Gavin Stewart, had a background of an Eton education and the family engineering firm of Stewart & Lloyd. Before the Second World War he had served at sea and engaged in a variety of occupations, including cattle-droving and olive-farming.

As the site of their first headquarters Mackenzie and Stewart decided against Delhi and chose Meerut instead. Later Force 136 acquired bases in both Calcutta and Ceylon. Its principal areas of operation were Malaya, Siam and Burma, but its activities extended to a number of other territories, including the Andaman Islands, where a former district superintendent of police named Denis McCarthy was successfully infiltrated with an operational party.

In 1942 it became known that a radio transmitter was providing German U-boats in the Indian Ocean with important information about Allied shipping. The transmitter was located aboard a German ship, *Ehrenfels*, in the harbour of Marmagoa in the Portuguese colony of Goa.

As Goa was neutral territory, an officer of the Royal Navy approached Lewis Pugh, a member of Force 136, who had served as a regular officer in the Royal Horse Artillery and later in the Special Branch of the Bengal police, and asked whether he could to anything to help. A conference was held in Force 136's offices in Meerut attended by, among others, Mackenzie, Stewart and Pugh. There it was decided that an attempt must be made to bribe the German captain of the *Ehrenfels* to desert. The attempt failed.

Stewart and Pugh then made their way to Goa, ostensibly as representatives of a trading company, kidnapped the German radio operator and his wife, and brought them to India. Shortly afterwards the transmissions began again, and it was clear that a new operator had been found.

Pugh therefore devised a more elaborate plan. This called for the co-operation of reserve officers in the Calcutta Light Horse, a body which members of the British business community in Calcutta traditionally joined, not in search of martial glory, but because of the social amenities offered. What followed has been vividly described in James Leasor's *Boarding Party. The Last Action of the Calcutta Light Horse*.

A number of the officers underwent secret training, and Pugh set about finding a vessel which could be made available to transport them to Goa. In the end he was given the use of a hopper barge, which had been built in 1912 and had a maximum speed of less than nine knots. In this Stewart, Pugh and a selected group from the Calcutta Light Horse were brought to Goa from Madras.

Meanwhile another Calcutta Light Horse member of the operational party named Jock Cartwright had been sent to Goa overland. His task was to ensure that as few men as possible would be aboard the *Ehrenfels* on the night chosen for the assault.

Cartwright did his job skilfully. He bribed a brothel-keeper in Goa to offer free services on that particular night to seamen of all nations. He then bribed a Goanese official to give a party and invite all officers connected with the port or who had ships in the harbour. When the party ended there were no taxis available to take the officers back to their ships.

Members of the operational group had been carefully rehearsed in their cover-stories. If their attack on the *Ehrenfels* failed they were all to say they had been enjoying a celebration party when the idea had suddenly been put forward that they should attack a German ship for the fun of it. Suitable apologies could then be made to the Portuguese authorities.

In fact the cover-story was not needed. The boarding party met with little opposition, and the *Ehrenfels*'s radio transmitter, which was the principal target, was quickly put out of action. More destruction was to follow.

In addition to the *Ehrenfels* there were two German ships and one Italian ship in Marmagoa harbour. Their crews, like that of the *Ehrenfels*, had been instructed to prepare for a possible attack by the Royal Navy, and their orders were to scuttle their ships rather than allow them to be captured. When the boarding party seized control of the *Ehrenfels* it was assumed that this was the beginning of the expected attack and the order to scuttle the ships was carried out.

Not only was the toll of destruction four enemy ships, but Allied losses at sea suddenly and sharply declined. The attack on the *Ehrenfels* took place in the middle of March 1943. Allied shipping losses in the Indian Ocean in the second half of the month, expressed in tons, were less than one twentieth of those recorded in the first half.

The raid in Goa had much in common with the raid led by Gus March-Phillipps in Fernando Po, although Cartwright's introduction of the brothel-keeper added a new feature. The total tonnage of enemy ships destroyed or captured through the undercover efforts of SOE in neutral ports was in fact appreciable, but for diplomatic reasons the facts could not be admitted at the time. Indeed after the Goa raid the story was successfuly planted that the scuttlings had followed disagreements among the crews about whether or not to make a dash for Singapore. There were also hints of differences between Nazis and anti-Nazis.

One member of SOE who organized the capture of a vessel off the African coast almost entirely on his own initiative was the son of an Afrikaner father, who decided he did not want to live in South Africa under British rule and chose to live in Latvia instead, and of a half-Lett, half-German mother. This was Leonard Manderstam, a man of exceptionally lively and inventive mind, whose profession was that of civil engineer.

While working for SOE in Angola Manderstam bribed the captain of a ship controlled by the Vichy government to surrender her to the Royal Navy. He made himself personally responsible for the £10,000 which had to be borrowed locally to pay the bribe and arranged for payment to be made by complex routes and in small denominations. The official citation which led to the award of the MBE to Manderstam for this exploit included the phrase 'sheer effrontery'.

The status of SOE in the south-west Pacific differed appreciably from its status in most other theatres of war. In the south-west Pacific the Supreme Allied Commander was General Douglas MacArthur, one of the most imposing and forceful of all American military figures. British influence was never more than secondary and usually less. Following the series of disasters involving Malaya, Singapore, Hong Kong and Burma Britain's military reputation was low. In Australia and New Zealand, from both of which countries servicemen had set off to fight in the Middle East and elsewhere, the concept of mutual aid within the Commonwealth had begun to seem a rather one-sided commitment.

Any British irregular force operating in the south-west Pacific area had therefore to overcome a certain scepticism about its ability to succeed. It was also liable to be suspect politically, not least because its theatre of operations must largely be territories which the British and the Dutch intended to retain as colonies once the war was over. It was not uncommon for Americans to translate the initials of the South-East Asia Command to mean 'Save England's Asiatic Colonies'. In the south-west Pacific area, where MacArthur's sway was almost absolute, similar attitudes to colonialism were to be expected.

The first SOE mission to be established in Australia after the fall of Malaya was set up by a man who served under St John Killery in Force 136 and who, like him, had commercial interests in the Far East. His name was Egerton Mott. Shortly before the fall of Singapore he had flown to Java with General Wavell and discussed with Dutch government representatives the possibilities of organizing stay-behind parties. The Japanese invasion was too swift and too successful for much to be achieved.

Mott escaped in a fishing boat, was picked up by an Australian corvette, and was landed in Fremantle on 10 March 1942. He reported his arrival to SOE in London and was instructed to set up an organization with the object of conducting clandestine warfare in territories which the Japanese had occupied.

Mott had an encouraging reception from the Australian Prime Minister, John Curtin, and the Commander-in-Chief of Australian Land Forces, General Thomas Blamey. It was agreed that the organization he intended to establish would be under Australian operational control, but that it could use its own ciphers for direct communication with London.

The mission based in Australia was known publicly by a variety of names, including the Services Reconnaissance Department and Z Force, but within SOE it was usually referred to as Force 137. As had happened in Cairo, the command of the mission was changed more than once, but continuity was maintained in the person of the principal General Staff Officer (Operations), J. E. B. (Jack) Finlay, who remained on the strength of Force 137 until the war ended and who brought to it considerable administrative skills. Finlay, who had been a civil servant before the war, was one of five Army officers who, after passing through the Staff College, were assigned to SOE for general staff duties in the Far East.

From modest beginnings, when it was accommodated in a private house in a suburb of Melbourne, Force 137 expanded until it had bases or training camps in Queensland, in Western Australia and at Darwin; an operational headquarters in Morotai in the Moluccas; and two advance headquarters in Balikpapan and Labuan Island. That such facilities were provided in a theatre of war where a British service presence had at first been little more than a source of curiosity was evidence both of the extent of American and Australian co-operation, and of the standing which SOE, in the shape of Force 137, had come to enjoy.

Serious respect began to be accorded to it after its early penetration of Timor, the large island colonized partly by the Dutch and partly by the Portuguese. Here the Japanese had assembled a large force of front-line troops with the intention of invading the mainland of Australia. The first SOE operational party in Timor landed there on 2 September 1942. It was led by a former officer in the Malayan police named Ian Wylie. After the Australian High Command lost contact with Timor SOE was virtually its sole source of military intelligence in an area of major strategic importance.

In time the number of SOE agents remaining in Timor was reduced to two, and it began to be feared that the Australian radio operator, who had remained in contact with SOE, had suffered the fate of Hubertus Lauwers in the Netherlands. Like Lauwers he indicated by pre-arranged code that he was acting under duress, and this time appropriate precautions were taken.

The radio operator was told when and where he would receive a drop of stores. A party was then parachuted in, of which he received no warning, whose members were able to observe how the stores were picked up. The radio operator was seen to be a prisoner of the Japanese, and from then on he was used as the recipient of a carefully regulated supply of information calculated to mislead Japanese intelligence.

SOE obtained most of its recruits in the south-west Pacific from Australian and, to a lesser extent, New Zealand volunteers. Indeed, though initiated by the British, it came to be regarded increasingly and rightly as predominantly an Australian fighting unit. Yet it continued to attract British volunteers, some of whom entered by unorthodox channels.

One of these was a regular officer in the Gordon Highlanders named Ivan Lyon. A thin, tense, silent man with exceptional powers of endurance, Lyon was a skilled small-boat sailor. Like Richard Broome and John Davis he had reached Ceylon by boat after the fall of Singapore, bringing a party of fifteen Europeans, a Chinese and a Malay.

Lyon was convinced that raids on Japanese-controlled islands could be more successfully mounted from Australia than from Ceylon and was persuasive enough to be allowed to go to Australia to investigate the possibilities. He talked to the Governor-General, formed his own small unit, and then met Egerton Mott, under whom he was happy to serve. In September 1943 Lyon led a raid on Singapore in which 40,000 tons of enemy shipping were destroyed.

As SOE's Force 137 was the only British military unit operating in parts of the south-west Pacific it received reports from time to time of the presence of people thought to be British servicemen in the area and was expected to take appropriate action. One such report, which came from the United States Navy, concerned two men who had been picked up from a boat near Zamboanga in the south-west Philippines, and who claimed to be escaped prisoners of war from northern Borneo.

One of the men, named Rex Blow, was unmistakably an Australian. He was later taken on to the strength of SOE and sent on an operational mission to Borneo. The other, whose name was Robert McLaren, was something of a mystery figure. He was in the Australian Army, yet was discernibly British. While he answered all other questions freely he was reluctant to give any explanation of why he had left Britain for

Australia. He asked only to be allowed to serve in any capacity, no matter how dangerous.

Finlay decided to put his trust in McLaren, having come to the conclusion that his reason for leaving Britain was probably of the kind which might have motivated a P. C. Wren character. McLaren had already shown himself to be a man of resource and courage. In the course of his prolonged escape he had found it necessary to remove his own appendix. He had used a mirror for guidance and jungle fibre for stitching the wound.

McLaren's opportunity to serve came when the Australian 7th Division launched an attack on Balikpapan on the east coast of Borneo, which was the site of the largest oil refinery in the Far East. The role of SOE in this operation was mainly one of deception. Large numbers of dummy parachutists were dropped which were fitted with time-switches. These let off reports at different times and gave the impression that the dummies were engaged in battle long after they had landed. The aim was both to harass the enemy and to mislead him about the direction of the attack.

A small number of men were needed to accompany the dummies, both to add to the confusion caused and to increase verisimilitude. One who volunteered and was chosen was McLaren. After landing McLaren rushed about in different directions, firing from as many places as possible in order to give the impression that a large force had landed near the Japanese headquarters, and in effect doing all he could to attract the enemy's attention to himself.

When he had completed his task he made his way to Balikpapan Bay by swimming, rowing, running and jumping. He was lucky enough to find a boat, which picked him up, and was then flown to SOE head-quarters, where he arrived on the afternoon of the day on which he had been parachuted in. In the course of the day he had made a round trip of 1,000 miles. He immediately volunteered to return to Balikpapan and twice repeated his near-suicidal exercise in deception.

In the south-west Pacific area SOE was responsible for 81 operations carried out behind the enemy lines. It raised and equipped some 6,000 guerrilla troops in Japanese-occupied territory. The official booklet which recorded its achievements contained the statement: 'It became quite apparent that the Japanese High Command had no answer to these activities.'

The activities referred to extended from New Guinea to the coasts of Malaya and China. Some of the most successful were conducted on the huge island of Borneo, in particular in British North Borneo and Sarawak.

One of the SOE officers sent to Borneo was a former rubber planter, F. G. L. Chester, who knew the territory well. Chester, who was generally known as Gort because of his physical resemblance to the Army commander of that name, was born in Johannesburg. He went to Borneo in 1927, but when the rubber industry suffered a slump he returned to South Africa for a time to work in gold-mining. He was in his early forties when war with Japan broke out.

Chester was infiltrated more than once into Borneo, being transported by American submarines. He succeeded in making contact with a number of the local inhabitants whom he had known in his rubber-planting days, established intelligence networks and coast-watching stations, and began the arming of resistance forces. On one of his missions he travelled some 250 miles through the interior of Borneo in one of the small folding boats which SOE had developed and which were known as 'folboats'. On another occasion he was infiltrated so close to the Japanese headquarters that he did not allow his radio operator to transmit, as the sound of the dynamo would certainly have been heard by the Japanese staff.

Finlay wrote of Chester that he could 'cut his way through close jungle quicker than almost any man alive'. He added that he had never known him walk more than a hundred yards in Melbourne without summoning a taxi. Chester died of blackwater fever soon after the war ended. The inscription on his grave in Borneo includes the words, 'a pioneer of victory in Borneo and a most lovable man'.

The leader of another operational mission, Tom Harrisson, was sent out from London by SOE to join Force 137 in Australia. Harrisson had taken part in the Oxford University expedition to Sarawak in 1932, although he graduated at Cambridge. He spent some two years on Pacific islands and acquired something of a reputation both as an anthropologist and as an ornithologist.

After returning to England he worked in Bolton as a cotton operative, a shop assistant and a lorry driver. He also met Charles Madge, a future professor of sociology, who was at that time a reporter for the *Daily Mirror*. Together they formulated the discipline and founded the organization known as Mass-Observation, which became the forerunner of countless sociological studies in subsequent decades.

After the outbreak of the Second World War Harrisson continued for a time to produce reports for Mass-Observation, mainly on the effects of bombing on civilian morale. He then served for a time in the King's

Royal Rifle Corps. His introduction to SOE came about, he afterwards learnt, as a result of a case of mistaken identity, but his qualifications for service in the Far East were soon recognized.

In Australia, where he studied all the relevant literature he could find in the Melbourne public library, Harrisson came to the conclusion that the prevailing assumption that the best approach to Borneo for SOE's purposes was by submarine might well be wrong. Borneo has the largest area of virgin rain forest, or jungle, outside South America, but there is a central area known as the Plain of Bah on to which, Harrisson thought, it might be comparatively easy to drop by parachute.

By this method, he reasoned, an SOE mission might be able to work its way from the interior outwards instead of, as hitherto, the other way about. He was also influenced by his memories of the people of Sarawak as he had known them under the hereditary rule of the Brooke family. They were, he wrote in his colourful book on his wartime experiences, *World Within: A Borneo Story*, 'devoted to, even loving towards, white men'. This he attributed, knowledgeably though unfashionably, to 'the goodwill built up in a century of White Rajah Brooke rule'.

As part of his preparations for his operational mission Harrisson visited an American geologist named Dr W. F. Schneeberger, who had been employed by the Dutch in Borneo and who advised him to take in, as currency, a supply of fish-hooks and needles. With estimable largesse SOE provided him with 50,000 fish-hooks and 250,000 needles. In fact, when he reached the interior, he found the prevailing currencies were salt, *borak* (rice wine) and buffaloes. Gold also changed hands for a time, but most of it ended up as fillings or decorations for teeth.

Harrisson was dropped from an Australian Liberator aircraft on 25 March 1945. He was accompanied by three Australian sergeants, whose names were Barry, Bower and Sanderson. They landed some ninety miles south-east of Brunei in the territory of a people known as the Kelabits. It was a country in which, for the most part, there was no such thing as an open or permanent track and men could become lost in seconds. The Kelabits measured the seasons by the habits of migratory birds. For some time Harrisson found nobody who could speak Malay, which was the *lingua franca* of Borneo and which he himself spoke well.

The first ally whom Harrisson acquired was a Kelabit named Lawai Bisarai, who pledged his support after an hour's talk and *borak*-drinking. Not long afterwards a man of some standing named Penghulu Badak, which meant Great Rhinoceros, made a journey of thirteen days across mountains to offer Harrisson his help. He was the first man who lived within easy reach of the Japanese to declare his allegiance to the Allied cause. He was also, in Harrisson's words, 'a wonderful naturalist, even by Borneo standards'.

One reason why Harrisson received such offers of support was what he described as the 'incredible stupidity' of the Japanese administrators, who treated the peoples of the interior with even more contempt than the coastal Malays did, and who had allowed the economy of much of Borneo to come almost to a standstill. Other reasons were that Harrisson brought with him arms, promised that more would be dropped from the sky, and indicated that it would now be lawful to use them. This was a clear reversal of the policy of the Brooke regime.

As an interim measure, until more arms could be parachuted in, Harrisson authorized the formation of groups armed with blow-pipes of the kind which the Kelabits traditionally used for killing monkeys, wild pigs, parakeets and flying foxes. These groups must surely have constituted the only blow-pipe force to serve under Allied command in the Second World War.

Harrisson's mission was followed by others which were also parachuted in. One was led by a New Zealander, Eric Edmeades, who after the war chose to live in Sarawak, as for a time did Harrisson. Others were led by Toby Carter, a New Zealand oil surveyor, and Bill Sochon, who was British and had been a police officer serving the Brooke regime.

The total number of the people among whom the SOE missions were able to move freely was estimated by Harrisson at about 100,000. Not one of them betrayed the missions to the Japanese, although the rewards offered for doing so were considerable.

The missions provided much of the military intelligence which facilitated the final successful landings by Australian troops. The forces which the missions raised were officially credited with killing 1,700 Japanese. In time the control they achieved in the interior of Borneo was such that Harrisson began to believe that, so long as there was an SOE presence, they could never be beaten.

After the atom bombs were dropped Harrisson did not accept the decree that fighting must cease. The consequences of doing so, as he afterwards expressed it, would have been 'not only to expose a fine people to devastation, but also to expose the good name of the British to undying contempt'. After coming out for discussions he insisted therefore on being parachuted into Dutch territory after the war with Japan had officially come to an end. On this occasion he found himself suspended by his parachute from a tree some 200 feet high, from which he had to be rescued with an improvised ladder. It was nearly three months after the dropping of the atom bombs that he finally accepted the Japanese surrender.

The history of SOE's active service in the Second World War may be deemed to have begun when members of a British military mission were retreating hastily from Poland to Roumania in September 1939. It may be thought to have ended when the first white man to be parachuted into Sarawak, and future curator of Sarawak's ethnological museum, accepted the surrender of Japanese forces on 31 October 1945.

Chapter 10

Retrospect

Professor M. R. D. Foot, one of the few serious students of the achievements of SOE as a whole whose work has hitherto been published, estimated that the total strength of SOE in manpower and womanpower, when it was at its highest, was approximately that of a weak army division. He added: 'No single division in any army exercised a tenth of SOE's influence on the course of the war.'

Another thoughtful student of guerrilla activities in the Second World War, Kenneth Macksey, after recording that about a quarter of the SOE agents sent to occupied Europe lost their lives, commented in his important work, *The Partisans of Europe in World War II*, that this was 'low by comparison with an infantry unit, which could suffer nearly one hundred per cent turnover in a few months' intensive combat, and of RAF bomber crews who lost ninety per cent in a tour of thirty missions'. With the obvious exception of the attempts to drop supplies during the Warsaw rising, losses of air crews and of aircraft in support of SOE activities were nearly everywhere accepted as being encouragingly low.

These analyses, added to the tributes of military commanders and resistance leaders, suggest that not only did SOE achieve much in the operational field, but that it did so with relatively small loss of human life and with minimal expenditure, by Second World War standards, of material resources.

Why then, it may be asked, did SOE not achieve more? The answer is mainly to be found in a contest which SOE must be deemed to have lost. It was the kind of contest which inevitably occurs when global war is conducted, the contest for supplies. In this SOE was consistently outmanoeuvred by representatives of other service interests, in particular RAF Bomber Command.

In the operational sphere relations between air crews, British, American, Polish and others, and SOE agents and liaison officers were nearly everywhere of the best. This was not surprising, for they were based on mutual respect. Numerous agents commented with admiration on the manner in which air crews, after piercing enemy defences,

222

were able to pick out a few dim lights laid out in a field and, in consequence, drop agents and supplies on target. Air crews were correspondingly impressed as they saw men or young girls drop through the floor or jump out of the side of an aircraft into enemy-occupied territory by night, singly or in small groups, armed with little more than a pistol for self-protection and the L-tablet as the final resort.

The mutual regard was perhaps even greater between agents and airmen engaged in pick-up operations, for here the relationship tended to be closer than it was when agents were being dropped. Most pick-up operations were carried out by Lysander, a single-engined, high-wing monoplane with a cruising speed of 165 miles per hour. Lysanders had been designed as spotter aircraft for the Royal Artillery, but they were such easy prey for German fighters that they were found to be almost useless for the purpose for which they were built. They were therefore made available for picking up agents of both SOE and SIS. As they could land and take off within about 500 yards they were, in the pre-helicopter age, the only aircraft which could touch down in enemy-occupied territory in the early years of the war with any degree of safety.

Hugh Verity, who commanded the pick-up flight of No. 161 Squadron from November 1942 to November 1943, provided a vivid account of how Lysander pilots sometimes had to navigate by holding a map open with one hand while flying the aircraft with the other. Lysanders would be tossed about in air currents so violently that even experienced pilots, such as he was, were airsick. To minimize the chances of capture or destruction the maximum time allowed on the ground for landing agents and stores and picking up other agents was three minutes.

One Lysander pilot, Robin Hooper, on landing in France, found his aircraft was so bogged down that he could not take off. A friendly farmer produced some bullocks, but they could not extricate the Lysander from the mud, and Hooper decided it would have to be burnt.

He remained for some time as a guest of the French resistance before he could himself be picked up. He later recorded that he had long been aware of the physical dangers of an agent's life: his own experience had now given him 'a faint idea of the psychological strains' to which agents were subjected.

Verity was apointed SOE's Air Liaison Operations Officer in Baker Street. Hooper, who was later to become British Ambassador in Greece, was posted to the Air Ministry, where, among his other duties, he was directly concerned with the problems of trying to send supplies to Warsaw during the rising.

These were ideal examples of how the talents of SOE and the RAF could be fused and of the co-operation which could be achieved when this happened. Unfortunately at the highest levels it rarely did.

It was understandable that the very existence of SOE, as an upstart organization, should be resented within some of the older established services and departments of state, not only in its formative months but as its power and importance increased.

It was in SOE that the successors of those whom T. E. Lawrence had described as 'intrusives' were mostly to be found, and members of the Foreign Office staff, for example, would not have been human if they had felt no annoyance on learning of the opportunities SOE officers had of influencing policy. When a certain official complained that SOE's 'young men in the Balkans' were dominated by the 'easy philosophy of action for action's sake', he was voicing a common Foreign Office opinion, and he may be forgiven for not explaining what the exact antithesis of that philosophy would have meant.

Within SIS, which had some claims to have been the father of SOE, albeit a rather reluctant one, it was natural too that the professional's resentment of the intrusion of the over-confident amateur should be felt and at times petulantly expressed. Sir Claude Dansey, one of the most influential figures in SIS during the Second World War, was once heard to announce his intention of blackballing any member of SOE who was proposed for membership of Boodle's. (Not that he seems to have been very successful.)

Such infighting was sometimes conducted at the highest level, as the testimony of Sir Alexander Cadogan, the Foreign Office's Permanent Under-Secretary of State from 1938 to 1946, who suffered the posthumous misfortune of having his wartime diaries published, makes clear. But this was a familiar feature of the business of state, which continues in war as in peace. SOE had to undergo it to survive, and it was certainly more successful than OSS was in the corresponding battles it had to fight with the American State Department and with certain area commanders.

SOE's relations with those who controlled the policy of the RAF were of much greater importance, for on them depended, to a large extent, its ability to carry out the tasks for which it was constituted. At no stage in the war did SOE succeed in gaining the full confidence of the air marshals.

From the outset some of the principal air marshals regarded SOE with a distrust which was in part instinctive and in part the outcome of deliberation. Fairly early in the war Sir Charles Portal, the Chief of Air Staff, wrote to Gladwyn Jebb: 'I think that the dropping of men dressed in civilian clothes for the purpose of killing members of the opposing forces is not an operation with which the Royal Air Force should be associated.' He went on to stress the 'vast difference in ethics' between this sort of thing and 'the time honoured operations of the dropping of a spy from the air'.

In retrospect it may seem difficult to reconcile Portal's adherence to traditions of chivalry in warfare, against which SOE clearly offended, and his subsequent endorsement of the policy of so-called 'area bombing' – that is to say, the deliberate mass slaughter of women and children. But the opinions he expressed to Jebb were no doubt sincerely held.

On the relative merits of bombing and sabotage as methods of attacking the enemy Portal's opinions were even more decisive. When considering the claims of SOE to a greater share of resources, he stated: 'My bombing offensive is not a gamble. Its dividend is certain; it is a gilt-edged investment. I cannot divert aircraft from a certainty to a gamble which may be a goldmine and may be completely worthless.'

In the years following the Second World War there has been much derogatory criticism of the policy and practices of RAF Bomber Command, of the huge losses of air crews, of the failure to halt German production, of the obsessive belief of its Commander-in-Chief, Sir Arthur Harris, in the possibility of defeating Germany by the bombing offensive alone. The criticisms on moral grounds of area bombing made during the war by the Bishop of Chichester, Dr George Bell, and others have been recalled and considered justified.

So damaging have the criticisms been that some of the critics may now be thought to have over-reached themselves. Britain and the United States were engaged in total war. For years their only major contribution on the continent of Europe was the bombing offensive. Nothing could have adequately replaced this, certainly not any activities organized by, or in association with, SOE. Nor is it politically realistic to suppose that the western Allies could have maintained credibility if they had both delayed the invasion of France until the summer of 1944, as they rightly did, and also refrained from conducting a major bombing campaign against Germany.

Nevertheless it must surely now be clear that for the purpose of attacking the enemy in the occupied territories some resources could have been switched with advantage from bombing, which was usually inaccurate, to the kind of sabotage which could ensure that targets were destroyed. If, when the RAF was first able to mount 1,000-bomber raids, another dozen aircraft had been made available to help SOE, the dividends which Portal sought might have been out of all proportion to the capital invested. That this did not happen must be accounted one of SOE's major failures.

In arguing their case before the Chiefs of Staff the senior representatives of SOE had a difficult task. For some time they had to base their arguments on hope unsupported by precedent, and it was only after the success of the attacks on such targets as the Gorgopotamos bridge and the Rjukan heavy water plant that they began to gain credibility. For this very reason, perhaps, they ought to have acted more subtly than they did in trying to enlist the sympathetic support of some of the air marshals.

There were few senior airmen in the service of SOE. This in itself was a disadvantage. Charles Hambro, while he was second-in-command of SOE, held the rank of squadron-leader. When he was promoted to succeed Sir Frank Nelson as the head of the organization he was made an honorary air commodore. This was characteristic of the relative indifference to rank to be found within SOE, but it was not calculated to impress professional airmen. (It was also perhaps characteristic of SOE that Hambro, like Sir William Stephenson, declined to accept any salary for his wartime service. So strongly did he adhere to his amateur status that while head of SOE he even retained his directorships of Hambro's Bank, the Bank of England and the Great Western Railway Company.)

Gubbins, Hambro's successor as head of SOE, did at least have a conventional military rank, but as it was never higher than that of major-general he could find himself outranked by corps commanders. For the advancement of SOE's interests at the highest political and service levels much, therefore, depended on the personality and authority of the Earl of Selborne, the man who replaced Hugh Dalton as Minister of Economic Warfare.

Selborne, who succeeded to the earldom at about the same time as he was appointed minister, was a Conservative politician, who had been known as Lord Wolmer. He had been closely associated with Winston Churchill in opposing disarmament. In appearance he was not impressive: he was of no more than medium height; he suffered from asthma; and he had a slight stoop and a quiet voice. In short, he was the complete antithesis physically and, indeed, in most other respects of Hugh Dalton. Among the causes to which he devoted much of his energies was that of the Church of England.

When Churchill chose him to be Minister of Economic Warfare Selborne was employed as head of the cement division in the Ministry of Works. From there he brought with him as his secretary a red-headed girl of abundant vitality named Patricia (Pat) Hornsby-Smith. She grew steadily in stature within the Ministry of Economic Warfare until she was appointed, against strong civil service opposition, the Minister's principal private secretary. After the war she was to become a Conservative politician of some repute.

Selborne could act with a firmness and a power of decision which his appearance belied. He showed this, for example, when he came to the conclusion that the right place for Gladwyn Jebb, who had been seconded from the Foreign Office to the Ministry of Economic Warfare, was back in the Foreign Office, and told him so.

Pat Hornsby-Smith had a vivid recollection of a scene which took place in her office after Hambro had had a personal interview with Selborne. A heavy wooden door had been placed between the secretary's office and the minister's to prevent Dalton's booming voice from carrying further than was necessary. On emerging from the inner office, Hambro, a man whom nobody could dominate, leant his huge frame against the wooden door and said. 'Don't ever let anybody tell you that's a weak man.' He added that he had never had such a dressing-down in his life.

Selborne fought tenaciously for the interests of SOE. He had the advantage of being on much friendlier personal terms with Churchill than Dalton ever was. But his power to influence policy was limited, largely because, unlike Dalton, he was not a member of the Cabinet and accepted his exclusion with characteristic modesty and good grace.

Soon after arriving in London Emmanuel d'Astier de la Vigerie sensed clearly what measures had to be taken to obtain more support for the French resistance. 'Without Winston Churchill', he wrote, 'there was nothing to be done.' By then he had tried, and failed, in his approaches to the 'polite and self-effacing Attlee', the 'affable Lord Selborne' and 'General Gubbins, the mysterious manipulator of the initials SOE'. From SOE the most effective approaches to Churchill came from young men who had just returned from the field, Deakin and Yeo-Thomas, whose activities carried their own romantic appeal.

Yet there were methods by which SOE could have obtained more support from the RAF and therefore more aircraft. The Air Force was the *parvenu* of the First World War and for this very reason, at least so far as its senior professionals were concerned, was the least likely of all the armed services to welcome SOE, the *parvenu* of the Second World War. If the nature of the relationship had been accepted; if the RAF had been given some measure of operational control, as later happened in the Balkans, while SOE retained detailed control in its own hands, aircraft might perhaps have been suddenly made available for other operational theatres, just as they were, latterly, for the Balkans.

To devise a satisfactory formula for bringing all this about a devious mind was needed. Selborne, Hambro and Gubbins all to some extent lacked deviousness. Perhaps deviousness was incompatible with their other qualities. But the upshot was that the total quantity of explosives received by the resistance in France, a favoured country in this respect, was, according to Professor Foot's calculations, less than the normal load carried by a single light bomber of the kind in service in 1944.

Had SOE operated on a much larger scale than it did, its nature would certainly have changed. Because its demands in manpower and woman-power were relatively small it was able to retain certain peculiar qualities, some of which distinguished it, for better or for worse, from other services. These would no doubt have been diluted with the access of numerous new recruits. Through being, numerically, a compara-tively small organization it was also able to apply the principle that only those who volunteered would be sent on operational missions.

In a foreword to the book in which Brigadier 'Trotsky' Davies described his experiences in Albania, *Illyrian Venture*, General Frank Simpson, who in 1943 and 1944 was Director of Military Operations at the War Office, wrote that missions of the kind which Davies com-manded 'attracted the very best type of officers and other ranks'. He added: 'Very few of the individuals employed in the many Allied missions ever came back to orthodox operations while the war lasted.'

This was a high compliment from a regular soldier to those who served in SOE, but it would be wrong to jump from this statement to the conclusion that SOE necessarily attracted the best fighting material. In practice the best strategists and the men who won the VCs were to be found in other services.

SOE did have officers of exceptional quality who would have been considered outstanding in any form of warfare. Such men, finding themselves in the trenches of the First World War, would probably have acquired individual reputations as daredevils, as, for example, Siegfried Sassoon did. Other types of men whom SOE attracted would probably, in conditions of trench warfare, have been considered mis-fits. One or two would have refused to fight at all. (Sasson nearly did this too.)

If a common quality is to be sought among those who served SOE in the field it will probably be found in individualism. SOE attracted, as by its very nature it was bound to attract, people who preferred making their own decisions to receiving orders from others; who operated better singly or in small groups than in large numbers; and who judged those they met by their personal qualities rather than by the status they enjoyed. General William Donovan, who had already made a study of SOE, summarized his requirements in those who were to serve in OSS succinctly when he stated: 'I'd rather have a young lieutenant with guts enough to disobey an order than a colonel too regimented to think and act for himself.'

Resourcefulness, as exemplified in an ability to fend for oneself when no rations are provided, was another essential ingredient in a successful SOE operator. Techniques for survival were, it is true, taught in the training schools, but only those judged likely to benefit were accepted for training in the first instance.

Successful SOE agents were nearly all people of unusual sensitivity. Not only was it sometimes a requirement for their survival that they should be able to make quick, instinctive, accurate assessments of the characters of people they encountered, but there were numerous recorded instances of telepathic warnings being given, received and acted upon.

Richard Heslop reported that he suddenly knew that his close friend and associate, Ernest Wilkinson, was 'in danger, deadly danger'. His presentiment was correct. Heslop attributed it to 'an instinct developed over the months'. Philippe de Vomécourt twice had a feeling that his radio operator, Muriel Byck, was in trouble, first when she narrowly escaped capture, second when she contracted meningitis and was taken to hospital. Hugh Dormer wrote of 'a certain intuition, a kind of sensitive antenna' which agents were able to develop in occupied territories and which guided them in deciding who could be trusted. Other examples could be cited.

The degree of sensitivity must have been related to the degree of fear experienced. Many SOE agents recorded their intense fear of parachuting during their training period. Jumping out of an aircraft is an unnatural procedure, and the mechanics and methods of jumping were more primitive and cumbersome in the early 1940s than they became later. Yet it is a pastime in which a number of people today indulge for their own pleasure. Some of the SOE agents to whom the thought of parachuting was most abhorrent were outstanding in their achievements.

The ability to understand and adapt to an alien culture was normally considered a necessary qualification before acceptance into SOE. After acceptance the discipline demanded was mainly self-discipline. In the field there were virtually no sanctions which could be applied, and for members of the staff, breaches of the Official Secrets Act apart, almost the worst threat which could hang over the head of anyone suspected of inadequacy was of being 'returned to the Army' (or the Navy or the Air Force).

The strength required, particularly in an undercover agent, was the strength of endurance, not of mere force. Courage was sometimes in itself not enough, for it needed to be sustained by faith in a cause for an agent to be able to overcome the tortures, the indignities and the hardships to which so many members of SOE were subjected and which so many endured without being broken.

The principal qualifications required for active service in SOE help to explain, to some extent, how the organization was able, in a manner unprecedented in the modern history of advanced nations, to use women in operational roles. Within SOE a new form of family service was even established, with brother and sister performing similar roles. Outstanding in this respect was the Nearne family, of which three members of the same generation served with distinction as agents of Buckmaster's section. Two were sisters, Jacqueline and Eileen. The third was their brother Francis.

Resourcefulness, sensitivity, endurance, courage, faith were qualities which a number of members of SOE possessed in high degree. They were supplemented, in a few at least, by another quality, that of undeniable authority. This was most manifest in those officers, some of them still in their twenties, who were able to sustain quasi-ambassadorial roles while cut off from communication with the outside world for weeks or even months, or who were in effect commanders of substantial forces with little more evident authority than the ability to organize an occasional parachute drop of arms.

In one or two the combination of all these qualities was suggestive, at least, of greatness.

Comparisons between the achievements of SOE and those of comparable organizations in other countries are not easily made. The body which most closely resembled SOE in structure and aims was certainly the American OSS. After the Second World War OSS was to provide the nucleus of the Central Intelligence Agency, which in later conflicts operated on a scale of expenditure and with a sophistication of techniques which in retrospect make the efforts of SOE seem modest and homespun. But in the Second World War the role of OSS was a restricted one.

The principal reason for this was the prejudice felt against it by two Army commanders, General Douglas MacArthur and General Joe Stilwell. Both stated clearly that they wanted OSS to have no part in their theatres of war, and both had the authority to ensure that their wishes were carried out. OSS suffered no such exclusion from the European theatre, but for the very reason that it began operations much later its role in Europe could never be more than complementary to that of SOE.

A detailed assessment of the achievements of the Soviet organizations which in one way or another corresponded to SOE is impossible for anyone without access to Soviet archives. In one limited sphere of activity a comparison can, however, be offered. This was the provisioning and support of guerrilla forces in Europe, towards which SOE and the RAF between them certainly made a greater contribution than the Soviet Union did. But in general in the conduct of clandestine and guerrilla warfare Soviet aims, techniques and long-term policies were so different from those of the British that comparisons must be largely irrelevant. Where they are not they redound almost wholly to the credit of the Soviet Union.

The Soviet Union had the immense advantage of having conducted world-wide clandestine activities for many years before the Second World War broke out. This became apparent when the Germans invaded the Soviet Union in the summer of 1941 and communist parties everywhere, some of which had long been operating underground, suddenly gave their support to the Allied cause.

In the territory of the Soviet Union itself partisan warfare was conducted behind the German lines on an immense scale and of a kind which the British did not even experience. As the war neared its end the long-sustained Soviet campaign of subversion of all pre-war governments in eastern and central Europe, whether liberal, conservative or dictatorial, reached its climax with the establishment of new docile administrations, a number of whose members had been trained for years in Moscow.

These achievements, brought about largely by clandestine methods, far surpassed any which Britain or other nations could claim. They were also of course beyond the authority and capacity of SOE even to emulate.

The clandestine services of Britain's European allies were so much concerned with the liberation of their own countries that they were understandably able to achieve little elsewhere. One exception was the Polish underground organization, which operated in Germany much more effectively than SOE did. Its successes even included some spectacular sabotage in Berlin.

Perhaps the most revealing, and certainly the most important, of the comparisons which can be made between SOE and other organizations are with those of its enemies. It is from these that it emerges with the most evident credit.

When Italy entered the war in 1940 there were millions of people of Italian origin, an appreciable number of whom were Italian citizens, living outside Italy. Yet there is no evidence that Mussolini's government successfuly organized them or anyone else for acts of sabotage or other para-military activity.

Both Germany and Japan established extensive intelligence networks in countries which they intended to invade. The number of Japanese in Burma shortly before the invasion was believed to be more than 30,000, an appreciable proportion of whom were certainly spies. Immediately before the invasion of Poland Germany had a number of agents operating in Polish uniform whose tasks included committing acts of so-called provocation against Germans. The belief was also sedulously and successfully spread that the Germans had a widespread fifth column in every country which they planned to attack, with the result that any English nun going peacefully about her business was liable to be suspected of being a parachutist. But in fact, once the immediate objects of a *Blitzkrieg*-type attack had been achieved, Germany had no effective organization for sustaining underground warfare. Nor had Japan.

That Germany achieved next to nothing through clandestine activities in Britain is not altogether surprising. SOE achieved next to nothing in Germany, in spite of the presence there of millions of forced labourers from occupied countries. SOE's policy, which of course failed, was based on the belief that only the Army could provide effective opposition to Hitler. This may have been true, but in retrospect it is difficult to decide which was the more astonishing, the number of German generals who were privy to the plans to overthrow Hitler and approved of them, or the incompetence with which the conspirators tried to translate their plans into action.

Where the full failure of Germany, and of Japan, in clandestine warfare was most evident, and, from their point of view, most disastrous was in neutral countries or in those territories where the Allies had a military or a colonizing presence.

Before the attack on Pearl Harbor Germany deliberately refrained from sabotage in the United States for fear that it might induce the American government to declare war on the Allied side. But even after Pearl Harbor the results achieved by the Germans in the western hemisphere were negligible. According to H. Montgomery Hyde, who wrote an admirable biography of Sir William Stephenson, *The Quiet Canadian*, and who was a member of Stephenson's wartime staff, 'not a single British vessel was lost or seriously held up by sabotage in a United States port throughout the war'. The damage inflicted by

Stephenson's organization alone to German property and nationals certainly exceeded the total damage caused by the Axis powers on the whole of the American continent.

In countries which had comparatively recent memories of bloody fighting against the British, such as South Africa and Ireland, the Germans scarcely caused the Allies inconvenience. In Egypt, even at the height of the German military threat, it was found feasible to leave internal security to the Egyptian army and police and so allow the British, Commonwealth, Polish and other forces to devote their energies to fighting the Wehrmacht. Perhaps most grotesque of all was the failure of the Germans and the Japanese to organize any effective resistance movement in the huge Indian sub-continent or to exploit the movements which already existed.

An Indian nationalist leader of some standing, Subhas Chandra Bose, did visit Germany in 1941 and offered his services in organizing a resistance movement against the British. He was subjected to a number of indignities and had the disconcerting experience of being told by Hitler that India would not be ready for self-government for a hundred and fifty years. He then went to Japan.

The principal effort made by the Japanese to mobilize Indian man-power was the creation of the so-called Indian National Army. This was formed from prisoners of war whom the Japanese had captured and was, arguably, the most useless military force in the history of the Second World War.

Looking back over a period of some decades, I find it curious, though it seemed wholly natural at the time, that I, like countless others, was able to walk in British uniform alone and unarmed, by day or night, in the streets of Baghdad or Jerusalem, Lagos or Gibraltar, and later of Naples or Rome, not only with impunity, but without even those slight twinges of anxiety I have subsequently felt as a civilian when walking in New York's Central Park, in Belfast and even in the King's Road in Chelsea, where I live. While we were doing this, in territories occupied by the enemy resistance forces were engaging whole divisions in battle.

These contrasting facts afford some measure of the differences in achievements in clandestine warfare of SOE and the nations against which it fought.

The legacy which SOE left was to prove, in a number of respects, disappointing. When the war came to an end there were some who felt that for many years to come, in little-frequented places in Europe such as mountains and islands, the picture which would be held to typify the

233

British would be of some young man or young men who had been parachuted in to help the resistance. The belief was soon to be shattered by the new phenomenon of mass travel.

The techniques of destruction which SOE had done so much to develop were before long to be used for purposes which had not been fully foreseen. In the words of Kenneth Macksey, 'it is the tragedy of our time that the organized lawlessness which eats into the freer societies bears close resemblance to partisan activity such as was propagated during the Second World War'. The causes for which its techniques were applied were, increasingly, those which the great majority of the men and women who had served in SOE found repellent.

When Henri Bernard, the Belgian historian and resistance leader, claimed that the international solidarity of resisters was 'the first real manifestation of the European idea', he was expressing an opinion to which a number of thoughtful Europeans subscribed. Members of SOE too looked forward to participating actively in the creation of a new united Europe and felt confident that Britain could, and would, again play a leading role. Their hopes were soon undermined as successive British governments chose to spurn Europe in favour of other preoccupations. When, some two decades too late, the decision was partially reversed, what was on offer and under consideration was no longer a common heritage, a common purpose, a common faith. It was nothing more than a common market.

Yet of what was done to sustain and defend the common heritage during the war the record remains. For most of the first half of the 1940s London was the spiritual capital of the civilized world more certainly than any other city, except Rome, has ever been in the history of the human race. It was a privilege and a challenge which the British had not known before and seem unlikely to know again. Rome apart, it is perhaps a phenomenon which can be expected to occur no more than once in a nation's history.

In providing the links between those who fought in the resistance and the seat of power in London the men and women of SOE played a significant part in determining how the privilege was enjoyed and the challenge was met. The manner in which most of them did so gives, and will continue to give, their descendents abundant cause to feel thankful and proud.

Bibliography

Amery, Julian, *Sons of the Eagle: A Study in Guerilla Warfare* (Macmillan, 1948).

Amery, Julian, *Approach March: A Venture in Autobiography* (Hutchison, 1973).

Amies, Hardy, *Just So Far* (Collins, 1954).

d'Astier de la Vigerie, Emmanuel, *Seven Times Seven Days*, trans. Humphrey Hare (Macgibbon & Kee, 1958).

Astley, Joan Bright, *The Inner Circle: A View of War at the Top* (Hutchinson, 1971).

Auty, Phyllis, and Clogg, Richard (eds), *British Policy towards Wartime Resistance in Yugoslavia and Greece* (Macmillan, 1975).

Barker, Ralph, *One Man's Jungle: A Biography of F. Spencer Chapman, D.S.O.* (Chatto & Windus, 1975).

Battaglia, Roberto, *The Story of the Italian Resistance*, trans. and ed. P. D. Cummins (Odhams, 1957).

Bernard, Henri, *La Résistance 1940–1945* (La Renaissance du Livre, Brussels, 1968).

Bleicher, Hugo, *Colonel Henri's Story: The War Memoirs of Hugo Bleicher*, ed. Ian Colvin (William Kimber, 1968).

Boulle, Pierre, *The Source of the River Kwai*, trans. Xan Fielding (Secker & Warburg, 1967).

Bowen, John, *Undercover in the Jungle* (William Kimber, 1978).

Braddon, Russell, *Nancy Wake: The Story of a Very Brave Woman* (Cassell, 1956).

Bruce, George, *The Warsaw Rising 1 August–2 October 1944* (Rupert Hart-Davis, 1972).

Buckmaster, Maurice, *Specially Employed: The Story of British Aid to French Patriots of the Resistance* (Batchworth Press, 1952).

Buckmaster, Maurice, *They Fought Alone: The Story of British Agents in France* (Odhams, 1958).

Burney, Christopher, *The Dungeon Democracy* (Heinemann, 1945).

Butler, Ewan, *Amateur Agent* (Harrap, 1963).

Cadogan, Sir Alexander, *Diaries 1938–1945*, ed. David Dilks (Cassell, 1971).

Calvocoressi, Peter, and Wint, Guy, *Total War: Causes and Courses of the Second World War* (Allen Lane, 1972).

Carton de Wiart, Lieut-General Sir Adrian, *Happy Odyssey* (Cape, 1950).

Christensen, Synnöve, *Norway is My Country* (Collins, 1943).

Churchill, Peter, *Of their Own Choice* (Hodder & Stoughton, 1952).

Churchill, Peter, *Duel of Wits* (Hodder & Stoughton, 1953).

Churchill, Peter, *The Spirit in the Cage* (Hodder & Stoughton, 1954).

Cline, Ray S., *Secrets, Spies and Saboteurs: Blue-print of the Essential CIA* (Acropolis Books, Washington, 1976).

Cookridge, E. H., *They Came from the Sky* (Heinemann, 1965).

Cookridge, E. H., *Inside S.O.E.: The Story of Special Operations in Western Europe 1940–45* (Arthur Barker, 1966).

Cooper, A. R., *Born to Fight* (Blackwood, 1969).

Cooper, Capt. Dick, *The Adventures of a Secret Agent* (Frederick Muller, 1957).

Cruickshank, Charles, *The Fourth Arm: Psychological Warfare 1938–45* (Davis-Poynter, 1947).

Dalton, Hugh, *The Fateful Years: Memoirs 1931–1945* (Frederick Muller, 1957).

Davidson, Basil, *Partisan Picture* (Bedford Books, 1946).

Davies, Brigadier, 'Trotsky' (Edmund T.), *Illyrian Venture* (Bodley Head, 1952).

Dayan, Moshe, *The Story of My Life* (Weidenfeld & Nicolson, 1976).

Deacon, Richard, *A History of the British Secret Service* (Frederick Muller, 1939).

Deakin, F. W. D., 'Great Britain and European Resistance' (paper presented to the Second International Conference on the History of the Resistance, Milan, March 1961).

Deakin, F. W. D., *The Embattled Mountain* (Oxford University Press, 1971).

Dean, Sir Maurice, *The Royal Air Force and Two World Wars* (Cassell, 1979).

Dedijer, Vladimir, *With Tito Through the War: Partisan Diary 1941–1944*, trans. Alex Brown (Alexander Hamilton, 1951).

Delmer, Sefton, *The Counterfeit Spy* (Hutchinson, 1971).

Djilas, Milovan, *Wartime*, trans. Michael Petrovich (Secker & Warburg, 1977).

Dormer, Hugh, *Diaries* (Jonathan Cape, 1947).

Dulles, Allen, *The Secret Surrender* (Weidenfeld & Nicolson, 1967).

Fielding, Daphne, *The Nearest Way Home* (Eyre & Spottiswoode, 1970).

Fielding, Xan, *Hide and Seek* (Secker & Warburg, 1954).

Fielding, Xan, *The Stronghold. An Account of the Four Seasons in the White Mountains of Crete* (Secker & Warburg, 1955).

Foot, M. R. D., *SOE in France: An Account of the British Special Operations Executive in France 1940–1944* (HMSO, 1966).

Foot, M. R. D., *Resistance: An Analysis of European Resistance to Nazism 1940–1945* (Eyre Methuen, 1976).

Foot, M. R. D., *Six Faces of Courage* (Eyre Methuen, 1978).

Frenay, Henri, *The Night Will End: Memoirs of the Resistance*, trans. Dan Hofstadter (Abelard, 1976).

Fuller, Jean Overton, *The German Penetration of SOE* (William Kimber, 1975).

Gage, Jack, *Greek Adventure: Six Months in the Life of a South African Officer in Occupied Greece* (Unie-Volkspers Beperk, Cape Town, 1950).

Garlinski, Jozef, *Poland, SOE and the Allies*, trans. Paul Stevenson (Allen & Unwin, 1969).

de Gaulle, Charles, *War Memoirs*, volume 1, *The Call to Honour, 1940–42*, trans. Jonathan Griffin (Collins, 1955).

de Gaulle, Charles, *War Memoirs*, volume 2, *Unity, 1942–44*, trans. Joyce Murchie and Hamish Erskine (Weidenfeld & Nicolson, 1959).

Bibliography

Gilchrist, Andrew, *Bangkok Top Secret* (Hutchinson, 1970).
Giskes, H. J., *London Calling North Pole* (William Kimber, 1955).
Gladwyn, Lord, *The European Idea* (Weidenfeld & Nicolson, 1966).
Glen, Alexander, *Footholds Against a Whirlwind* (Hutchinson, 1975).
Goldsmith, John, *Accidental Agent* (Leo Cooper, 1971).
Gubbins, Major-General Sir Colin, 'Resistance Movements in the War' (lecture to the Royal United Service Institute, January 1948).
Guthrie, Duncan, *Jungle Diary* (Macmillan, 1946).
Hamilton-Hill, Donald, *SOE Assignment* (William Kimber, 1973).
Hamson, Denys, *We Fell Among Greeks* (Jonathan Cape, 1946).
Hansson, Per, *The Greatest Gamble*, trans. Maurice Michael (Allen & Unwin, 1967).
Harrisson, Tom, *World Within: A Borneo Story* (Cresset Press, 1959).
Hauge, E. O., *Salt-Water Thief*, trans. Malcolm Munthe (Duckworth, 1958).
Haukelid, Knut, *Skis Against the Atom*, trans. F. H. Lyon (William Kimber, 1954).
Heslop, Richard, *Xavier* (Rupert Hart-Davis, 1970).
Howarth, David, *The Shetland Bus* (Nelson, 1951).
Howarth, David, *We Die Alone* (Collins, 1955).
Howarth, Patrick (ed.), *Special Operations* (Routledge & Kegan Paul, 1955).
Hutchison, Sir James, Bt, *That Drug Danger* (Standard Press, Montrose, 1977).
Hyde, H. Montgomery, *The Quiet Canadian: The Secret Service Story of Sir William Stephenson* (Hamish Hamilton, 1962).
Ind, Colonel Allison, *A History of Modern Espionage* (Hodder & Stoughton, 1965).
Irwin, Anthony, *Burmese Outpost* (Collins, 1945).
Ivanović, Vani, *LX: Memoirs of a Yugoslav* (Weidenfeld & Nicolson, 1977).
J. E. A., *Geoffrey: Major John Geoffrey Appleyard, DSO, MC and bar, MA of the Commandos and Special Air Service Regiment* (Whitehead & Miller, Leeds, 1945).
Johnson, Brian, *The Secret War* (BBC, 1978).
Johnson, Stowers, *Agents Extraordinary* (Robert Hale, 1975).
Jones, R. V., *Most Secret War* (Hamish Hamilton, 1978).
Jones, William, *Twelve Months with Tito's Partisans* (Bedford, 1946).
Jullian, Marcel, *H.M.S. Fidelity* (Souvenir Press, 1957).
Karski, Jan, *Story of a Secret State* (Hodder & Stoughton, 1945).
Kemp, Peter, *Mine Were of Trouble* (Cassell, 1957).
Kemp, Peter, *No Colours or Crest* (Cassell, 1958).
Kemp, Peter, *Alms for Oblivion* (Cassell, 1961).
Kipling, Rudyard, *Kim* (Macmillan, 1901).
Knight, Frida, *The French Resistance 1940–1944* (Lawrence & Wishart, 1975).
Kovpak, Major-General G. A., *Our Partisan Course*, trans. Ernst and Mira Lesser (Hutchinson, 1947).
Lampe, David, *The Savage Canary: The Story of Resistance in Denmark* (Cassell, 1957).
Lampe, David, *The Last Ditch* (Cassell, 1968).
Langelaan, George, *Knights of the Floating Silk* (Hutchinson, 1959).
Laqueur, Walter, *Guerrilla: A Historical and Critical Study* (Weidenfeld & Nicolson, 1977).

Lassen, Suzanne, *Anders Lassen, V.C.*, trans. Inge Hack (Frederick Muller, 1965).

Lawrence, T. E., *Seven Pillars of Wisdom* (Jonathan Cape, 1935).

Leasor, James, *Boarding Party: The Last Action of the Calcutta Light Horse* (Heinemann, 1978).

Leber, Annedore, *Conscience in Revolt: Sixty-Four Studies of Resistance in Germany 1933–45*, trans. Rosemary O'Neill (Mitchell, 1957).

Le Chêne, Evelyn, *Watch for Me by Moonlight: A British Agent with the French Resistance* (Eyre Methuen, 1973).

Leigh-Fermor, Patrick, *A Time of Gifts* (John Murray, 1977).

Lett, Gordon, *Rossano: An Adventure of the Italian Resistance* (Hodder & Stoughton, 1955).

Lewin, Ronald, *Ultra Goes to War* (Hutchinson, 1978).

Macksey, Kenneth, *The Partisans of Europe in World War II* (Hart-Davis, MacGibbon, 1975).

Maclean, Fitzroy, *Disputed Barricade: The Life and Times of Josip Broz-Tito, Marshal of Jugoslavia* (Jonathan Cape, 1957).

Macrae, R. Stuart, *Winston Churchill's Toyshop* (Roundwood Press, 1971).

March-Phillipps, G., *Ace High* (Macmillan, 1938).

Marshall, Bruce, *The White Rabbit: From the Story Told to Him by Wing Commander F. F. E. Yeo-Thomas, G.C., M.C.* (Evans, 1952).

Martelli, George, *Agent Extraordinary: The Story of Michel Hollard, D.S.O., Croix de Guerre* (Collins, 1960).

Masson, Madeleine, *Christine: A Search for Christine Granville, G.M., O.B.E., Croix de Guerre* (Hamish Hamilton, 1975).

Masterman, J. C., *The Double-Cross System in the War of 1939–1945* (Yale University Press, New Haven, Conn., 1972).

Mastny, Vojtech, *The Czechs Under Nazi Rule: The Failure of Nazi Rule, 1939–1942* (Columbia University Press, New York, 1971).

Maxwell, Gavin, *The House of Elrig* (Longmans, 1965).

Michel, Henri, *The Shadow War: Resistance in Europe 1939–1945*, trans. Richard Barry (Andre Deutsch, 1972).

Milazzo, Matteo J., *The Chetnik Movement and the Yugoslav Resistance* (Johns Hopkins University Press, Baltimore, 1975).

Millar, George, *Maquis* (Heinemann, 1945).

Millar, George, *Horned Pigeon* (Heinemann, 1946).

Minney, R. J., *Carve Her Name with Pride: The Story of Violette Szabo* (Collins, 1964).

Moen, Lars, *Under the Iron Heel* (Robert Hale, 1941).

Moravec, Frantisek, *Master of Spies* (Bodley Head, 1975).

Morrison, Ian, *Grandfather Longlegs: The Life and Gallant Death of Major H. P. Seagrim, G.C., D.S.O., O.B.E.* (Faber & Faber, 1947).

Moss, W. Stanley, *Ill Met by Moonlight* (Harrap, 1950).

Mulgan, John, *Report on Experience* (Oxford University Press, 1947).

Munthe, Malcolm, *Sweet is War* (Duckworth, 1954).

Musard, François, *Les Glières* (Laffont, Paris, 1965).

Myers, E. C. W., *Greek Entanglement* (Rupert Hart-Davis, 1955).

Nicholas, Elizabeth, *Death be Not Proud* (Cresset Press, 1958).

Olsen, Oluf Reed, *Two Eggs on My Plate*, trans. F. H. Lyon (Allen & Unwin, 1952).

'Passy, Colonel' (André Dewavrin), *Missions secrètes en France* (Plon, Paris, 1951).

Peers, William R., and Brelis, Dean, *Behind the Burma Road* (Robert Hale, 1964).

Philby, Kim, *My Silent War* (McGibbon & Kee, 1962).

Phillips, C. E. Lucas, *The Raiders of Arakan* (Heinemann, 1971).

Piquet-Wicks, Eric, *Four in the Shadows* (Jarrolds, Norwich, 1957).

Pochard, Jean, *Le Savoie sous l'Occupation 1940–1944* (Comité d'histoire de la deuxième guerre mondiale, Chambéry, Haute Savoie, privately printed, n.d.).

Quayle, Anthony, *Eight Hours from England* (Heinemann, 1945).

Raczynski, Count Edward, *In Allied London* (Weidenfeld & Nicolson, 1962).

Raine, Kathleen, *The Lion's Mouth* (Hamish Hamilton, 1977).

Rake, Denis, *Rake's Progress* (Frewin, 1968).

Rendel, A. M., *Appointment in Crete: The Story of a British Agent* (Allan Wingate, 1953).

Romans-Petit, Colonel Henri, *Les Maquis de l'Ain* (Hachette, Paris, 1974).

Rootham, Jasper, *Missfire: The Chronicle of a British Mission to Mihailovich 1943–1944* (Chatto & Windus, 1946).

Salvadori, Massimo, *The Labour and the Wounds: A Personal Chronicle of One Man's Fight for Freedom* (Pall Mall, 1958).

Saraphis, S., *Greek Resistance Army: The Story of E.L.A.S.*, trans. Marian Pascoe (Birch Books, 1951).

Seth, Ronald, *Anatomy of Spying* (Arthur Barker, 1961).

Seton-Watson, Hugh, *The East European Revolution* (Methuen, 1950).

Slessor, Marshal of the RAF Sir John, GCB, DSO, MC, *The Central Blue* (Cassell, 1956).

Smith, R. Harris, *OSS: The Secret History of America's First Central Intelligence Agency* (University of California Press, Berkeley, 1972).

Spencer Chapman, F., *The Jungle is Neutral* (Chatto & Windus, 1949).

Stead, Philip John, *Second Bureau* (Evans, 1959).

Stevenson, William, *A Man Called Intrepid: The Secret War 1939–1945* (Macmillan, 1976).

Sweet-Escott, Bickham, *Baker Street Irregular* (Methuen, 1965).

Sykes, Christopher, *Troubled Loyalty: A Biography of Adam von Trott zu Stolz* (Collins, 1968).

Tevet, Shabtai, *Moshe Dayan: The Soldier, the Man, the Legend* (Weidenfeld & Nicolson, 1972).

Thomas, John Oram, *The Giant-Killers: The Danish Resistance Movement, 1940–5* (Michael Joseph, 1975).

Tickell, Jerrard, *Odette: The Story of a British Agent* (Chapman & Hall, 1949).

Tickell, Jerrard, *Moon Squadron* (Mann, 1956).

Tilman, H. W., DSO, MC, *When Men and Mountains Meet* (Cambridge University Press, 1946).

Tolstoy, Nikolai, *Victims of Yalta* (Hodder & Stoughton, 1977).

Trenowden, Ian, *Operations Most Secret: SOE: The Malayan Theatre* (William Kimber, 1978).

Usborne, Richard, *Clubland Heroes* (Barrie & Jenkins, 1953).

Verity, Hugh, *We Landed by Moonlight* (W. H. Allen, 1978).

'Vercors' (Jean Bruller), *The Battle of Silence (Le Silence de la mer)*, trans. Rita Barisse (Collins, 1968).

de Vomécourt, Philippe, *Who Lived to See the Day: France in Arms 1940–1945* (Hutchinson, 1961).

Walker, David E., *Adventure in Diamonds* (Evans, 1955).

Walker, David E., *Lunch with a Stranger* (Allen Wingate, 1957).

Williams, J. H., *Elephant Bill* (Rupert Hart-Davis, 1950).

Wilson, John S., *Scouting round the World* (Blandford, 1959).

Winterbotham, F. W., *The Ultra Secret* (Weidenfeld & Nicolson, 1974).

Woodhouse, C. M., *Apple of Discord: A Survey of Greek Politics in their International Setting* (Hutchinson, 1948).

Woodhouse, C. M., *The Struggle for Greece 1941–1949* (Hart-Davis, McGibbon, 1976).

Zawodny, J. H., *Nothing but Honour: The Story of the Warsaw Rising, 1944* (Macmillan, 1978).

Zuckerman, Solly, *From Apes to Warlords* (Hamish Hamilton, 1978).

Composite works

Special Forces Club Newsletters, 1946–79.

The Unseen and Silent: Adventures from the Underground Movement, narrated by Paratroops of the Polish Home Army, trans. George Izanek-Osmecki (Sheed & Ward, 1954).

Proceedings of a Conference on Britain and European Resistance 1939–1945, organized by St Antony's College, Oxford, 10–16 December 1962.

Resistance in Europe 1939–1945, based on the Proceedings of a Symposium held at the University of Salford, March 1973, ed. Stephen Hawes and Ralph White (Allen Lane, 1975).

Editors of the *Army Times*, Heroes of the Resistance (Dodd, Mead, New York, 1975).

For the convenience of British readers I have included in the above list English editions or English translations in preference to the originals; place of publication is London unless otherwise stated.

Index

Index

Index